The Ultimate Home Style Guide

The Ultimate

Home Style Guide

KATHERINE SORRELL

·SEVEN· ·DIALS·

First published in the United Kingdom in 1998 by
Ward Lock

This paperback edition first published in 2000 by
Seven Dials, Cassell & Co
Wellington House, 125 Strand
London, WC2R 0BB

Distributed in the United States of America by
Sterling Publishing Co., Inc.
387 Park Avenue South,
New York, NY 10016-8810

A CIP catalogue record for this book is available
from the British Library

ISBN 1 84188 059 0

Edited by Caroline Ball
Designed by Harry Green
Printed & bound in Italy by Graphicom

Contents

Introduction

When reading about interior design it's easy to get the impression that there is a set of rules that one is obliged to follow, some sort of list of prerequisites for getting it right – put this here and that there, add a touch of such-and-such and everything will be perfect – and that when it's done, you mustn't alter a single thing, move a book, add a side table, reposition a vase, in case it will then be 'wrong'.

This book is not about that. I firmly believe that decorating a home is a matter of purely personal preference, a means of expressing one's own style, taste and individuality and, most of all, something that should be done for pleasure and enjoyment rather than any sense of obligation. And I also believe that it is important to recognize the everyday constraints that affect most ordinary people when it comes to decorating our homes. Huge budgets and blank canvases are often out of the question, with most of us limited by time, money and the presence of existing furnishings, so that the process is one of working with what we already have and using ingenuity and creativity to make the best of it – a process that can, however, be enormously satisfying.

In this book you will find descriptions of some of the most interesting and achievable styles of interior decoration, with explanations of how and why they evolved and guidelines on creating a similar look in your own home. Those who wish to reproduce a historically authentic interior, or a highly accurate global 'look' will, I hope, find enough information here to give you at least a very good start. More details can be found in the many excellent books which specialize in the areas that I have outlined here (Further reading, page 220). For those who are happy simply to emulate the feel or spirit of a certain period or place, I hope that this book covers most of the essential areas, giving inspiration and ideas for you to develop that will suit your own taste and lifestyle.

The emphasis of this book is, necessarily, on the rooms which are the most likely candidates for decorating in a particular 'style' – sitting rooms, bedrooms and dining rooms. Tips on creating the look in kitchens and bathrooms are given where appropriate, as are some hints for hallways, stairs, studies, children's rooms, conservatories and so on. I hope, however, that the ideas here will provide a starting point for you to develop as you feel appropriate, to decorate any room in your home.

Historical styles

If you are lucky enough to live in an old building, then decorating in a complementary style is often the best option. On the other hand, owners of modern homes may find that adding period touches is a wonderful way to provide extra character and interest. An historical theme may vary from an utterly authentic recreation of a certain era, perhaps at some expense, to the evocation of atmosphere with a few junk-shop finds.

This book aims to give enough ideas to enable you to create the look of a particular period to whatever level of detail you prefer, while at the same time recognizing that the demands of modern life may mean a few compromises along the way. While we wouldn't want to live without efficient plumbing, electricity, hi-fis and TVs, for example, such contemporary conveniences won't immediately fit in with many historical styles. The key is to disguise as much as you can – by hiding the CD player and videos in cupboards or cabinets, covering fitted carpets with rugs, boxing in radiators, adding loose covers or throws to furniture and painting over inappropriate architectural detailing – and then to give an overall impression using colour, fabrics and a variety of accessories.

ABOVE Every detail in this dramatic Georgian-style dining room has been carefully thought out, from the rich crimson walls down to the tiered fruit stand and classical bust.

It is amazing how a sympathetic feel for a period can be just as effective in transforming a room as bundles of cash and a complete makeover: even the most fitted of kitchens, for example, can be altered beyond recognition by a fresh coat of paint, a change of cupboard doors, adding a dresser and including some finishing touches such as plate racks, hanging rails, a butcher's block or pastry table and period glassware or crockery displayed on open shelves. The same goes for bathrooms, too, where replacement taps and other fittings, whether salvaged or repro, will give a new lease of life to a standard suite, and more atmosphere can be added by curtains or blinds, shelving, cupboards, towel rails and shower screens, and by displaying, say, a large pitcher and bowl and some suitable plants.

Another important consideration to bear in mind is that styles do not begin and end at neatly prescribed times. The wealthiest, most fashionable households, usually in large cities, embraced each and every new fashion as it occurred, but it could take decades for the 'latest' styles to reach middle-class, provincial homes, while peasants' cottages were almost totally unaffected, remaining essentially the same in style (if you could even call it that) for centuries. And, just as today we might furnish our homes with both modern and antique pieces, so in the past home-owners mixed contemporary styles with those from previous eras. Many even enthusiastically adapted revivalist designs – the Victorians reinvented Medieval Gothic, the Edwardians loved the Georgian look, while as recently as the Sixties there was a taste for the florid colours and sinuous lines of Art Nouveau. These 'looks within a look' are covered in each chapter introduction, but in general, when creating a style it is best to stick to the 'typical' in order

LEFT There's no harm in mixing styles if that is what appeals: here, bold colours and patterns reminiscent of India or Mexico are combined with curly French wirework and a bath that is eminently Victorian. The result is an assured look that is highly individual.

RIGHT The furniture in this pretty room is authentically Scandinavian in style, but the overall look also owes a great deal to thoughtful finishing touches – the seat cover, a narrow rug, even the row of pots at the window.

to avoid confusion. That said, the fluidity of evolution of new historical styles does offer a certain amount of freedom when creating your own look: there's no reason why an Edwardian bedroom shouldn't contain Victorian chairs, for instance, or a Fifties sitting room be equipped with Art Deco lights. Or you could be bold and deliberately juxtapose two completely different periods, where the unexpected contrasts can be surprising and very pleasing. Georgian and contemporary spring to mind as one fortunate pairing, but you might equally put Medieval with Arts and Crafts, or Modernist with Fifties. Such unusual schemes

need careful planning in order to avoid an awkward muddle, so consider unifying elements such as colour, shape and material in order to arrive at a deliberate, co-ordinated and attractive look.

Global styles

The desire to decorate is inherent in all of us, whether we live under the grey skies of northern Europe, near the snowy fjords of Scandinavia or in the perpetual sunshine of the tropics. And emulating a style from another part of the globe is a marvellously exciting way to transform a home and to transport ourselves, mentally, emotionally and spiritually, into an entirely different world. The permutations of these different looks are endless, and they can be adapted to any location and to suit any budget; what's more, they are often exceptionally easy to achieve. Appropriate fabrics, colours and a few accessories can evoke a style, whether the aim is to go the whole hog with an entire scheme or simply give a flavour of a place.

The styles outlined here are, essentially, timeless rather than belonging to one particular period in a nation's or region's history. Generally, they have evolved through the ages, owing a great deal to indigenous arts and crafts and affected by factors such as climate, lifestyle, religion and immigration. The one important exception is Shaker style, which developed from a very particular set of circumstances and which I have included in this rather than the historical section because it is a look that has remained basically unchanged for almost two centuries and, therefore, owes more to its place of origin than any particular era.

When recreating your look, then, there is no duty to authenticity other than your own interests and desires. Equally, just as historical styles don't begin and end at specific times, so global styles tend not to stop at man-made political boundaries. So you have a choice of whether to stick to a pure, unadulterated style, or to create your own mix – Scandinavian with Shaker, Mediterranean with North African or Mexican with Caribbean, for example. Design elements from one region are often found replicated in another – just think of the Spanish conquistadors' influence in Latin America, or the geometric patterns common to Islamic nations – and you may prefer to choose a look that combines harmonious colours, patterns and materials regardless of their provenance.

Do avoid, however, the 'junky' ethnic look, in which cheap and tacky holiday souvenirs are cluttered around indiscriminately. Instead, explore the wealth of beautiful crafts and furnishings from around the world and use your instinct to display pieces in an individualistic way, whether it is in a typically understated, minimalist Japanese style, or with exuberant and abundant Mexican kitsch.

Creating your look

The intentions of this book are to inform and to inspire, giving you the basic ideas from which to develop your scheme. How you interpret the styles is up to you, and will vary according to the architecture of your home, the amount of time you have to spare, your budget and your individual preference. Here is some further information that relates to the sections within each chapter. The rest is up to you …

Walls, floors and lights

The architectural character of walls is essential to an historical style, but if your home suffers either from the 'wrong' architectural detailing or from having none at all, there are ways to remedy the problem. To start with, never rip out old cornicing, dados, panelling and so on unless you are absolutely certain that they are of no significance. Instead, if such details look inappropriate, 'wash' them out by painting the same colours as walls or ceilings, and then simply decorate around them. If you need to add such components, choose either the genuine article, to be found in salvage yards,

or reproductions made by specialists or found off the peg in high street DIY shops. Alternatively, you can create wonderful architectural effects, fake wood panelling and stonework with trompe-l'oeil wallpapers and borders.

Suitable paintwork can make all the difference to walls in both historical and global styles. Colourwashing, for example, in which one thin layer of emulsion is brushed roughly over another, gives a superb visual depth and interest which is suitable for many ethnic styles and also the earlier historical eras. Other effects, such as ragging, stippling and sponging, can be employed to the same purpose. If the walls in your bathroom, kitchen or any other room are tiled, an inexpensive way to alter their look is by using specialist tile paint – some careful preparation and application is needed, but the results will be worth the effort.

Laying a new floor or floorcovering may prove to be the costliest element of your decorative scheme. If you have the funds to choose the most suitable type – be it marble, wood, tiles or carpet – all well and good. If not, aim to make the best of what you already have. The cheapest option is to lay loose rugs – if you're clever, you can

disguise the whole room very effectively in this way; you could even make your own hooked rug or painted canvas floorcloth, choosing appropriate colours and designs customized to your individual scheme.

Vinyl flooring imitates the look of wood or stone, while linoleum laid in black and white checks comes close to marble at a fraction of the cost. Reclaimed flooring often makes an ideal choice: brick pavers, terracotta tiles and extra-wide wooden boards all have an authenticity that is hard to beat using modern products, although prices may not be much lower than for their brand-new counterparts. When buying new wood, ply boards are inexpensive and can be painted with a suitably coloured floor paint, as, indeed, can any timber or concrete floor which you need to disguise. For carpets, the best option is a neutral colour with either no pattern or just a speckled effect that won't show the dirt. Whether wool, synthetic or a combination of the two, this provides a perfect understated backdrop for most schemes. As an alternative, natural mattings – jute, sisal, coir and rush – are increasing in popularity, and are very reasonably priced. They make a versatile option which fits in with many different styles, though you may find, initially at least, that they're a little prickly on bare feet!

The importance of lighting should never be underestimated – it really can make or break a room as much as (if not more than) any other aspect of its decoration. The presence of lamps, sconces, pendants and other fittings that are full of character will go a long way towards establishing a style, whether global or historical, while overall levels of light make all the difference between an uncomfortable and unattractive environment and one that is both functional and enjoyable to live in. A successful scheme requires a combination of general, task and mood lighting, and in an ideal world all these would be planned before any of the decorating is done, in order to cater for all activities, highlight attractive features and provide a good balance of light through the room without the need for multiple adapters and trailing cables. If, however, you are forced to consider lighting at a later stage, much can be done by moving existing fittings or sockets, and by plugging in extra lamps – making sure any new connections are both tidy and safe. Avoid over-lighting, which gives an uncomfortable glare and can make you feel as if you are living in a lamp shop.

When creating a period style, the use of modern fittings is unavoidable. This should not, however, present too much of a problem as long as you keep them as discreet as possible. Spotlights recessed within a ceiling, small highlighters in the corners, plain wall-mounted uplighters and lamps in neutral styles can all contribute to levels of light without making their presence felt too strongly, while candlesticks, torchères, lanterns, oil lamps or whatever is most appropriate can be added, more for atmosphere than practicality. While a wide range of reproduction lighting is available today, antique lighting can often be converted for use with electricity – buy fittings ready converted from a reputable dealer or ask a qualified electrician to do the job for you, ensuring that the result has an insulated cable and is earthed to comply with international standards.

Soft furnishings, accessories and colours

Fabrics make an invaluable contribution to any scheme, and can be used creatively to achieve all sorts of different styles. It is not necessary to spend an exorbitant amount of money – it is just as easy to create the impression you want through pattern, colour and texture as it is by buying expensive textiles. If you want the look of luxury curtains, for example, an inexpensive cotton or wool will do, used generously, gathered, perhaps trailed on the floor and held by tasselled tie-backs; the same is true of elaborate bed-hangings, which can create the look of a sumptuous four-poster

without the bulky framework. A swathe of muslin draped around a curtain pole or a mosquito net suspended from a coronet above a bed both have an instant, dramatic effect at little cost, while simple canvas or ticking loose covers can completely disguise furniture that's upholstered in the wrong fabrics or that looks overly contemporary.

To evoke time or place with startling immediacy, choose pattern – blowsy florals for English country, restrained checks for Shaker, Morris birds and flowers for Arts and Crafts – and colour with care. Bear in mind the importance of synthetic versus natural dyes, and remember that interesting effects can be achieved by mixing different textures within the same colour range. Historical and ethnic fabrics can be sourced through auctions and specialist dealers, but if you don't want to go to such lengths look out for the many excellent reproduction prints and weaves available in high street stores. Also, bear in mind that you don't have to restrict yourself to buying fabric off the roll – use ready-made curtains to save time and trouble, while old tablecloths, tea towels, sheets and even items of clothing can all be adapted, as small blinds, cushion covers, basket linings, picture frames and hat box covers, for example. And then, of course, there are the trimmings – whatever the fabric, don't forget that lace, braid, fringing and tassels can all be employed for fabulous stylistic effect.

The use of colour can express your personality, your creativity and your emotions; it can also send out strong signals as to style. Colour is powerful but also versatile: putting up a bright picture, throwing a length of fabric over a sofa and, especially, giving a wall a fresh coat of paint are instant ways to transform a room without going to great expense. Plan colour combinations with swatches of fabric, scraps of wallpaper and sample pots of paint, using key colours from elements of your scheme – antique tapestries or ethnic cloth, for example, or ceramics or pictures. Remember that lighting plays a major part in the appearance of the colours you choose – standard tungsten bulbs make them more yellow, fluorescent brings out the blue tones, while halogen makes everything harsh and flat.

COLOURS Even within a similar range of colours, alterations of shade can make all the difference in terms of evoking a particular style.

Now that in-store paint mixing can create almost any hue imaginable, it is really simple to emulate any global or period style through colour. and ready-mixed historic or 'ethnic' ranges by a growing number of manufacturers make it even easier. Even if you don't choose from these ranges, bear in mind that bright, synthetic white is wrong for any historical scheme before the Sixties, and also that the very bright colours used in some hot countries can look garish or odd under greyer, cooler skies. Experiment with different combinations until you reach one that evokes the correct ambience and with which you feel comfortable. Your choice of finish, too, can make all the difference – shiny gloss would look completely wrong in a Shaker interior, for example, but is just right for a funky Sixties feel.

Finishing touches are the very essence of decorating in different styles. They can be as elaborate or as inexpensive as you like, and may range from folk crafts to crockery, paintings to pewterware. Whether such accessories aspire to the grand title of a 'collection' or are simply an assortment of items which have taken your fancy, suitable pieces will create an invaluable feeling of period or place. And the way in which you display them is as important as the objects on show – one Zen-like oriental jar on a plinth, perhaps, or a wall-full of black-and-white Georgian silhouettes, would make a marvellous impression in the right setting. And don't forget that house plants, scented candles and music will also go a long way towards achieving a particular atmosphere.

Furniture

Hunting out the perfect pieces of furniture is all part of the fun of creating your style, and although just the right item may be found in high-class auctions or a pricey antiques shop, it could also come from a jumble sale, a friend's loft or the junk shop

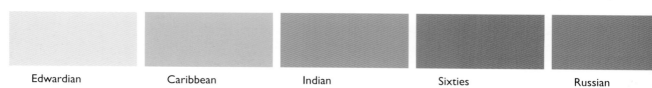

Edwardian   Caribbean   Indian   Sixties   Russian

RIGHT Simple, country-style furniture is not expensive to buy and can be adapted to suit many different looks – the pieces don't even have to match unless you want them to. Stencilled patterns can transform wooden tables and chairs, while quirky items, such as the little side table with a wavy apron, will add interest to any scheme.

down the road. Fine antiques have their place, but you can do without if you want, remembering that period styles can be evoked by rustic, country pieces that have their own inherent appeal. Take advantage, too, of the various revivals that have taken place over the years, and buy Victorian-Medieval, or Edwardian-Georgian – it's a lot cheaper than the original and creates the style just as effectively.

Develop an eye for a bargain – second-hand pieces such as chests of drawers, tables, chairs, wardrobes and so on can be 'tarted up' with ease once you know how: stripping off old paint can be a revelation, or you could use a 'distressed' paint technique for a wonderfully worn and aged look, or create stencilled or free-painted patterns using acrylic paint. Fix on new knobs or handles, add mouldings, replace panelled doors with frosted glass, chicken wire or ruched fabrics, and you'll have a fabulous piece of furniture with a new lease of life that really evokes a certain style. You'll also have the satisfaction of knowing that you have

saved a fortune and achieved all this with your very own hands!

Last, but by no means least, allow comfort to be a priority rather than any over-the-top notions of pristine authenticity. Many historical styles, and some global ones, owe far less to considerations of comfortable seating than we do today – as you will find just by sitting on an upright Georgian chair for more than a few minutes. Convenience, then, will probably persuade you to add one or two more upholstered pieces than is strictly authentic, and if this is the case, look for plain lines and unobtrusive styles (revealing a wooden framework is often appropriate) and cover with suitable loose covers, throws and cushions. After all, designing to a style is one thing, but this is a look that you have got to live with, so ensure not only that you have followed the style to the degree which suits you, but also that it is practical, relaxing and appropriate for your lifestyle. Adapt and adopt the ideas that follow, be inspired and, most important of all, enjoy yourself.

Moroccan   Mediterranean   American Settler   Medieval   Victorian

1 Introduction
This opening page describes the essential character of each style. It details how and why the style arose, looks at the key figures in its development and summarizes any other influences – of history, geography or lifestyle.

2 Creating the look
This opening paragraph sums up at a glance which are the essential elements of each style. It gives, in broad terms, ideas on how to create the look in a modern home, and outlines which main features it is important to emphasize.

3 Walls, Floors, Lights
The practical sections on the next five pages offer advice and inspiration on how to achieve a look that evokes the spirit of a style. Suggestions for different treatments for walls and floors and ideas for lighting are given first of all.

4 Colours
Six colour swatches and a brief description provide a useful visual reminder of the key shades – whether used for paintwork or carpets, fabric or furniture – that play such an enormous role in creating the feel of an era or place.

FABRICS

For the epitome of country charm a broad mix of fabrics is desirable – the aim is for them to work well together without looking too co-ordinated. Choose cosy tweed and chenille, strong tartans and pretty lace for a variety of colour, pattern and texture, adding checks and, of course, a few floral patterns, all in nature-inspired, soft and faded colours.

LEFT A delicately pretty country bedroom, with bedlinen and curtains that mix pale floral designs for an informal look.

RIGHT The bold, all-over rose pattern and deeply frilled valances of this plump armchair and footstool are echoed in the festoon blind at the window of this welcoming, comfortable room.

look, while plain fabrics can be decorated using stencils or stamps with a countryside theme. Over-all, aim for an eclectic mix of lights that don't quite match, and you'll be well on your way to creating a friendly, informal and relaxing effect.

Soft furnishings
Patterns and colours that look too well matched are wrong – aim for an unstudied mixture, using inexpensive new fabric and pieces picked up in second-hand shops and jumble sales, or unpicked from old clothes. If they look gently worn that is all the better, and anything that appears overly bright and new can be soaked overnight in cold tea for an instant ageing effect.
The fabric that is most closely associated with the country look is chintz, with its colourful, complex designs of full-blown roses, parrot tulips, peonies, lilies and other flowers. Too much chintz, however, can be overpowering, and it's not suited to the more elemental, hard-working country look. You might also want to consider tweed, with its natural colours and interesting weave, tartans,

which are bright and warming, or plain and simple ginghams, or a selection of narrow stripes and tiny spots. Or how about paisley and other 'ethnic' fabrics; tapestry and crewel-work; fruit patterns; or plains in linen, wool, fleece, chenille, velvet, mohair and cashmere? And don't forget the last word in home-made pleasure – knitting and crochet. Even beginners can get instant gratification from making small squares in different colours and sewing them together.
Window treatments should, essentially, be fairly simple – just a pair of curtains, with a lace or muslin net underneath, generously gathered or pleated and perhaps with frilled edges. Pelmets suit grander, larger rooms; otherwise just use a wooden or wrought iron pole with pretty, understated finials. If your windows are draught-proof, leave the curtains unlined for a light, casual effect. As an alternative, you could use prettily ruched Austrian blinds, while the decorative potential of roller blinds can be increased by adding a contrast border, a shaped bottom edge or stencilled patterns. Soften the look with a shaped pelmet or sham curtains.

With this style there's no harm in upholstery that's a little worn, even sagging, and loose covers in chintz, corduroy or simple, plain canvas will do wonders to disguise a modern suite. Cover every sofa and armchair with piles of cushions, preferably with ones that don't match at all – use covers made from remnants, knitting, old blankets, kilims and so on. They should be as plump as possible, and if made of flowery fabric, you might want to add frilled edging. Then layer on a few throws, in the form of blankets, patchwork, paisley shawls or whatever takes your fancy. Cover side tables with floor-length fabric and use shirred material (gingham is especially nice) to replace the doors of cupboards and wardrobes. Bedlinen, too, looks best when it's piled layer upon layer. For the full effect,

start with flowered or coloured sheets, then add embroidered, lace-edged or flowery duvet covers, soft blankets and pillowcases with old-fashioned button- or tie-fastenings. Finally, top with a knitted bedcover or a pretty patchwork quilt.

Accessories
There are any number of extra touches that will transform most homes into a comfortable, cosy cottage. Piles of ancient hard-backed books, or even old Penguin classics, add an informal literary touch, and on the walls hang framed needlepoint samplers, hunting prints, watercolour landscapes and wood-block illustrations. On all available surfaces gather family photographs in silver or wooden frames. You could arrange floral or blue and white china,

ABOVE A dresser, however simple, allows you to display country-style crockery in assorted colours and styles. Distressed paintwork adds to the effect.

creamware or spongeware on shelves and dressers in rows or attractive groups. Display home-made jams, chutneys and pickles, along with jelly moulds, copper pans, cider jars and bread crocks. Gardening equipment can be attractive as well as useful – consider trugs, a cast iron wellington boot remover, a metal watering can and a besom broom, for example. Use wicker baskets of all sizes and shapes for storage – fruit, magazines, logs for the fire; show off any old-fashioned toys such as a rocking horse or a doll's house; use boxes and bowls to hold pine cones and pot pourri and, finally, arrange plenty of fresh flowers in simple containers – jam jars or enamel ewers, for example – to give you a scent of the country, wherever you happen to live.

Furniture
English country furniture is hard-wearing, honest and effortlessly attractive. The essential look is a combination of Georgian and Victorian, updated with more recent pieces – simple, sturdy and not too delicate. The aim is a handed-down, faded appearance that looks both well-loved and lived-in, so you can mix antiques with junk-shop finds, old with new. Arrange them around the fire or in casual groups, and if things get a little knocked-about, don't worry. Mend rather than replace, and cover anything that's badly battered with a layer of paint.

Avoid materials that are too twentieth-century – matt black, chrome and plastic should be banned – and try to find old pine rather than new as it is so much more solid and good-looking. Oak, elm, mahogany and cane are also appropriate. Look for comfortable, squashy sofas in timeless styles, mixed with armchairs that have room enough to curl up in, rocking chairs, ottomans, and plain wooden settles and stools. Dining chairs can have ladder, splat or spindle backs, and are best gathered around a huge, scrubbed-pine table, while a large, open dresser is pretty much an essential.
There are various ways to cheat in order to achieve this style, and if you haven't got a dresser a good idea is to hang rows of shelves above a wooden cupboard. Distressed paintwork is most effective for an instantly worn-out (but attractive) surface finish, and limewashing has a similar feel. Further tricks include lining the insides of cupboards with floral or polka-dot wallpaper, and replacing solid doors with chicken wire or gathered, checked fabric. Good quality pieces, however, should always be left untouched.
In the bedroom, a wooden four-poster or a Victorian metal bedstead are really attractive and in keeping, but a modern bed can easily be disguised with layers of flouncy bedlinen. Bathrooms benefit from the unfitted look – a deep, cast-iron roll-top bath is perfect, but modern bathrooms with standard suites can be transformed by the clever use of fabrics, accessories and the odd piece of free-standing furniture such as a wooden towel rail or a washstand complete with pitcher and bowl.
In the kitchen, choose cupboards with plain or panelled doors, large metal hinges and round, wooden or ceramic knobs. The most appropriate worksurfaces would be made of wood or tiles, complemented by a butcher's block, splashbacks made of brightly coloured ceramic tiles (farmyard scenes are particularly suitable), a large Belfast sink with brass taps and a wooden plate rack. Hang mugs, pans and implements from hooks and, if there's room, a central rack. If you are lucky enough to have a range oven, make the most of it, as it really does epitomize the country style.

For an idyllic English cottage look, there's nothing better than pale colours, floral patterns and a comfortable arrangement of unpretentious furnishings.

Summing up the style

1 Creamy walls are relaxed and attractive, and complement the soft colours of the furnishings.

2 A soft carpet underfoot can be essential for warmth and comfort in this type of interior. Dark floorboards are also very appropriate.

3 This hanging light is simple and charming; the table lamp on the chest of drawers to the left has more obvious prettiness. The fact that they don't match is an advantage rather than a problem.

4 A patchwork throw combined with floral upholstery is nicely informal and the cushions fit in well without looking deliberately co-ordinated.

5 These dining chairs are of a totally timeless 'farmhouse kitchen' style. Neither they, nor the old-fashioned armchair, the dresser or the chest of drawers match, giving a sense of family furniture collected over the years.

6 A collection of crockery displayed in a cabinet is really appealing. Other lovely touches are the prints, the basket and pitcher (in the background) and jugs of fresh garden flowers.

5 Soft furnishings, Accessories
Continuing with practical advice and inspiration, information on soft furnishings includes window treatments, upholstery and bedlinen. Accessories looks at the finishing touches that really help make a style work.

6 Fabrics
A selection of fabric swatches form another visual reminder, this time offering examples of the types of fabric, and the colours, patterns and textures, that can be used in order to build up a particular look.

7 Furniture
Rounding off the practical advice section is a guide to choosing the furniture that creates a style, with regard to comfort, convenience and budget – as well as ideas for dealing with 'awkward' rooms such as bathrooms and kitchens.

8 Summing up the style
Concluding each chapter is an easy-to-follow yet exciting and inspiring annotated photograph that sums up all the important elements of a style, showing how they can be realistically combined for an authentic and attractive effect.

Historical styles

Medieval

Interiors across Europe were largely similar during the Middle Ages, influenced in style by the French court and the powerful church; indeed, domestic decoration differed only from that of places of worship in its greater emphasis on warmth and comfort.

Many homes consisted of just one room, and even in those large enough to provide separate quarters for kitchens, store rooms, servants and animals, all day-to-day activities took place in one large, central hall, including eating and even communal sleeping – it was only in the second half of the twelfth century that a few of the grander houses began to feature a private room, called a solar, for the lord and his family.

Open to the timber arches that supported the roof, the great hall was cold and draughty. The focal point in this all-purpose room was the fire, placed in the centre of the room, where smoke escaped as best it could through gaps in the roof. At one end of the hall was a platform on which stood a high, fixed dining table, for the more important members of the household. Behind them were hangings, for added warmth, and above the chair of the highest-ranking person was a canopy, symbolic of his status but also, perhaps, originating in the need for protection from bird droppings! At the opposite end of the room was a large, heavy, wooden screen, probably painted and often highly carved, similar to those found in churches of the period. This screen served a very practical purpose: to block the cold winds which would otherwise have whistled in constantly through the doors behind it.

Windows in medieval homes were small, which was just as well because glass was extremely expensive and rooms were frequently left open to the elements. In better-off households, however, the lower halves of windows were protected with

Providing warmth was the focus of life in a medieval home, and although furniture was sparse and relatively plain, painted walls, bright hangings and rich fabrics gave comfort and colour, making for a feeling of robust vigour and earthy simplicity.

iron bars and shutters and the upper portions glazed, using small panes in a removable frame. The ability to pack up and move their furnishings was essential to the medieval gentry, who spent much of their time visiting widely scattered strongholds and whose household could number up to a hundred. The risk of theft was great when owners were absent, so pieces of furniture tended either to be built-in – benches, wardrobes or tables attached to the walls – or easily dismantled so that they could be packed into chests and transported by horse and cart to another property. Thus arose the French word for furniture, *meubles*, meaning anything movable.

Such a peripatetic lifestyle resulted in the emphasis being placed on textiles rather than furniture to create a comfortable interior. By arranging tapestries, hangings, cushions, seat covers and carpets, a home could instantly be transformed upon its owner's arrival, turning a draughty, often damp, building into a welcoming home full of rich textures and glorious colours.

CREATING THE LOOK

Medieval style is highly appealing for its simple furniture, strong colours and luxurious textiles. Even side by side with today's modern comforts, it is still possible to recreate the essential elements of this way of life, combining wood, wrought iron and rich fabrics, all with familiar heraldic and Gothic motifs, to result in a satisfyingly vibrant atmosphere.

Walls

Medieval walls were often highly decorated and covered with wall-hangings made of tapestry or plain or painted cloth (see Soft Furnishings for further details). For a really authentic look, start by skimming walls roughly with plaster, then cover with chalky white, warm red, ochre, soft green or blue paint – avoiding too perfect a finish. This surface, particularly in the more important rooms, would have been decorated in a variety of ways. You could mark it out with thin red lines to represent stonework, or paint repeated patterns, extended freely across beams, doorways and window frames, using typical medieval motifs such as shields, crowns, rampant lions, griffons, fleurs de lys, roses and quatrefoils. Or you could emulate the Gothic lettering of illuminated manuscripts, painting Latin words confidently around

ABOVE Striking stone-block walls could easily be emulated with a clever paint technique or the use of *faux* wallpaper. Huge candlesticks, too, are not hard to find these days.

the tops of the walls. Wallpaper, if printed with suitable motifs, makes a good substitute for hand-painted designs.

The really adventurous may want to try their hand at a mural – representational pictures were often painted straight on to walls, even in the humblest homes – based on biblical, historical or pastoral themes. Alternatively, use wood panelling (widely used for insulation throughout northern Europe at this time), painted in a bright colour, perhaps green – a favourite of Henry III – blood red or gold. Finally, if you prefer a plainer effect, off-white or stone-coloured paint would work equally well as a backdrop to this style.

Floors

The simplest of medieval floors was basic beaten earth, covered with rushes and bents (sweet-smelling wild plants) that were watered regularly to keep down the dust. Wealthier homes had hard plaster flooring, while stone slabs and wide wooden boards, usually oak, were found in grander properties. Broad reclaimed boards, with their patina of age, make a particularly nice choice today. Tiling became widespread in the fourteenth century, and often consisted of red tiles inlaid with white in various patterns. Plain, square, modern unglazed tiles look very appropriate – black, red, white, yellow and blue are all suitable.

For a little more comfort underfoot, larger medieval houses sometimes used 'Egyptian matting', made of rushes plaited together. This look can easily be copied with any of the modern natural floorcoverings – sisal, coir, jute or rush. This is the best option if you like wall-to-wall carpets as, generally speaking, floor carpeting as we know it did not exist in the Middle Ages. Instead, such carpets as did exist, imported from Persia and Turkey, were almost always displayed draped over tables, chests and sideboards – an interesting touch if you want to maintain a true period feel.

Lights

Candlelight makes the most appropriate setting for a medieval-style interior. The great hall of the Middle Ages was lit mainly by its central fire, together with brands soaked in oil or pitch which were mounted in cressets, iron baskets on the

ABOVE This atmospheric fitting shows how even the most medieval of looks can be achieved while retaining the convenience of electricity.

walls. The poorest people made do without any artificial light, though farmers used rushes dipped in tallow, a fatty product extracted from sheep and cattle. Wealthy households were able to afford beeswax candles. The first floor-standing candle holders, ancestors of our standard lamp, were in the form of a tripod-based spike, called a pricket. Then came torchères, which could display up to 20 candles in iron rings of descending size. Similar constructions, though made centuries later, can be hunted out in antiques shops today, or you could commission a craftsperson to make one to your own design. They look very impressive, but do ensure the base is heavy, so it cannot be knocked over easily. For overhead lighting, candles were fixed on to iron spikes set in a rough wooden

COLOURS

The medieval interior was extremely rich, using deep hues that gave a sumptuous impression. Although colours were produced from natural dyes, they could still be startlingly bright. Warm russet red, ochre yellow, strong green and vivid blue should predominate, offset with natural stone and a little black plus, of course, gold for a dazzling accent.

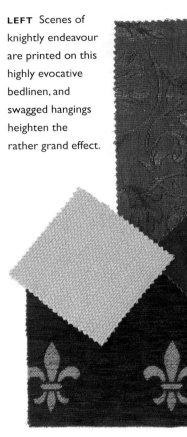

LEFT Scenes of knightly endeavour are printed on this highly evocative bedlinen, and swagged hangings heighten the rather grand effect.

beam, a crude invention that developed into an early chandelier, made from a square or circle of iron and hung by chains from the roof. These styles were still made in the nineteenth century and you will often find something similar in the shops today, perhaps conveniently wired for electricity. In general, look out for candle holders in the simplest of designs, made of iron, wood, brass, bronze or pewter. To supplement overall levels of light, choose simple, wood or metal fittings and table lamps with an old-fashioned air, or use the most unobtrusive modern lights you can find.

Soft furnishings

Textiles were the most important element of a medieval home, easy to transport, essential for warmth and comfort and also providing a very welcome air of luxury.

The wealthier the household, the more expensive the fabric, of course, and the richest houses made great use of lavish tapestry wall-hangings. Depicting scenes of battle and courtly love, Bible stories and histories, or sometimes with a *mille fleurs* (thousand flowers) pattern, they mostly originated in France and the Low Countries, the most famous coming from Arras in Artois, northern France. Ready-made tapestries in various styles are available today, as are tapestry-prints and kits with which you can stitch your own.

Hangings weren't just made from tapestry, however. Other fabrics were frequently used, from the roughest canvas to the finest silk, either left plain or painted with simple patterns or scenes – when they were called 'stayned cloths'. This allows for a great deal of flexibility when aiming for a similar look – choose your cloth to suit your pocket, keep

FABRICS

Deep, rich colours and heavy, luxurious fabrics are what make medieval style so vibrant and sumptuous. Plain velvets and chenilles in bold, strong hues mix happily with the more complex pictorial patterns of tapestries and twining floral designs to create an authentic look, while gold fleurs de lys and printed text (in Latin) add to the overall effect.

to medieval colours, and you can't go wrong. Either attach the hangings to the walls with metal rings, or suspend them from wooden or metal poles, covering just one wall or maybe even a whole room.

Hangings were also used around beds, hung from wooden rails and gathered into bags at the corners when not in use. This look is relatively easy to copy, and can be emphasized with the addition of quantities of sheets, blankets and pillows to emulate the piles of bedlinen that would have been used in a well-off medieval home. The same desire for comfort also gave rise to large numbers of feather-filled cushions on stools, chests and chairs, while seats were also covered with pieces of loose material, called bancoves or bankers, and their backs sometimes hung with lengths of fabric known as dorsars. In this vein,

add a touch of luxury to your medieval-style room by buying or making cushion covers or seat hangings in damask or velvet, with patterns of fleurs de lys, heraldic animals and quatrefoils, and perhaps embroidered with metallic thread or embellished with gold braiding, piping and tassels.

The medieval hall owed its integrated appearance to its soft furnishings: a collection of all these hangings, covers, cushions and curtains was known as a chamber and the fabrics and colours were carefully mixed to create a pleasing effect. To complete your look, create suitable window treatments. Though curtains as we know them did not exist in the Middle Ages, it would be appropriate to use just a single curtain, simply gathered or tab-headed and hung from rings on a wooden or metal pole with fleur de lys or spearhead finials. Velvet, brocade and silk damask look wonderfully rich and fine, but the fabric need not necessarily be expensive – plain wool or linen, if heavily draped and held back with a huge tassel will still appear suitably sumptuous.

Accessories

Decorative items were not a priority in the Middle Ages, when possessions reflected wealth and importance rather than personal taste. There are, however, some finishing touches that you can add which will give a period feel without going over the top. Though your savings are more likely to be in a bank account than in the form of tableware, you can echo the medieval custom of displaying wealth by arranging metal plates, cups, flagons and dishes on open shelving. Complement these with plain earthenware jugs, bowls and vases, and eating and drinking vessels made of turned wood, especially sycamore, ash or cherry. Cooking pots in brass, bronze and iron also make a good display, along with bunches of herbs hung from the ceiling and iron implements by the fire. Hang tassels, which were used as adornments on church vestments, for curtain tie-backs, and arrange giant wood or metal candle holders around the room. Heraldic devices – rampant lions, crowns, spheres, shields and stylized flowers – look good on any accessory, as do the Gothic pointed arch and trefoil and quatrefoil shapes, while gargoyle figures – the grotesque carvings used as waterspouts on churches and other medieval buildings – always add an element of wit and humour.

Furniture

Furniture in the Middle Ages was basic by today's standards, but the simplicity of the style means that unfussy wooden furniture made in different eras will often fit in well, and the end result is a suitably plain, elemental feel.

ABOVE A tapestry hanging and display of pewterware provide suitably medieval embellishments to this solid, dark and heavy reproduction furniture.

Simple stools, chests, benches and trestle tables were the staple items, arranged in a haphazard fashion or pushed back against the walls to create space. Stools were either in the common square shape or the x-shaped folding version. Chairs were rare, used only by the head of the household, and tables were often just wooden boards on trestles, with benches for the diners. A simple planked construction was the norm for all these pieces, although in later years the Gothic style of architecture that swept across Europe was echoed in furniture design, and carving became more common in wealthier homes. Today, antique or new 'country style' furniture, preferably of oak and keeping to the simplest possible shapes, makes the best choice.

Chests and coffers, usually brightly painted and often embellished with ironwork, were used extensively during the Middle Ages. In a modern home, large wooden chests make excellent storage for blankets, linen or clothes, or even for work files, little-used crockery or children's toys. And, with a plump cushion on top, they can double as extra seating. Other types of medieval storage to emulate are the hutch, a long side table with a cupboard underneath; the aumbry, or armoire, a free-standing or built-in cupboard with doors and sometimes shelves and/or drawers; and the buffet, which had stepped, open shelves used to display plate or for serving wine. This type of open shelving – literally a 'cup board' – a visual reminder of the household's wealth, is the easiest to copy today, and is highly effective when filled with a collection of medieval-style tableware.

Although most medieval furniture was roughly treated, the bed was treasured as an important indicator of prestige. While most people had to make do with a straw-filled mattress on the floor, the next step up was a basic, easy-to-take-apart structure, and the wealthiest owned a wooden bedstead with carved or turned posts. Hangings and tapestries were suspended from rails around the bed for privacy, and in the thirteenth century a canopy, or tester, was slung above it to indicate high rank. Eventually the curtains and canopy became attached to the posts, and so evolved the four-poster bed. Today, hangings made from suitable fabrics around and above your bed (see Soft Furnishings) will create an instant medieval effect. Keep other bedroom furniture to a minimum, using chests, chairs and simple cupboards in the same style as other rooms in the house. Remember that sleeping arrangements in the Middle Ages were basic, to say the least – in fact the only other item of furniture to be found in a medieval bedroom (when such a separate room existed, which was rare) was a 'perch', or rod, on which to hang clothes. Sometimes there might even have been two perches – the other for the owner's falcon!

The plank door with its heavy metalwork and the flagstone floor set the scene in this large hallway. The result is medieval in feel, but comfortable to live with.

Summing up the style

1 Roughly plastered walls painted in a warm stone colour provide an elemental background.

2 Large stone flags are both hard-wearing and good-looking. Unvarnished wooden boards, tiles or natural matting would also be appropriate.

3 A simple lantern, though not strictly medieval, is in an appropriate style.

4 The medieval hall was hung with rich-looking fabrics in vibrant colours – an essential for warmth and comfort. This gathered drape makes a dramatic contrast to the adjacent bare wall.

5 A plain wooden chest is typical of the basic furniture used in the Middle Ages. Chests like this can be used for all sorts of storage, and also as extra seating. The chair is relatively grand for this style, but does not seem out of place.

6 Antique antlers mounted on shield-shaped backs make an excellent finishing touch. Also very much in keeping would be a display of metal plates and flagons, or earthenware bowls and jugs.

Tudor

Political stability and international trade brought increased prosperity for many in the sixteenth century and, as the merchant classes grew richer, an unprecedented building boom took place. Extra storeys were added to homes, thanks to the fact that the fireplace – instead of venting through the roof – was now set against an outside wall or had an internal flue. So arose, for the first time, rooms that served separate functions. Correspondingly, new types of furniture were designed for these new sitting rooms, dining rooms and bedrooms, including the draw-leaf table, ornate four-poster beds, several types of comfortable chair and varieties of cupboards.

The fact that rooms were no longer blackened with soot led directly to the introduction of the decorated ceiling. Suspended ceilings were first introduced in the late fifteenth century, when the undersides of floor joists were covered with thin, plastered boarding, sometimes with a cornice to cover the join. Even poor households decorated their joists with mouldings, while the well-off employed ornamental strapwork, a form of carved or moulded plaster that imitated cut leather in a series of interlacing, strap-like bands. Originating in Antwerp, strapwork patterns were widely used in the sixteenth century, not just for ceilings but also for fireplaces (a focal point for decoration, reflecting the household's status and wealth), staircases and wall paintings.

The increased availability of glass resulted in one of the most recognizable elements of the sixteenth-century house: windows with transoms (horizontal bars) and mullions (vertical posts) within which small panes of blown glass were held by lead bars, usually in rectangular or diamond shapes. Stained glass also became very popular, often featuring heraldic motifs. Homes were now much lighter

Dramatic changes took place in people's homes during the Tudor period. There was a new emphasis on comfort, convenience and decoration – overall, rich colours, elaborate patterns and ornate furniture created a bold and impressive effect.

and brighter, bringing a new incentive to devise more sophisticated decoration.

Much of the inspiration for interiors of this time came from the ideals of the Renaissance, the revival of interest in ancient Greek and Roman culture which began in Italy and spread throughout Europe (aided by the invention of printing) in the fifteenth and sixteenth centuries. Homes began to adopt classical ornamentation, including columns, acanthus scrolls, vases and vine leaves. Such designs extended from murals, furniture and textiles to metalwork, pottery and jewellery, and were at their purest in the large Italian trading cities. From there they spread to France and the Low Countries and, for a short while, to England. When Henry VIII broke with Rome in 1535, however, first-hand experience of new developments was denied to English designers, who had to rely on immigrant craftspeople and pattern books by German and Flemish engravers. The English style of Shakespeare's time was, therefore, rather different from that of the rest of Europe, combining an individual interpretation of Renaissance decoration with the continued use of forms popular since the Middle Ages.

CREATING THE LOOK

The Tudor home was bare by our standards but enlivened with rich upholstery, tapestry, hangings and carpets. Furniture was both sturdy and well-designed, often featuring elaborate inlay, gilding and carving. Create the look with nineteenth-century or modern reproductions, emphasizing warm and welcoming colours and an ornate style.

Walls

In this period walls were often largely composed of timber panelling. Use square or rectangular panels, made of thin oak boards, extended to dado, frieze or ceiling height – they can be plain or carved in linenfold, arabesque, foliage or strap-work designs. Alternatively, apply moulded battens to create geometric shapes, inlay woods of contrasting colours or stencil the panels with swirling patterns or classical motifs. Leave a gap above the panelling for a painted frieze, featuring arms and heraldic devices, your initials or the five-petalled Tudor rose. If the panelling reaches only to dado level, suspend embroidered wall-hangings or tapestries (see Soft Furnishings for more ideas) or else paint the plasterwork. Plain red, blue or green would be appropriate, as would intricate geometric patterns interspersed with flowers, landscapes and hunting scenes, historical stories or a trompe-l'oeil effect simulating cloth, hardwood, marble or stone.

A more basic background can be achieved by

ABOVE Faded rugs and coir matting laid on a hard floor are earthy and ancient in appearance. Thick beams stand out marvellously against distempered walls.

using chalky whitewash – a slightly off-white modern paint will do – or maybe a warm red, stone, soft blue or green. Alternatively, create the look of mellow oak woodwork using paint effects or one of the trompe-l'oeil wallpapers now available. A minority of houses at this time had walls papered with black and white woodblock prints, in the form of imitation fabric, heraldic motifs or repeated shields, vases and flowers. An original look in this spirit can be achieved by using enlarged photocopies from a copyright-free source, and colouring them in by hand as was the sixteenth-century custom.

Floors

Rushes were sprinkled over floors well into the sixteenth century, but more typical was rush matting, stitched in lengths and nailed at the edges.

This look can easily be achieved with a modern natural flooring such as sisal or coir, available both as wall-to-wall carpets and as rugs. You could add one or two oriental rugs, remembering that they were still a rare luxury, and were most frequently used as table and cupboard coverings and for wall-hangings. On the rare occasions that they were laid on the floor, however – as is evident from the fact that a distinction was made between 'borde' carpets and 'ffote' carpets – it was often beside the bed. More common as a floorcovering, however, was dornix, a woollen cloth with stripes or a small pattern that can be imitated today with any simple woven rug in suitable colours.

For the flooring itself, use brick, tiles – boldly patterned, glazed or plain – or flags made of stone, including York stone, granite, slate, sandstone and marble. Flags in varying colours were occasionally laid in patterns, and when worn it was common to turn them over and re-use them. Upstairs, wood was the norm, usually oak, but sometimes elm or imported fir. Try to find boards that are wider than normal (reclaimed flooring is a good option), and don't be overly concerned about dents, marks or scratches – they only add to the character.

Lights

Lighting had developed little since the Middle Ages, and rushes or tallow candles, erratic, smoky and foul-smelling, were still usual – unless you were very poor, in which case you rose and slept by the sun. The only important change was that candles were no longer pushed on to a spike, but were held within a stick. Designs were simple at first – a circular base with central support – and then developed into more elaborate branched affairs which could hold a number of candles at once, spreading their light further around the

ABOVE A metal coronet provides a stand for five 'candles', which give off a reasonable amount of soft light.

room. Choose simple shapes in wood, iron, pewter, brass, bronze or silver for chandeliers, wall sconces, table lamps and floor lights, or perhaps plain ceramic bases, with very simple parchment or fabric shades. Huge, church-style candlesticks are very suitable, or you could look for fittings which feature classical designs such as vines, acanthus leaves, urns or columns.

COLOURS

Rich, jewel-like colours are one of the elements that make this style so enjoyable to live with. Uninhibited use of lavish paintwork and sumptuous fabrics make for an interior that is highly ornate, featuring bold combinations of crimson, orange, yellow, turquoise, indigo, sky blue, pink, purple, green and mid-brown, highlighted by glittering gold and silver.

Soft furnishings

Textiles in this era were not as vital a part of the decorative effect as they had been in the Middle Ages; nevertheless, they continued to be extremely important, and are one of the easiest ways to emulate this style in a modern home. Favourite fabrics in the sixteenth century were damask, velvet, silk and brocade, and there is a wide choice of patterns: hunting scenes, fables, mythological and Bible stories remained popular, and a newly developed interest in gardening and botany meant that a great many Elizabethan fabrics featured naturalistic or stylized flowers, fruit and foliage.

Wall-hangings were used everywhere, taking various forms according to the wealth of the householder. Tapestries, produced in England, France and, especially, Brussels, were a popular status symbol in better-off homes – Henry VIII owned more than 2000 – and it is possible today to obtain contemporary prints which imitate the look, as well as ready-made tapestries and sew-it-yourself kits. Flamestitch fabrics, with dramatic zigzags of graduating colours, are also appropriate. On a simpler level, however, linen painted in imitation of tapestry featured widely as a cheap decorative device in less well-off homes, as did woollen cloth with a twill weave, which was known as say. Wool, linen, or any other inexpensive cloths are a good alternative for wall-hangings or, equally, used for curtains.

Such window treatments as did exist in this era were very plain and basic. To emulate them, use a length of fabric, gathered or tab-headed, on a pole with spherical, fleur de lys, arrow-shaped or scrolled finials, pulled to one side and held with a tassel or wrought iron tie-back.

Other forms of sixteenth-century fabric treatments included embroidery, appliqué and crewelwork (the last widely available again today), all of which were frequently employed for bed-hangings. A sumptuous bed is an important element of this look, and while expensive fabrics were popular at the time, cheaper cloth will do just as well if thickly draped and bordered with tassels and fringes. For authenticity, create matching cloth panels, called bed valances, to hide the rails from which the hangings around your bed are suspended.

During this period it became more common for the fabrics, colours and patterns of wall-hangings, bed curtains and upholstery to be matched in order to produce an integrated look. Upholstery was still far from being as comfortable as it is today, but seats were often padded and covered with leather, velvet, worn tapestries or an imitation of Turkish rugs known as turkeywork. Seats were embellished with fringes and tassels, and topped with square cushions, while large floor cushions were also much in use – Elizabeth I is recorded as having once spent four days reclining on hers. To recreate this elegantly over-the-top effect, co-ordinate richly coloured fabrics, especially velvets, silk damasks and brocades, and fill your rooms with well-padded cushions of all shapes and sizes, adding silver or gold tassels and piping or deep fringing for a true touch of luxury.

Accessories

The small touches that will help create the look of a Tudor home should feature a combination of medieval motifs, such as heraldic images, fleurs de lys, trefoils and quatrefoils, and Renaissance ornamentation, including strapwork, acanthus and vine leaves, mythological creatures, vases, dolphins, Corinthian columns and medallions surrounded by wreaths. The main display of possessions consisted of open shelves lined with drinking vessels,

FABRICS

Many Elizabethan fabrics featured flowers, fruit and foliage; a Tudor rose, as here, is particularly appropriate. Flame-stitch and crewel-work, too, are very evocative of the sixteenth century, and these intricate patterns can be balanced with small geometric repeats and plains. Fabrics are heavy and sumptuous – velvets and wools, for example, would make good choices.

plates, spoons, bowls and candlesticks made of pewter, brass or silver. A collection of just three or four pewter plates makes an instant impression, while modern recycled glass is a wonderful substitute for the thick green cast glass of the era, which was usually to be found arranged on top of buffets. Earthenware glazed in black, green or yellow was common, while wealthier homes may have had a little Islamic pottery or Chinese porcelain. Small, many-drawered spice chests provide handy storage, and you can reflect candlelight in mirrors with carved gilt frames. Use heavy gold frames, too, for naïve animal paintings and portraits of historical figures. Thick, leather-bound books look wonderful arranged in casual piles, and wrought iron gives a suitably period feel, in the form of a fire basket and hearth accessories, or large hinges,

ABOVE Sometimes old, knocked-about furniture is better at creating a style than new pieces, as this rugged table-top demonstrates. The carpet on the sideboard is a nice touch.

locks and straps on doors and chests. You could also add one or two metal pomanders, their filigree decoration allowing sweet scents to permeate the room.

Furniture

As furniture achieved greater status in the newly prosperous homes of this era its quality and quantity increased. It was now considered a true part of a room's decorative scheme and, because it no longer had to be packed away and moved at regular intervals, it became both more solid and more sophisticated, featuring joinery, turning and carving, inlays, gilding, painted patterns and strapwork.

In Italy, where the Renaissance was at its height, furniture was at its most ornate, and techniques were developed such as elaborate carving, gilding, intarsia – inlaid ivory or bone, and *pietre dure* – inlay using marble, pebbles, lapis lazuli and other stones. Mother of pearl, silver and tortoiseshell were also incorporated into furniture, and the fashion for such luxuries spread throughout Europe.

Such extravagance, however, is not absolutely necessary in order to recreate the style of the period. The average home still contained little in the way of luxury, especially in the British Isles, where the excesses of the Renaissance were tempered by lack of direct contact with Italy. This is

the style on which it is best to concentrate. Look for suitable reproductions, either nineteenth-century or modern-day, made of native woods such as oak, walnut, chestnut or beech. Really well-made pieces are expensive but will last a lifetime; if, however, your budget cannot stretch that far, disguise cheaper furniture with a mid-brown stain, paint it red, blue, green or black, or use some judicious gilding (or gold paint) for a more sumptuous look.

The most highly prized item in every household remained the bed, now usually a feather-filled mattress within a wooden four-poster with heavily carved, bulbous footposts – often in the shape known as cup-and-cover – and wainscoted headboard supporting a canopy and curtains. Cardinal Wolsey had 280 beds at Hampton Court and, in fact, beds were considered such a status symbol that people often received guests while lying in them! If you can afford such an eye-catching bed it will create a marvellous effect; a less expensive option, however, is to surround a standard bed with luxurious fabrics hung from rails attached to the ceiling (see Soft Furnishings for more ideas).

Other furniture came in the form of settles, high-backed wooden benches; court cupboards, two- or three-tiered open shelves for displaying crockery and glassware; and presses, tall cupboards with doors, for clothing, bedlinen, books and valuables. Seek out pieces such as these, then add some chests, carved and fitted with iron studs and hinges, a selection of simple stools, not necessarily matching in style, and a fixed-leg dining table, which had replaced the movable trestle. For a little more comfort, high-backed, carved and panelled chairs are authentic, in various forms including the x-shape, the *caquetoire*, or gossip chair which had a trapezoid seat and wide arms to fit ladies' skirts, and the back stool, or farthingale chair, which had no arms but a padded back and seat. Chairs were often upholstered in silk or velvet, trimmed with gold or silver fringe and topped with cushions, and the use of rich fabrics – in the form of a loose cover to disguise a piece that doesn't quite fit in – is a good short cut to creating the right impression in a modern-day scheme.

By now, rooms had become both more comfortable to live in and noticeably more sumptuous in appearance – as is evident from this warm and inviting dining room.

Summing up the style

1 A chalky, off-white paint colour on roughly plastered walls always looks appropriate when creating the effect of a centuries-old style.

2 This oriental rug in rich, deep colours has a grand, luxurious look. Underneath, uneven flagstones are absolutely typical.

3 Simply shaped metal wall lights with plain, parchment-coloured shades make a good choice for Tudor style. Adding candles in wooden or wrought iron sticks would increase the atmosphere at night.

4 Padded upholstery became more widespread in this period, and fabrics were often matched to provide a co-ordinated look. Heraldic patterns such as this add to the overall feeling of opulence.

5 Nothing could be more typical of the Tudor age than this cupboard with doors below and a display area above. Its sophisticated turning and carving are echoed in the matching table and chairs.

6 'Plate' displayed in a cupboard or on a shelf is a perfect accessory; the coloured glassware on the table, in an old-fashioned style, is another nice touch.

Baroque

The Baroque style first developed in Rome after about 1620, as part of the attempt by the Catholic church to regain ground lost to the recent rise in Protestantism. Dramatic, expressive paintings and sculptures and splendid new buildings were intended to reinforce the power and authority of the church, but the style soon became as much a setting for earthly glorification as spiritual inspiration, developing into an extravagant means for families to display their secular wealth.

Imaginative, vigorous and extreme, Baroque was designed to surprise and impress. Its theatrical grandeur made great use of the art of illusion, featuring jewel-like colours, trompe-l'oeil paintwork and the dazzling glitter of silver, gilt and crystal. Furniture was amazingly opulent, its swelling curves and massive forms enhanced by gilding, marquetry and inlays. Textiles were luxurious and expensive, draped and swagged to emphasize their richness, while typically exotic decorative effects included acanthus leaves, shells, cherubs, garlands of fruit and flowers, crowns, dolphins and swirling scrolls. Far Eastern artefacts played a major part in these schemes, the European nations having recently developed trading links with China and India, and few well-off households were without several items of lacquerware and chinoiserie, adding yet another element of the exotic to these already sumptuous interiors.

Baroque gradually took hold throughout aristocratic Italy and elsewhere, finding its most magnificent expression in Louis XIV's palace at Versailles, where the interior was designed by Charles Lebrun between 1671 and 1681. Bringing together the finest native and foreign talents, Lebrun's efforts resulted in new standards of taste and craftsmanship that were copied by every other court in Europe. He designed much of the furni-

Baroque art, architecture and interiors were highly prized throughout Europe in the seventeenth century, the name arising from the Portuguese term *barocca*, describing an irregular pearl – implying a flawed beauty, something precious and yet decadent.

ture, fabric, silver and sculpture himself, resulting in a unity of decoration deemed highly desirable.

The influence of Baroque reached the British Isles in the last quarter of the seventeenth century. Charles II's exile in France and Holland had given him a liking for luxury and comfort, and after his Restoration to the throne in 1660 Baroque splendour was embraced not only by his young, lively and forward-looking court, but also by the aristocracy and better-off merchants – no doubt it was seen as a pleasant antidote to the rigours of the Puritan era. Acceptance of the Baroque was aided by the fact that this was a time of growing national prosperity, with building and furniture-making carrying on apace (especially after the Great Fire of London in 1666), and immigrant craftsmen from Europe helped to disseminate the style's main features. It fell out of favour with the triumph of science and reason at the end of the seventeenth century, but not before its final flowering during the reign of William and Mary, whose continental tastes made sure that Baroque's dynamic, curvilinear forms and rich ornamentation featured in many of the greatest houses of the era.

CREATING THE LOOK

Although many stately homes are decorated in Baroque style, you don't need a huge palace to emulate the look.

A little inventiveness can transform even the smallest flat – start with some heavy, carved or gilded furniture, and then use colours, fabrics and reflective surfaces to achieve a glittering effect.

Walls

Baroque interiors were the first ever to be concerned with design and comfort, and it was during this period that rooms came to be seen as grand settings for social events. Consequently, only the poorest houses had plain walls. There are several choices of wall coverings that would suit the grand Baroque style. Wood panelling with an ornamental cornice was widespread, fitted above and below a dado rail, in square or rectangular shapes that were sometimes used to frame paintings or lacquer or leather panels. In common with the desire to exaggerate wealth and splendour, pine and fir were painted to resemble oak, oak to resemble walnut and many woods to look like marble or tortoiseshell. You could achieve this look by applying mouldings to a smooth plaster wall and painting with a *faux* finish of your choice, or by using a trompe-l'oeil-effect wallpaper that resembles wainscot, marble or fabric.

ABOVE These grandiose wall mouldings could be copied with clever paintwork, while suitably patterned vinyl or lino would give the look of marble flooring. A concentration of gilt gives an immediately Baroque feel.

Alternatively, paint a geometric design, with bold curlicues or flowers, a moral or heraldic theme or scenes of classical architecture, using glowing colours on a dark background. For a different look, you could use richly coloured and exotically patterned tapestry or fabric hangings, as were favoured by wealthy households, either continuous or in separate panels that are bordered in contrasting material and trimmed with fringing (see Soft Furnishings for more fabric ideas).

Floors

Flooring can continue the Baroque theme of strong colours and dramatic looks. At ground level, use stone flags, bricks or tiles, perhaps arranged in combinations of two or more colours to create a pattern. Black and white marbled floors were highly fashionable, and an easy way of copying this look at less expense is to use marbled lino tiles.

Upstairs, wooden floors are most suitable, in oak, pine or fir. Use plain boards or, again, several colours to create interesting patterns. Parquet would have been polished, but boards were cleaned with sand and water to show off the grain; use a modern matt sealant for a similar appearance without the effort. A popular treatment for wooden floorboards was to paint them with border patterns known as broderie: geometric designs which echoed those of contemporary parterre gardens. Rush matting and plain rugs in coarse materials look good in less formal rooms, while rich oriental carpets are suitable for more luxurious surroundings. In this era they were placed underneath the furniture as they were considered too expensive to be walked on – an arrangement which would allow you to show off your floorboards to their best advantage.

Lights

At this time, the poorest people still used rushes dipped in fat and held by a clip, the middle classes had tallow candles, but the wealthy employed wax candles, which gave a more constant light and smelt a great deal less pungent! Today, a theatrical Baroque feel can be greatly enhanced by the right choice of lighting – dim and flickering, it should be reflected from mirrors, metalwork and gilding.

COLOURS

This era favoured an unrestrainedly rich effect, created by sometimes startling combinations of deep red, indigo, dark green, raspberry, ochre yellow, purple, strong blue, umber and a range of earthy tones. Most essential, however, are plentiful touches of gold, which can be added everywhere in the form of gilding and will greatly enhance your desired atmosphere of intensity and grandeur.

Choose elaborate candle stands and branched candelabra made from turned or carved wood, brass, bronze, pewter or silver. A typical style featured a circular or flared, trumpet-shaped base, with a turned-effect stem and a drip tray mid-way down. A little extra light can be added with several sconces fixed to the wall. They could be silver or brass-coloured (metallic paint works wonders on cheaper fittings) with a metal or mirror back-plate

ABOVE An elaborate reproduction pendant candle holder in gleaming brass has the element of theatricality that is required for true Baroque style.

to reflect a gentle glow; while for pendant fittings fix a central chandelier in silver, brass, crystal or carved and painted or gilded wood. Hung low from the ceiling, one of these will create a wonderful atmosphere for an intimate dinner party.

Soft furnishings

This is a style where lavish hangings and upholstery can contribute enormously to the overall appearance: choose from a huge variety of textiles, from cotton, wool and leather to silk damask, velvet and brocade.

European trade with India and the Far East had a huge impact on the fabrics that were used in the seventeenth-century home. Indian cotton was a revelation because it was not only colourful but also colour-fast. It came woven in stripes or checks, or printed in vivid, multicoloured floral patterns – when it was known as pintadoes or chintes, from the Hindi word *chint*, meaning variegated. Western manufacturers soon began to reproduce similar block-printed designs, and cotton chintz became very popular for bed-hangings because it could be washed easily. Wealthier homes continued to use hangings of tapestry, velvet or silk damask, while the very richest householders preferred leather, which was stamped, tooled and occasionally gilded. Using these types of bold fabric for a Baroque scheme has an instant effect, while crewel-work on a linen background, featuring floral or arabesque patterns in softly coloured twisted wool, is an equally good, and very distinctive, alternative.

Other fabric patterns were generally exuberant and on a large scale: look for those featuring chinoiserie designs of dragons, winding trees, exotic flowers and leaves, birds and butterflies. The strapwork motifs found in plasterwork of the previous century were another popular fabric motif, especially for tapestry borders, appliqué and embroidery. Plenty of fabrics employed the gleam and glitter of metallic threads to great effect.

Beds were as extravagantly decorated as could be afforded. To create the right look, suspend hangings all around and cover the bed post finials with the same fabric. Trim with fringes or tassels and, if you want to really go over the top, place a cup on top of each post containing plumes of feathers. Add an upholstered headboard in matching fabric, and cover dressing tables in a floor-length, fringed cloth, with a smaller, protective toilette of washable linen, edged with lace, on top.

Although at the beginning of the seventeenth century curtains were still less usual than internal shutters, they gradually came into general use. Pairs of curtains took over from a single piece of fabric and, later, pull-up or festoon curtain made the most of sumptuous fabrics. Towards the end of the century the pelmet was introduced, and this was seen as a marvellous opportunity for yet more decoration. This, then, is a style where your window treatments can be fairly grandiose. You could choose a rectangular pelmet with side drapes, a wavy-edged pelmet with tasselled trim, a braided ruffle, or a pole swathed in two contrasting lengths of fabric.

Co-ordination was the latest fashion of the Baroque era, so you should aim to use the same fabrics, perhaps in different colourways, for your wall- and bed-hangings, table linen, curtains and upholstery. Matching cushion covers, perhaps embroidered with silver and gold thread, and with a large tassel at each corner, would round off the effect perfectly.

FABRICS

The deep colours and intricate patterns of crewel-work remained popular in this era, as did woven designs featuring fruit, flowers and other botanical themes. Silk damask, wool, linen and cotton are authentic, and large-scale designs predominate for a flamboyant look. These are bold schemes, matched by the boldest of soft furnishings.

Accessories

Three types of accessory are pre-eminent for the Baroque style. First, choose chinoiserie, or any objects, real or false, that have the look of the Far East. Lacquered boxes of various sizes, porcelain and figurines make wonderful displays, especially when grouped together for emphasis. Second, groupings of blue-and-white Delftware (originally made in imitation of Chinese Ming porcelain and all the rage throughout Europe in this era), are extremely effective. Pile different pieces on to chests, shelves and wall brackets, or arrange them along the stretchers under a cabinet – large vases and ginger jars are especially impressive, and also

look good in an unused fireplace. Third, silver, an abundant feature of Baroque thanks to the comparatively wealthy times, adds greatly to the atmosphere of riches and luxury; you could display teapots, plates and urns, for example.

The seventeenth-century mania for collecting meant that many other items were also put out on show, including precious stones, shells, geological specimens, manuscripts, coins and medals. Alongside these, decorative andirons in the fireplace, sturdy earthenware or salt-glazed jugs in generous, bulbous shapes, classical busts and brass cooking pans will fit in well. For complete accuracy hang your pictures and mirrors (in elaborate, gilded frames) so they are leaning forward – the better to reflect low, shimmering light and contribute to a room's atmosphere of sensuous vitality and unrestrained luxury.

Furniture

This was the first era in which furniture came to be seen as decorative and comfortable as well as useful. Typically heavily carved, painted and gilded, and frequently inlaid with expensive materials such as silver, ivory, tortoiseshell, mother of pearl and ebony, it was monumental in size, shape and form, intended blatantly to impress – and sometimes to shock, too.

Many Baroque pieces would be impossible to reproduce today without spending a fortune. Fine veneers and marquetry, silver and brass inlays, throne-like chairs and marble table-tops, with supports in the shape of cherubs, mermaids, titans, dolphins or eagles – none of them are exactly easy to come by. But don't worry. What's important is to stick to the spirit of the style in terms of shape and colour, giving an impression of luxury that may be out of all proportion to the amount of money you have actually spent. And you can fill in any gaps by emulating the plainer furniture that was used in less well-off households, in country homes and by those who weren't interested in fashion; solid and cubic in form, it was dark and utilitarian, and should blend in well with one or two more eye-catching items.

One typical piece of furniture that was developed in this era, and is still in widespread use today, is the Knole sofa. With high, cushioned arms that could be raised and lowered to form a day bed, it was one of the first examples of full upholstery, heralding a move towards greater comfort in the home. Though much seating was in the form of hard stools and benches, chairs were often upholstered, in velvet, leather, needlework, turkeywork (the imitation of Turkish rugs) or plain coarse cloth, with fringes attached by gilt nails. Try to find chairs with low, wide seats, high backs and scrolled arms, preferably made of oak or walnut, and highly polished rather than painted, and use a rich, heavy fabric to cover the seat and back. Wing chairs are suitable too, and so are chairs with caned seats and backs, a new fashion thanks to recent oriental explorations.

Lacquerwork, another import from the east, had an even greater impact on the Baroque interior. Lacquer cabinets were displayed on gilded or silvered stands, while screens were sometimes cut up to make other items of furniture such as tables, chairs and mirror frames. An imitation of lacquer, known as japanning, was all the rage, and became a suitable skill to be practised by well-bred young ladies. If you can find any examples of lacquered or japanned furniture it will add enormously to your effect.

Other pieces to look out for are gate-legged or draw-leaf tables, dressing tables, swing mirrors, writing desks and wardrobes, all of them new appearances during this century. Another new invention arose from the fact that people often placed smaller boxes inside a storage chest to make it easier to find things. Eventually the front of the chest was removed and the boxes pulled out (teardrop-shaped brass pulls were fashionable) along carved grooves – resulting in the chest of drawers. Beds still had pride of place, in four-poster or half-tester form, but since their woodwork had come to be completely covered with fabric, you can rely on flounced, fringed and tasselled cloth hangings to create the right look with minimal outlay.

This gilded room captures the dramatic, over-the-top effect that makes the Baroque style so distinctive.

Summing up the style

1 As a sign of social status, wallcoverings became more elaborate in the seventeenth century; these bold stripes have the appropriate amount of bold impact.

2 A richly coloured and patterned rug such as this is the obvious choice for a Baroque interior. Laid on top of honey-coloured flooring it is especially authentic.

3 Lighting in this style should be suitably theatrical, and the soft, dim glow of this large lamp, with its striking base and pleated silk shade, is just right.

4 An elaborate window treatment such as this is perfect. The effect of luxury can be achieved by using inexpensive fabrics in abundance, with plenty of gathers, drapes and trims.

5 Baroque furniture was imposing and impressive, much like this gilded wall table with its bulbous, curving legs and elaborate decoration. The same feel is achieved by the chair on the other side of the doorway.

6 Gilded mirrors are almost an essential to this look. Overall, the slightly oriental feel of the room is highly appropriate, while the huge blue-and-white jar under the table is another excellent accessory.

American Settler

Having crossed the Atlantic to escape poverty, war and religious persecution, the American settlers were greeted by inconceivably harsh conditions. In a vast and uncultivated land, where the weather could be fierce and communities were completely isolated, famine, disease and hostile native Indians were ever-present dangers. Security, then, was the first priority, and early homes were thrown up rapidly, in the form of wigwams, dug-outs, huts and wattle-and-daub cabins. But soon more substantial dwellings were built, made of a timber frame covered with lengths of overlapping planking – named clapboard due to the sound it made during construction – and with shingle roofs of white cedar. Initially homes were rectangular, then, as time and prosperity allowed, many householders added a lean-to extension, creating the familiar asymmetrical shape with a gable roof longer on one side than the other, called a saltbox house due to its likeness to the wooden salt container found in every colonial kitchen.

A typical New England house had low ceilings with exposed joists and beams, a central chimney and panelled doors and walls. Small windows, which were often positioned asymmetrically, were covered with oiled paper or wooden shutters, though grander houses featured casements with leaded panes of glass. The fireplace, often large in size, was the decorative focus of the living room, with a wooden frame, a brick hearth and cupboards on either side, planked so as to match the walls.

The settlers brought with them skills and traditions from all over Europe, and at first the interiors of their homes tended to replicate the familiar furnishings and decorations of their native countries. Gradually, however, the different styles of England, Germany, Scandinavia, Switzerland, the Netherlands, Ireland, Scotland and others were

When the colonists landed in North America in the early seventeenth century, little did they know that the distinctive interior style they developed, born of necessity but fuelled by creativity, would survive the centuries to inspire future generations.

intermingled, aided by journeying painters, carvers and decorators who transferred patterns, colours and techniques from one settlement to another, until eventually a unique look emerged – that of the New World.

Sturdy furnishings, uncomplicated and unpretentious, were made by the families themselves, who, while not necessarily being highly skilled, soon learnt how to adapt the materials available to their own tastes and requirements. There was an emphasis on practicality but, far from being stark and austere, the settlers' surroundings were frequently enriched with folk art and crafts: Scandinavian marriage gifts, German painted tinware, English quilting and weaving, and French and Italian glassware helped beautify these homes, as did the German tradition of carving and painting furniture. The settlers' creative impulses produced a wide variety of patterns, applied in bright colours to all sorts of furnishings and accessories. Two motifs, in particular, were widely used: the tulip, celebrated in Holland and Germany, and the heart, a symbol of love employed by Scandinavian rural art in particular.

CREATING
THE LOOK

The unfussy good looks of
American settler style
beautifully complement simple
contemporary furnishings and
suit any room in the house,
especially living rooms, kitchens
and children's bedrooms.
Sixteenth- and seventeenth-
century country-style
furnishings are the basic
elements, with settler colours
and folk motifs or naïve art for
decorative effect. There are
plenty of shops which sell
American folk crafts, but you
may enjoy making your own.

Walls

Plastered walls covered with whitewash are ideal
for this period, as is panelling, either left bare or
painted with suitable colours. Remember that
dados and cornices were not part of a settler interior; if you have such architectural details you can
make them less conspicuous by painting them the
same colours as the walls.

Paints in these times were usually home-made,
made from earth and vegetable pigments mixed
with linseed oil or soured milk curd – the latter
was known, unsurprisingly, as milk paint. Paint
took a long time to prepare and was a luxury
item, so was usually applied in just one thick coat,
worked in with a bristle brush to give depth and
character. The surface was not usually very even,
and graining and marbling were popular techniques to disguise its streakiness. Use these and

other paint techniques – stippling, ragging or glaz-
ing, for example – to imitate this look, or find
dragged or sponged-effect wallpapers as an alternative. For added decoration, put up ready-made
borders featuring folk motifs, such as hearts,
tulips, fruit, baskets, cockerels and oak leaves, or
paint your own stencilled designs in bright colours
on a pale background.

Floors

Early settler houses often contained floors made of
compacted earth, either covered in straw or decorated with a scratched design. Brick floors could be
found in cellars, and stone floors in porches or in
halls, laid in diagonal checks. Most common of all,
however, were wide, smooth pine or oak boards –
which makes the best type of flooring for a modern
scheme of this type. Leave them bare to best reflect

the light, cover with floor paint in settler colours, or perhaps border with stencilled folk motifs.

Carpets at this time were rare, and only the richest homes possessed woven or knotted oriental floorcoverings. To protect their wooden floors the settlers employed floorcloths, often made of sail canvas, painted in imitation of eastern carpets or else featuring marbled diamond patterns. You can

LEFT Settler walls need not be too perfectly finished – slightly uneven plasterwork only adds to the effect. The quarry-tiled floor is very practical, and its colour gives a lovely feeling of warmth.

RIGHT The patterns crimped and punched on to these tin sconces are taken from the folk art of northern Europe. The backing plates help reflect candlelight into the room.

easily make your own floorcloth by painting a length of canvas with acrylic primer, a matt emulsion base coat and then your own design in acrylic paints, finished with several coats of varnish. Rush matting, either as rugs or fitted wall-to-wall, is a suitable alternative. It was during the eighteenth

century that home-makers began to create rag rugs. Probably developed from a Scandinavian craft, it was typical of the waste-not, want-not attitude of the settlers in making good use of worn clothing. Alternatively, flat-weave rugs in straightforward, broad stripes also provide a simple design that works just as well in a bathroom or a study as in a living room or bedroom.

Lights

A wonderfully homely colonial atmosphere can be created by the use of warm, low lighting. Modest hanging candle holders in wood or metal are suitable, especially iron chandeliers with several curving arms. Look out, too, for brass or pewter candlesticks with a circular or pyramidal base, and boat or saucer-shaped lamps (known as Betty lamps) filled with oil. Supplement these with wall sconces made of tinned sheet iron. These were composed of a holder and a backing plate in various shapes, sometimes concave or mirrored to best reflect the light, and often crimped around the edges and punched so as to create pretty embossed patterns. Today, a wide variety of light fittings can be found in this style, featuring hearts, flowers and stars, for example. Modern fittings in plain wood or wrought iron that echo these features will fit in well, with shades made of checks or plain fabrics. If you are feeling adventurous, you may want to stencil, stamp or paint freehand your own motifs on to shades – use acrylic paints and don't worry about creating too perfect a finish, as their charm is in their hand-made appearance.

COLOURS

The colours used by the American settlers are instantly recognizable, in particular their 'barn red', made using red oxides from soil, in various shades from brown to russet. Other popular colours were straw yellow, buttermilk, stone and cream, earthy browns, verdigris, grey, dark green, indigo and a lovely soft blue. Don't be afraid to use several colours at once – they always work well together, giving a wonderful air of warmth and energy.

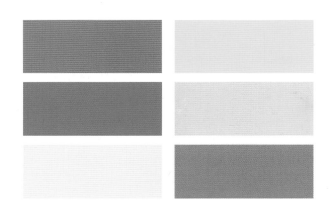

Soft furnishings

Colourful fabrics contributed greatly to the settler home, softening its rather functional appearance and adding comfort and vibrancy. Soft furnishings were home-made by the women of the household (when they weren't darning, patching or mending) and the fabrics used tended to be simple and practical – making it an inexpensive look to copy today. Generally, keep fabrics as unfussy as possible – plains, checks, plaids and stripes are all suitable, in down-to-earth linen, wool, cotton or calico. Vary the scale of patterns and the fabric colourways to create simple yet effective overall schemes that don't look too deliberate, yet nevertheless work well as a whole.

Beautiful patchwork quilts are an intrinsic part of this style, and were used not just as bed covers but also to wrap valuables when travelling, to pad the insides of wagons, as baby blankets and even burial cloths. The earliest were English in origin, using remnants of chintzes that were a new import from the east. Plain fabrics were also used to great effect, particularly by the Amish settlers, whose quilts are renowned for their bold hues and striking patterns. Making quilts was originally a form of recycling, using pieces of cloth from old clothing or worn furnishings. Eventually, however, it became an art form, and an inevitable part of young women's education.

There is a wide choice of ready-made American-style patchwork quilts in the shops, but if you have the time and inclination, piecing your own is a highly satisfying process. You can use leftover fabric or buy kits containing ready-cut pieces – don't forget, however, that an especially fine quilt could contain as many as 12,000m (40,000ft) of stitches!

Simpler bed covers make a plainer alternative to patchwork quilts. A throw of checked fabric, for example, is exceptionally nice, and you could even make some matching, modest bed-hangings, to go with plain linen sheets and woollen blankets.

Keep window treatments simple: most rooms had interior shutters made of wood and only the best rooms in a settler house would have featured curtains. Yours should be made of plain cloth (muslin in the summer and wool in the winter, for

FABRICS

American Settler fabrics were wonderfully colourful but extremely unfussy – simple practicality is the key to this look. Cotton, wool and canvas are ideal choices, in unbleached naturals or plains, stripes and checks. You can create extra interest by varying the scale and texture of these unpretentious weaves.

example, although a patchwork design would also suit this style very well), with a gathered, tab-headed or pencil-pleated heading, hung from a wooden pole with either a very plain pelmet or just one simple swag.

There are plenty of other home sewing projects that suit this homely and pretty style: making seat and cushion covers with frilled edges and fabric ties, covering shoe- and hat boxes with gingham or fabric featuring folk motifs, covering flat picture frames with cloth in tiny checks, or lining a wicker basket with striped fabric. Nursery linen, too, is absolutely charming made from fabrics in this style. Cloth torn into strips was either plaited and coiled, then stitched to create a flat, circular rug, or else hooked through holes in a backing canvas, sometimes forming pictures of flowers or animals. Rag rugs kits are available in the shops, but are relatively easy to make from scratch.

RIGHT Many different types of accessories can make a contribution to this style, including dolls, hanging baskets, lavender bags and even a clock.

Accessories

The settlers' artistry was always put to good use, and decorative folk motifs tended to be added to objects that were already practical in themselves. Carved and painted wood was a principal element: look for oval bentwood boxes in all shapes and sizes; butter moulds, decoy ducks, geese and other birds; hanging salt boxes; candle boxes with a sliding lid, and elegantly simple, turned-wood plates and bowls. Metalwork was also important, and you can include it in your scheme in the form of punched or painted tinware; iron door pulls, hinges and keyhole surrounds; wrought iron trivets in folk shapes, and perhaps even a weather vane in the shape of an arrow, a scroll, an animal or a human figure.

For crockery, choose creamware in thick white or off-white glazes and pieces painted with naïve designs and floral shapes. You could add glassware adorned with multicoloured designs in enamel paint; cross-stitch samplers; enamel kitchen equipment; large wicker baskets filled with dried flowers, and naïve portraits – in plain wooden frames – of people or farmyard animals. The final touch would be a few toys: a Noah's ark, a hobby horse, a whirligig or some rag dolls – which are, perhaps, the most charming examples of the settlers' creativity and craftsmanship.

Furniture

Since the settlers, on the whole, brought little with them except a few basic tools, they were forced to make their furniture from scratch, using the native timber – cherry, maple, cedar, elm and hickory – that was easily to hand. They were not generally followers of fashion, so their creations tended to echo the appearance of European furnishings designed several decades earlier, and even then were often simplified in style due to lack of time and resources. Though furniture was initially rough and ready, as time went on the colonists developed pride in their craftsmanship, and by the beginning of the eighteenth century their handiwork was quite fine.

ABOVE A grouping of simple pieces of furniture can have huge effect without costing the earth. This room has a plain, serene quality that would work very well in a modern home.

The religious beliefs of some of the groups who had travelled to the new world discouraged decoration purely for its own sake, but many others, in particular the Pennsylvania Dutch (who were, in fact, Deutsch – German), brought with them traditions of making furniture that featured complex carvings and brightly coloured paintwork. Chests and cupboards, for example, would be embellished with strips of moulding and bosses, or shallow carvings of flowers and leaves. Carvings sometimes featured on chairs, too, and woodwork of all types was frequently painted with intricate folk motifs, including tulips, hearts, stars, trees, garlands, vines, birds, pinwheels and zigzags. The plainest furniture was simply stained in red, blue, green, brown, grey or black.

Create your own versions of these vibrant pieces by stencilling patterns on to country-style furniture such as chests of drawers, plank-fronted wardrobes, rudimentary bookshelves and large dressers. This is a look that works especially well in the kitchen, and you can complement it with peg rails, hanging cupboards, a stone sink and old-fashioned brass taps. Solid, plain tables are perfect for decorating with stencilled borders, as are trestle, folding and frame versions with a detachable top, used by the settlers to create extra space. Look for seating in various forms, including stools, benches, panelled chairs, rocking chairs and chairs with ladder, splat or banister backs, with seats made of solid wood or covered in padded leather or cloth. The most popular of all was the curving, stick-back Windsor chair, which has now become an American classic. These were invariably painted, usually in green, but also in black, white or other colours, and one or two in this style will bring instant authenticity to a room.

When it comes to beds, you may wish to emulate the German settlers' custom of built-in bedsteads, or choose a free-standing style – either a heavy, panelled bed with turned posts, or a lighter version with spindles in a frame. Either can be embellished with fabric hangings, or left plain and simply covered with a pretty patchwork quilt (see Soft Furnishings for information on quilts).

Though very down to earth and practical, this bedroom is full of colour and life, thanks to the vivacious textiles and a mix of traditional accessories.

Summing up the style

1 The matt surface of milk paint is ideal for an American Settler bedroom, as here, where walls have been given the simplest of treatments.

2 A rug featuring stylized, nature-inspired patterns in bold colours is full of impact. Underneath, dark wooden boards are authentic.

3 The rustic charm of this bedside lamp makes an effective contribution to the overall scheme.

4 Piling the bed high with colourful patchwork quilts, gingham bedlinen and heart-shaped cushions is a wonderful way to recreate this style. Note the mini patchworks above the bedhead and the framed panels of pretty lace.

5 The simple but decorative carved corner cupboard is very suitable in a room of this type. The unpretentious stool and towel rail fit in well here, too.

6 This old-fashioned wooden birdbox is a typical example of American folk craft, making a beautiful ornament.

Georgian

In a reaction to the drama of Baroque, early Georgian style emphasized proportion, symmetry and restraint. It followed the ideals of sixteenth-century Italian architect Andrea Palladio, which themselves emulated ancient Roman architecture. Thus arose the principles of room dimensions based on the square, the circle and the cube, and of a revival of the classical orders.

As this new style matured under a confident and secure aristocracy and a prosperous middle class, speculative builders developed streets, crescents and even whole towns in the style with which we are now so familiar: a stuccoed facade; tall sash windows and a six-panelled front door painted dark green or black, with a semi-circular fanlight. Inside, spacious reception rooms had high ceilings, fine plasterwork, crisp joinery and imposing columned fireplaces.

In the 1730s and 40s several new influences began to make themselves felt, including Rococo, a leading French style which was adopted enthusiastically throughout Europe. Graceful, delicate and light-hearted, it featured shells, leaves, birds, ribbons and asymmetrical, scrolling lines in pale, fresh colours. In Britain, a renewed fascination with medievalism resulted in the introduction of 'Gothick gimmicks' such as the pointed arch, trefoil and quatrefoil. Added to these was a fascination for things Chinese – porcelain, lacquerwork and bamboo-effect railings on chair backs and table edges. The combination of these three resulted temporarily in an atmosphere of fantasy and frivolity.

During the 1740s the excavation of such settlements as Herculaneum and Pompeii provided models for a new system of architecture and decoration led by the French and British: neo-classicism. Robert Adam, England's most successful architect in the latter part of the eighteenth century,

The Georgian house is, for many, the archetypal style. This was the Age of Elegance, and the look was light, uncluttered and sophisticated, with a regard for classicism, colour and detail. The result? A simple refinement that is absolutely timeless.

softened the earlier Palladian style by using delicate mouldings, walls that were plastered instead of wainscoted, and unified schemes of decoration: sofa and chair backs echoed the shapes of the wall panelling, stools fitted into window embrasures and soft furnishings were closely co-ordinated. Houses were refined and graceful, with elegant, classical forms applied throughout.

The classical style began to reach the colonies in North America in the mid eighteenth century. Here, its character was relatively restrained – Rococo never really caught on. After the Declaration of Independence in 1776, the new United States used as a basis for their own Federal style first Adamesque neo-classicism and then the final flowering of the Georgian period in Britain – Regency style.

Influenced by the French Empire style, Regency style favoured dramatic Chinese colours, severe classical shapes, informal arrangements of light, easily movable furniture and an elaborate use of textiles, finding its most exotic application in the Brighton Pavilion completed by John Nash for George IV (the former Prince Regent) in 1823.

CREATING THE LOOK

This is a style that can suit any room in the house, from a formal dining room to a practical study, a comfortable living room to a bright conservatory. The effect can be simple or as dramatic as you dare, and a subtle sophistication can be achieved by mixing clean-lined modern furniture with period pieces. Overall, aim for symmetry, detail, proportion and a sense of good taste.

Walls

Though modest houses featured plaster walls washed with a distemper colour, anyone who was anyone in the Georgian era aimed for a grand effect with one of the new designs for wallpaper that had recently become available. Thanks to the number of reproductions around today, this means that it is relatively easy to achieve an authentic look. Seek out flocks in one or two colours, imitation marble, patterns featuring architectural shapes such as urns, columns and niches, naturalistic sprays of flowers, simple repeating motifs such as stripes or diamonds, and Chinese designs with birds, fishes, flowers or landscapes.

Georgian walls were divided into three areas. At the top was a cornice and frieze, with moulded motifs such as egg-and-dart, acanthus leaves, swags and ribbons or classical urns. In the centre was the 'field' area and below that was a skirting board, a wainscoted dado and a chair rail. If you're not lucky enough to have originals, modern prefabricated mouldings are inexpensive and easy to put up, and should be painted either in the same colours as the wall itself, or picked out in white or, for a very opulent look, gilt. Cover the dado part of the wall in a restrained white, stone, olive or brown paint. The field, as the largest area, can be treated in a variety of ways: painted a stone or pastel colour, panelled with wood, hung with a stretched fabric such as damask or toile de Jouy or, as was most common, covered with wallpaper.

Floors

The 'below stairs' flooring in a Georgian house would have been composed of edge-on bricks, thick slate tiles or plain stone paving, with perhaps a floorcloth protection in the kitchen – a modern substitute would be linoleum or vinyl. Servants' quarters, hallways and stairs were often covered with flatweave carpets, while druggets, made of heavy baize, serge or haircloth, protected fine floors in wealthy homes. In your Georgian scheme, pale-coloured flagstones or black and white marble are the most desirable for entrance halls, while wooden planks are best everywhere else. Remember that the Georgians never used varnish, so finish boards by painting (in a solid colour or marbled) or limewashing – unless the wood is of very good quality, in which case you can leave it untreated. Carpets can be used just to cover the centre of the room or wall-to-wall; in the latter case a border in a complementary design adds an authentic touch. Look for neo-classical and oriental patterns with a loop or cut-pile or else Turkish-style, knotted versions. Alternatively, you could use rush matting, which was a fashionable element of the chinoiserie style and employed by both George Washington and George IV.

Lights

At the start of the Georgian era homes were very poorly lit, but by the turn of the century there had been great advances in technology. Candles were still prevalent, but new gas and oil lighting (though prone to the occasional explosion) meant that, at least for some, dim rooms were a thing of the past.

Original Georgian lighting is hard to find and prohibitively expensive, so you will probably want to combine subtle modern lights with a few reproduction pieces. Candlesticks and candelabra are most effective, made of silver, pewter, brass, glass

LEFT A glimpse into the past: Georgian walls were sometimes painted in surprisingly bright hues, though the bare wood of panelling and untreated floorboards somewhat tempers the effect here.

RIGHT The incredibly delicate decoration on this lyre-shaped wall sconce is typical of painstaking Georgian craftsmanship.

or porcelain, in the shape of a fluted classical column with a pyramidal, octagonal or domed foot. Brass and glass oil lamps or enclosed lanterns, free-standing or wall-mounted, can be found in a variety of styles ranging from a simple cylinder to the highly ornamental. Rococo-style wall sconces, in brass, silver, wood (gilded or silvered), pewter or tin, with a reflective back-plate, are extremely attractive, and can be used in sets of two, four or more to achieve the symmetrical balance so important for this style. And a sense of intimate luxury can be achieved with a wood, brass or glass chandelier, featuring six or more curving arms, hung just above head height. Blue and white oriental-style ginger jars make good lamp bases, while modern lamps with a classical column shape and an unadorned, understated paper or fabric shade will also blend in nicely.

COLOURS

Today we associate Georgian interiors with muted shades, and it's true that the so-called 'common' colours included white, stone, grey, buff and chocolate, often used with pea green, olive, eau de nil and pale blue. As technology improved, however, brighter shades became more widely available. Red, 'Chinese' yellow and even touches of pink, lemon, orange, deep green or vivid blue would not be out of place for this look.

Soft furnishings

Fabrics became less expensive with the advent of industrialized manufacturing in the last quarter of the eighteenth century, and printed designs were finer, thanks to new copperplate printing techniques. While leather, velvet and silk damask were still in use, cottons and linens became extremely popular, being not only cheap but also easily washable. Many Georgian fabric designs are widely reproduced today: look for naturalistic flower sprays, chintzes with large, brightly coloured floral patterns, bold stripes, Chinese scenes and, especially, toile de Jouy.

Toile de Jouy, a monochrome print, usually in blue, purple, red or sepia on white, originated in France and is intimately associated with the Georgian style. Toile is easily found in a range of patterns and colours today, and can be used for all sorts of soft furnishings – chair covers, table linen, curtains, bed-hangings, even as framed pictures hung on walls. It is best displayed relatively flat in order to show the story depicted, so avoid heavy gathers. One particularly nice effect is to use a

toile scene as a cushion front, with piping in a matching tone. Whole toile rooms look amazing, but if you prefer a less intense look, it can be easily co-ordinated with checks, stripes and plains.

Although hinged wooden shutters were the norm in a Georgian house, by the 1730s the addition of impressive window treatments was essential for any well-dressed interior. Making curtains is an economical and enjoyable way to recreate a Georgian look. One of the most popular styles was the festoon, or Austrian, blind: one or two pieces of fabric that drew up vertically to create a series of looping gathers. Its near-relation was the drapery curtain, in two parts, which was drawn by the same principle but left heavy swags at each side of the window, sometimes fastened to the wall with a metal pin. If you choose either of these styles, hang them between the top of the window and the cornice so as to obscure as little light as possible.

By the 1780s, French rod curtains, which drew horizontally, had surpassed the festoon in popularity. These consisted of two pieces of fabric that were attached to a rod above the architrave by wooden or brass rings – forerunners of the typical twentieth-century window treatment. Finish windows with a scalloped, curved or arched pelmet, made of gilded wood or pleated fabric with a piped or narrow-frilled border. For a really opulent effect in a large room, you could even emulate the Regency practice of 'continuous drapery', in which a pole was hung across the tops of several sets of windows and fabric wound around it loosely; this is doubly effective if you use a contrasting lining. Heavy fringes and tassels are appropriate for all

styles of curtain, and you can increase the elaborate look by following the Georgian practice of dressing the window with several layers – adding either a wooden Venetian blind or a plain fabric roller blind, together with a muslin sub-curtain.

Accessories

The epitome of Georgian style is the print room, which can be easily recreated. Use either real pictures (silhouettes in black frames and landscapes were popular, while classical architectural drawings would be appropriate) or photocopies, pasted close together directly on to the walls. Add ready-printed borders, cords and bows to simulate the effect of elaborate hangings. An intense yellow or red background sets off this feature beautifully.

Another desirable finishing touch is blue and white china, either of oriental or European origin, placed in groups on wall brackets, shelves or in niches. It won't matter if some pieces are less than perfect – the effect depends on the symmetrical grouping rather than individual quality. You could also display silver tea and coffee services, classical busts or statues, romantic porcelain figures, and Wedgwood pieces such as cream-coloured Queen's Ware, bas-relief Jasper Ware and Black Basalt, all of which originated in the late eighteenth century. Final details could include a lacquerwork screen, mirrors framed in Rococo designs, and a pier glass (a tall, thin mirror) placed between two windows to enhance the sense of light and space.

FABRICS

Georgian fabrics can encompass a wide range of styles, from a large-scale, hand-blocked chintz to a much more muted olive and cream stripe – the choice depends very much on the other elements of your scheme and the desired overall effect. Toile de Jouy is very typical of the eighteenth-century look, especially in blue and cream, as are delicate trellises and twining florals.

Furniture

The eighteenth century was the era of the master cabinet-maker, when English furniture was in demand all over the world. Pieces were fine, small and light, in walnut, mahogany, rosewood, satinwood, maple or other rich woods, often with decorative marquetry, lacquer, gilding or stringing (a contrasting wood inlaid in narrow lines).

ABOVE Much Georgian furniture was specially designed for social rituals – receiving visitors, playing cards, listening to musical recitals and, as here, drinking tea.

Furniture shapes varied according to the prevailing fashion, influenced by the trio of great designers. The first of these was Thomas Chippendale, who favoured the curves of Rococo mixed with Chinese and Gothic designs. George Hepplewhite's designs exemplified the swing back to Robert Adam's delicate, smooth and streamlined classicism, while the excellence of late Georgian cabinet-making was demonstrated in the pattern books of Thomas Sheraton, featuring stricter classical forms, straight lines and compact, often multi-functional pieces.

Dining was an important social activity, and the most popular Georgian dining table in Britain was in three sections, with D-shaped ends. It may be easier, however, to copy the French fashion, which was simply to cover a wooden board with a good white cloth. Dining chairs may have openwork square or shield-shaped backs, or perhaps medallions with carved Prince of Wales feathers, wreaths, Chinese fretwork, sprays of flowers or ribbons. Legs can be cabriole-shaped, with scrolled or claw-and-ball feet, sabre-shaped, or straight and tapered, ending on plinth or spade feet. For relaxing, look for low, upholstered armchairs, perhaps with wings, couches with scrolled ends and chaise longues – always a good way to create a sense of luxury. Add a few typical pieces such as chests of drawers with brass drop-handles, console tables, small sideboards, library shelves and corner cupboards with panelled or glazed doors. One common arrangement was to flank a side table with pedestal cupboards, each topped with a classical urn. Beds should be canopied, in the form of a four-poster or, perhaps, with drapes hung from a circular ceiling ring, while in the kitchen a sturdy dresser with graduated shelving would be perfect, teamed with worksurfaces on turned balusters and plain but elegant joinery. New pieces of furniture that came into common use in this period included the kneehole and roll-top desk, round tea table with tripod base, bow-fronted sideboards, dwarf bookcases, nests of tables, chiffoniers (a pedestal cupboard with shelving behind a pair of doors), tallboys, hanging wardrobes and the sofa table, which was placed against the back of the sofa to hold sewing equipment, books and so on.

If genuine Georgian furniture is beyond your budget, look for cheaper reproductions from the Victorian or Edwardian periods. Disguise pale pine or cheap woods with a dark stain, and use loose covers to hide unsuitable modern pieces – it was usual in this period to protect furniture with plain, striped, checked or toile de Jouy covers that were only removed on special occasions.

Finally, the placement of furniture will also go a long way to creating the right atmosphere – keep it relatively sparse and, when not in use, push it back against the walls, making sure there's an emphasis on symmetry.

Sophisticated elegance sums up this room. Every element, including the sash windows, panelled dado and the fireplace, adds up to a classical refinement.

Summing up the style

1 Appropriately, the walls are divided into white-painted, wainscoted dado below and yellow 'field' above. This vivid 'Chinese' yellow was just one of a number of bright hues that were in use, particularly in the Regency era.

2 This floor treatment is typically Georgian – wooden floorboards with a central oriental-style carpet.

3 When choosing lights, look for candlesticks or candelabra such as this, made of metal, glass or porcelain.

4 This is a relatively restrained window treatment for a Georgian room, though the gathered style of the blind is extremely appropriate. Many rooms would have added more drapes and swags, together with an elaborate pelmet.

5 Although this sofa is not as fine as some Georgian furniture, its scrolled arms, tapering legs and streamlined, compact form are essential elements. The wall table behind it is more delicate.

6 The symmetrical grouping of ornaments on the mantelpiece and the Rococo-style mirror above the fireplace make for a very Georgian feel. The prints reflected in the mirror are also very appropriate.

Victorian

The nineteenth century saw change in more spheres – social, political, industrial and scientific – than any previous period in history. And when the Victorians weren't transforming home affairs, they were travelling the globe, returning with artefacts and ideas from all corners of the Empire. For the rapidly expanding middle classes, interior decoration was the perfect opportunity to display newly acquired wealth and cultural knowledge. The result was exuberant, eclectic, and sometimes downright over the top.

Status was everything in the Victorian house, revealed by the differences in decoration between grand public areas and the meanest of servants' quarters. A large porch and imposing entrance door was typical, while inside the size and complexity of plasterwork mouldings denoted the importance of a room. Newly developed plate glass led to the ubiquitous bay window and a craze for conservatories. There was a fireplace in almost every room, made of marble, slate or wood, and woodwork was stained dark or painted to resemble marble or expensive hardwoods. A profusion of patterned wallpapers, elaborate trimmings and arrangements of knick-knacks made for a feeling of crowded extravagance.

The high Victorian style was a riot of revivalism, with different periods mixed indiscriminately. The Elizabethan look was extremely popular, as were Italianate, 'Louis', Egyptian and Queen Anne Revival. But the real Battle of the Styles was between 'Greek', covering every phase of classical architecture and decoration, and 'Gothic', employing any style reminiscent of Olde Englande. Gothic was the eventual favourite, riding on a tide of nationalism and romanticism stirred by the novels of Sir Walter Scott. Its most famous exponent was Augustus Pugin (who refurbished the Palace of Westminster in the 1830s) but his crafts-

The typical Victorian home had a style that was at once confident and cosy. Inspired by many different periods and cultures, dark and cluttered rooms were filled with solid furniture and bric-a-brac, creating a look that was as distinctive as it was comfortable.

manship was often lacking in the crude and overly decorated copies found in many homes.

In the 1870s and 80s a lighter, less formal look developed among artists and designers influenced by arts and crafts from Japan. This Aesthetic movement – closely associated with Oscar Wilde, James McNeill Whistler and the Liberty store, which opened in Regent Street in 1875 – featured oriental artefacts and prints, peacock feathers, wicker and bamboo furniture and hand-crafted 'art' furniture, often in black and gilt.

The Victorian style spread throughout the British Empire, and in the United States, too, the era was characterized by a mix of styles, ranging from Gothic, Romanesque and American Queen Anne to the Stick style (inspired by English half-timbered houses), Shingle (from the plain, shingled surfaces of New England homes), colonial Revival and imitation Swiss chalets. Though similar to their cousins across the Atlantic, American houses were more often timber-built, with large porches, double doors and complex roof-lines, combining a recognizable Victorianism with typically robust American individuality and inventiveness.

CREATING THE LOOK

The Victorians mixed colour, pattern and decorative styles with abandon, and anyone aiming for this look needn't be afraid to put old with new, or to combine a number of different themes. High Victorian colours were rich and flamboyant, but you may prefer the lighter shades of the early period, or a country style with frills, lace and simpler furnishings. There are many sources of Victoriana, including auctions, antiques dealers and junk shops, and good reproductions are available from both specialists and large department stores.

Walls

Wallpaper came into its own as the predominant wallcovering in Victorian times. Today, many companies have reprinted archive designs, while others produce patterns that fit well with the style, making it easier than ever to achieve the look.

Walls should be divided into three with a dado and picture rail. Below the dado, use an embossed paper such as Anaglypta or Lincrusta, which were predominant during the 1870s and 80s. Dark colours are best, and you can varnish the paper for extra durability. Above, strongly coloured, maybe even gilded, wallpapers are ideal. Early Victorian prints were small, with frequent repeats, but as printing technology became more sophisticated a profusion of patterns developed, based on panelling or architectural mouldings, diamonds, medieval motifs or, most popular of all, flower

ABOVE Multicoloured floor tiles are an ideal choice for this Victorian hall, complemented by a tiled dado in deep green and stained glass insets in the sturdy front door.

designs. The latter were either realistic and three-dimensional in appearance or, according to another school of thought, stylized and flat, like those of the influential designer William Morris (see next chapter).

In response to a new attention to efficiency, health and hygiene, tiles were frequently found on the walls of halls, kitchens and bathrooms. Today, reproduction Victorian tiles are easy to come by and look stunning. Where walls are neither papered or tiled, use paintwork to create a marbled effect, or else a broken finish such as ragging, spattering, colourwashing or sponging, plus a stencilled or wallpaper border featuring suitable motifs.

Floors

Tiles were popular for Victorian floors as well as walls, and colourful, patterned tiles were used to create a grand impression in the entrance halls of the better-off. Look for the typical encaustic tiles in red, buff, brown, green, black, white and blue – though even a geometric arrangement in black and white is very effective. In the kitchen, and other utilitarian areas, go for plain quarry tiles or stone flags, while linoleum – introduced in the latter part of the nineteenth century – can be used for bathrooms, corridors and small rooms such as pantries. Patterns were available, but plain brown or green were the favoured lino colours. Living rooms and dining rooms look marvellous with a dark-stained and highly polished wooden floor, covered by a central carpet featuring large, bold patterns of flowers and leaves, swags, festoons or geometric designs. The same effect can be created with a wall-to-wall carpet topped by an oriental or needlework rug. On staircases, a runner carpet held by brass stair rods is ideal.

Lights

The nineteenth century saw a flood of inventions in the field of lighting, from the further development of the oil lamp to gas and, at the end of the century, electricity. Numerous elaborate and ornamental styles came on to the market and today original fittings, which can often be converted to electricity, are reasonably priced, while any number of reproductions are available. Look for lamps with an iron, china, silver-plate or brass and

ABOVE A typical Victorian combination: swan-necked wall lights with flower-shaped glass shades set against blowsy pink chintz wallpaper.

copper base, with a central chimney made of glass, either clear, opaque, coloured, etched or painted. Tulip-shaped shades are typical, too, while plain glass globes might be disguised with an outer shade of linen, silk, parchment or paper, adorned with beaded fringes, bows, rosettes and artificial flowers. China lamps were covered with floral sprigs, and sometimes bases were in the form of classical figures, children, cupids, soldiers or animals.

A swan-necked, brass or copper wall lamp with a flower-shaped glass shade is very Victorian, and coloured glass lanterns add a bright touch. Brass and cut glass can be used for wall sconces and central chandeliers, and a metal rise-and-fall pendant lamp is an efficient and very appropriate way to diffuse light to the desired area.

COLOURS

The essential colours of this period are rich and vivid, sometimes used in unusual and striking combinations. Deep shades, such as crimson, claret, bottle green, sharp yellow, purple, mahogany, terracotta and Prussian blue, were preferred for sitting rooms, dining rooms and studies; paler and fresher hues, including pink, grey, pale blue and soft green, were thought more suitable for bedrooms.

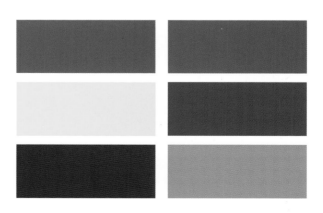

Soft furnishings

Victorian fabric designs were frequently inspired by the various revivalist styles that went in and out of fashion. Gothic, classical, Middle Eastern and oriental patterns all featured strongly, though the most consistently popular were floral designs, especially roses, dahlias and the many new varieties that were being introduced. Ribbons might twine among the flowers, while birds occasionally made an appearance, and bright stripes or scenes of children, animals or landscapes were other favourite choices. Improvements in printing and dyeing meant fabrics were often brightly coloured, and all-over-print cottons were used extensively.

You should not have much difficulty in finding Victorian-style fabrics today. Look for patterns like those described above, in luxurious fabrics including velvet, satin, silk damask, wool, chintz and chenille. If you are on a tight budget, however, use inexpensive, plain material in suitable colours, trimmed with deep fringes and large tassels.

Begin with elaborate window treatments, layering first a lace or muslin undercurtain and then a roller blind (perhaps with a false 'view'). Finish with a pair of curtains. In general, heavily gathered, swagged and draped styles are best suited to this look – a goblet-pleated heading looks beautifully bold. Hang from a brass or wooden pole, which could either feature ornate rings and finials, or else be hidden by a grandiose shaped pelmet. Cover with fabric or paint in complementary colours, even adding some gilding if you wish. Add heavy bullion (gold-thread) fringes to curtains and pelmets, or use the lining as a contrasting trim. Secure with ropes, gilded tie-backs, pins or scroll-shaped fittings.

Especially useful in a draughty house is another Victorian habit – hanging heavy room-dividing curtains, or *portières*, over doorways. Use velvet, serge, damask, tapestry or even a plain wool, and tie back with a tasselled rope, or perhaps a plait made from narrow lengths of the same fabric.

For upholstery, the ideal choice would be velvet, glazed cotton, chintz or a corded silk or wool rep, in any of the patterns mentioned above, tartan, or a plain colour from the era. Sofas and chairs covered in paisley and kilims also follow Victorian fashion, and you can always cheat by throwing over a tasselled, Indian-print shawl. Most importantly, however, finish the upholstery off with ruching, cords and deep fringes, and complement it with an excess of drapery: fabric-covered side tables, trimmed mantelpieces, embroidered and tasselled cushions, antimacassars laid over chair backs and lace-edged shelves, all of which increase the impression of enjoyable excess.

Accessories

The Victorians considered bare rooms to be in poor taste, and their houses were filled with knick-knacks, *objets d'art* and collections. The arrangements of these displays came close to being an art form, and today a few groupings of such typical items will go a long way towards creating the Victorian feel. You could start by making a *découpage* screen, tray or covered box by pasting down images cut out from magazines, books of old prints or even wallpaper, and protecting with a layer of varnish. Hang gilt-framed landscape paintings and black-and-white miniatures, and cover clocks, figurines and wax flowers with glass domes. Collections could include oriental fans, porcelain and lacquered boxes; shell-covered picture frames and boxes; scent bottles; colonial exotica; samplers; family photographs in silver frames; toby jugs; lead soldiers and wooden toys. Finally, add brass or china door knobs and finger plates, dot around plenty of potted plants, including aspidistras, ferns and palms, arrange fruit on a tiered, cut-glass stand, and find some old-fashioned implements for the kitchen. The Victorians loved labour-saving devices such as spice graters, fruit slicers, apple corers and coffee grinders but, hopefully, you won't need one 'appliance' which was used to catch cockroaches at night – a hedgehog kept in a box!

FABRICS

Striking, sometimes shocking colour combinations are typical of Victorian fabrics, and these authentic examples, in silk and cotton with gold thread, are a superb demonstration of this rather florid style. The popular medieval motifs are also apparent. Velvets, especially in bottle green and claret, epitomize the look – but in a more restrained way.

Furniture

The Victorians tended to overfill their homes with numerous pieces of furniture, not necessarily matching and often encompassing a wide range of styles. Rococo was popular, as were both Near and Far Eastern, Gothic, 'Louis', olde English and something called 'fat classical', which was neo-classical with additional carved ornamentation.

Because there's so much choice, it should be relatively easy to find Victorian pieces to suit your taste. Generally, furniture was solid and in swelling forms, and the best examples were made of mahogany, walnut, rosewood or satinwood. Typical of the era would be balloon-back chairs, massive sideboards, corner cupboards, rectangular dining tables with bulbous legs, small writing desks, elaborate coat, hat and umbrella stands, chiffoniers, whatnots (stands with three or more tiers), circular occasional tables and, of course, a piano and a long-case clock.

ABOVE Every single item of furniture in this bathroom has a Victorian appearance. The *faux* marbling below the dado is particularly effective.

It was the upholsterer, however, rather than the cabinet-maker, who had most influence over the Victorian interior. Thanks to the invention of coil springing in the 1820s, comfortable seating had a new prominence. All sorts of upholstered furniture was widely used; look for styles with the typical curving shapes and deep buttons, and remember that it doesn't matter if they don't match. Disguise modern pieces with a thrown-over paisley shawl and some plump cushions with huge gold tassels.

Upholstery was not, however, the only new art in furniture-making. In Austria, for example, Michael Thonet perfected a technique for bending beechwood to produce his now classic café chairs, while metal bedsteads were introduced to Britons at the Great Exhibition of 1851. Made of brass and iron, and often quite ornate, they can be bought today either from specialist outlets or in reproduction form. Other experiments included papier mâché, employed for fire screens, trays, boxes, bedheads and even small chairs and tables; cast iron, fashionable for garden and conservatory seating; and many types of ingenious 'patent' furniture, particularly popular in the USA.

The kitchen, inhabited mainly by servants, was the plainest room in the house. Strictly speaking, all kitchen furniture in a Victorian-style home should be free-standing, but adding a plate rack, open shelving, a linen press and perhaps a small marble-topped pastry table will reduce the fitted feel. As for bathrooms, until the 1870s all ablutions took place in the bedroom, at a wooden washstand equipped with bowl and pitcher, or in a tin bath in front of the fire. But with the introduction of indoor bathrooms came some distinctive sanitaryware: basins were large and often colourfully decorated, while baths were enamelled roll-tops on ball-and-claw or scroll feet. Many Victorian bathroom bits can be found in a good salvage yard, although there's a wide variety of reproduction suites around, too, while adding some free-standing furniture, such as small tables, towel racks and chairs, will increase the Victorian feel – even if your suite is more recent in origin.

This bedroom has a very Victorian feel. Colours are paler than those of living rooms, dining rooms and studies, where the look would be heavier and more cluttered.

Summing up the style

1 The pretty pattern of this wallpaper and complementary borders strikes just the right note of Victorian femininity.

2 A pale rug laid over wooden boards is soft underfoot and perfectly complements this delicate scheme.

3 Glass globes on a brass base make this pair of bedside lights typical of the era. Avoid too high a wattage of bulb to maintain an air of cosiness and to emulate the softer glow of an oil lamp.

4 Layers of flouncy bedlinen are appropriate soft furnishings for a Victorian style. The lace-edged pillows are especially nice and the overall effect is comfortable and attractive.

5 Deeply buttoned upholstery was favoured by the Victorians, and this armchair is a perfect example of the most popular style of furniture. The metal bedstead, too, sums up the look immediately.

6 The Victorians filled their homes with all sorts of accessories and knick-knacks, and a dressing table set such as this is just one good example.

Arts and Crafts

While most Victorians eagerly greeted the proliferation of cheap and eclectic furnishings that resulted from new machine processes, a few lone voices expressed their disillusionment with the changes brought by the Industrial Revolution, seeing not only overcrowded homes filled with badly made and mismatching styles, but also slums, pollution and dreadful working conditions. Since the 1830s, Augustus Pugin had been advocating a return to what he saw as the honest values of the Middle Ages, and his call was taken up by the leading design critic, John Ruskin.

Ruskin influenced a whole generation of reformists, of whom the most important was William Morris, designer, writer, poet, weaver, typographer, scholar, radical socialist and driving force behind the Arts and Crafts movement. The first example of Morris's new approach was his own Red House, built in 1860 by the architect Philip Webb in modest English vernacular style. At a time when excess was all, the house featured a shockingly simple combination of medieval and seventeenth-century features, and was furnished by Morris and his friends with wall tapestries, sturdy oak furniture and hand-made textiles.

In the following year Morris set up his own company, producing fabrics, wallpaper, ceramics, stained glass, metalwork, furniture and carpets by traditional methods. His ideals were truth to materials and techniques – showing peg joints, the grain of wood or hammer marks on metal, for example – high quality and individual craftsmanship, which he felt was life-enhancing for both maker and user. Morris firmly believed that beauty could be found in everyday things and that good design could go hand-in-hand with moral and social reform; it was a constant source of disappointment to him that his furniture, however

'Have nothing in your houses that you do not know to be useful, or believe to be beautiful.' William Morris's words aptly summarize the ideals of Arts and Crafts design, a radical alternative to the conventional Victorian interior.

plain in appearance, was for too expensive for working-class people.

This paradox did not, however, prevent Arts and Crafts becoming one of the most influential design movements ever, generating debate over the purpose of design and the merits of craft versus machine. Morris's philosophy was taken up by many prominent designers and architects, including Charles Ashbee, Walter Crane, William Lethaby, Charles Voysey and M. H. Baillie Scott. Arts and Crafts principles were even used in the building of early twentieth-century housing developments such as Letchworth Garden City and Hampstead Garden Suburb.

The movement was given its name when the Arts and Crafts Exhibition Society was founded in 1888. The style was particularly well-received in the USA, where it flourished alongside a keen sense of individualism, self-help and a revived interest in the colonial past. The Arts and Crafts philosophy was propagated by publications such as *The Craftsman*, whose founder, Gustav Stickley, had established the Craftsman Workshops near New York in the late 1890s. Stickley's simply styled, hand-made furniture gave the movement its American title – Craftsman style.

CREATING THE LOOK

Arts and Crafts was more an attitude to life than a set of rules, and its principles can be interpreted in different ways: one interior might have been very plain while another employed much greater decorative detail. Aim to create a harmonious whole, putting your emphasis on craftsmanship and quality, natural colours, warmth and welcome, using high quality but informal materials such as oak, copper, plain-woven wool and stoneware.

ABOVE For an Arts and Crafts-style hallway, polished wooden boards topped by a simple woven runner are perfect. The patterned wallpaper is extremely evocative.

Walls

Wall treatments contribute one of the most important decorative elements of an Arts and Crafts room. Whitewash, wallpaper, tapestry, mosaic and fresco were all approved by its exponents, as long as it was of good quality and did not attempt to represent something other than itself – historical fakery and *faux* finishes were abhorred.

If you prefer painted walls, choose whitewash, creams or earthy colours, perhaps with a high picture rail or plate shelf for added interest. A more complex effect can be achieved by adding a wallpaper border, stencilling a frieze of typical motifs (such as tulips, roses, leaves, birds and hearts) around the top of the wall, or hand painting patterns, scenes or figures such as medieval knights. For children's rooms a confident artist may want to copy the charming book illustrations from the era by the likes of Walter Crane and Kate Greenaway. Simple wainscoting or tongue-and-groove boards covering the lower part of the wall – left bare if the wood is good enough, or else painted a muted shade such as cream or sage green – are equally appropriate. The wall above can be covered with either paint or wallpaper. Many of the beautiful, nature-inspired papers produced by Morris and the Arts and Crafts masters are still widely available, their hand-blocked, flat and subtly coloured patterns of twining leaves and flowers, animals and birds making a strong background for a room in this style.

Floors

Wooden parquet or boards are the perfect Arts and Crafts-style flooring. They should be polished but not varnished, and covered with a rug (piled or flat-woven) in an Arts and Crafts pattern and with a co-ordinating border, or a faded oriental carpet. In the USA, striped Navajo rugs were popular, and these suit a bright, open, American-style Arts and Crafts house, such as those built in California by the brothers Greene and Greene. A good alternative would be a natural matting such as sisal, jute or coir, or a pale-coloured, fitted wool carpet. Avoid over-bright, unnatural shades or realistic plant designs underfoot: these were anathema to members of the movement. Stone flagging or earth-coloured ceramic tiles are perfect for entrance halls, with more tiles – sensible, hygienic and waterproof – in plain colours or an Arts and Crafts pattern in the bathroom. Lino or cork in a muted medieval shade provides a functional flooring for the kitchen.

Lights

Electricity, although by no means widespread, was gradually being introduced to the domestic interior during the last years of the nineteenth century. By 1900 its novelty had resulted in some bulbs being shaped like flowers or flames, used deliberately without a shade. Some Arts and Crafts designers welcomed the chance to work with this new invention; others preferred to stick to tried-and-tested styles from antiquity.

By now the massive central chandelier was becoming an outdated form of lighting, replaced by more sophisticated, smaller fittings spread around the room. That said, a central pendant or medieval-style wooden fitting would not be out of

RIGHT Brass and glass lights are particularly appropriate for this style – shapes are graceful but still practical, and the workmanship very fine.

place in your Arts and Crafts scheme, supplemented by a series of lamps hung from the wall at frieze height and a variety of table lamps and candle holders. Shapes should be both practical and graceful, employing simple but stylized details such as insets of small squares, spirals or flower outlines.

Typical materials to use are brass, wrought iron and hammered copper, perhaps with delicate, twisted-metal decoration. Vaseline glass, which was a glowing shade of yellowish-green, was one common type of shade, often in a simple flower shape, while stained glass was popular, too. Lights were frequently shaped like a lantern, or perhaps a corona – the medieval look was very much in favour, and using simple, Gothic-style wrought iron lighting, such as branched lights and sconces, would be an excellent way to emulate this look.

COLOURS

Morris and his fellow reformers abhorred the chemical dyes which had recently been invented, preferring instead to use natural pigments reminiscent of the Middle Ages. Warm and earthy colours, such as deep red, mossy green, indigo and ochre, are best suited to the Arts and Crafts style, offset by plenty of cream, ivory or stone to make them stand out.

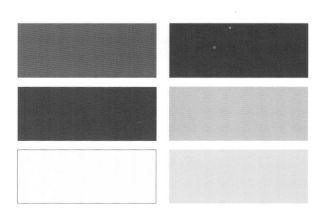

Soft furnishings

Arts and Crafts textiles are dramatically different from the masses of machine-made fabrics which dominated the market in the late nineteenth century. Featuring flattened patterns of wild and country flowers and muted, harmonious colours, they can be combined in different colourways and scales to produce highly effective results. And, of course, no Arts and Crafts-style home would be complete without at least one or two fabrics by the master himself, William Morris.

Always a perfectionist, Morris taught himself dye techniques, carpet knotting and tapestry weaving in order to improve his work with fabric, and the result is a series of versatile designs that are at once ordered and dynamic, a rhythmic evocation of the natural world using wonderfully balanced vegetable shades. Many of Morris's designs, and some by his colleagues, are still in production as upholstery-weight fabrics for purchase by the metre, and they can work extremely well in a modern context.

Morris is best known for his printed cotton chintzes ('Willow', 'Vine' and 'Strawberry Thief' are classic examples), but he also enjoyed the varying characteristics of other fabrics, including silk, wool, linen, damasks and velvet. For this look, mix Morris patterns with plain-coloured materials such as cotton, wool, linen or felt. Whatever the fabric, there is no need to add any further embellishment in the form of tassels or fringes.

Window treatments in this style are a complete contrast to the heavy, draped-and-fringed look of the high Victorian period, seen as gloomy and degenerate by Arts and Crafts practitioners. Their philosophy emphasized sunlight, fresh air and the outdoors, so curtains were designed to reveal rather than obscure the view, without pelmets or excessive gathers. Hang unlined, window-length curtains in pairs from a wood or brass pole, adding, if you wish, finials shaped as hearts, Gothic spears or simple spirals. Curtain fabric should be very sheer and plain, the better to filter the maximum amount of light, perhaps with a border and panels of embroidery or appliqué such as hearts, trefoils or twining ivy. Arts and Crafts fabrics may also be used very effectively as simple Roman or roller blinds.

Upholstery should be similarly restrained, with none of the excessive buttoning, fringing and braiding so beloved of the less 'artistic' Victorians. Choose dark leather, tapestry, velvet, cotton or wool, the latter two either plain or printed with plants, animals and flowers or with medieval motifs. Loose covers should be made up in relatively plain, tailored shapes. Bedcovers and table linen made from hemmed rectangles of Arts and Crafts-style cotton are very attractive and, if you have the time, inclination and patience, creating your own hand-embroidered cushions from one of the kits available in Arts and Crafts designs will be a source of enormous satisfaction as well as a wonderful way to evoke this era.

Accessories

It's important not to fill an Arts and Crafts-style room with too many items of furniture and decorative bits and pieces, as one of the chief differences between this look and the prevailing Victorian taste was a lack of fuss and clutter. 'It was as if spring had come all of a sudden,' said Belgian designer Henri Van de Velde about the work of Charles Voysey, and Arts and Crafts interiors were surprisingly light and bright compared with the typical nineteenth-century room. In fact, their unpretentious simplicity gives them an almost modern appearance, and certainly makes it easier to reproduce the style today.

Metalwork with a hand-beaten, medieval look is characteristic of the Arts and Crafts designer-makers. Choose a few articles made of pewter, iron, copper, bronze or even silver: lamps, vases, jugs, goblets, bowls, teapots, mirror and picture frames, plates, door furniture and candle sconces are all suitable. Hand-crafted ceramics with interesting glazes, or earthenware painted with natural images, can make an attractive display on a dresser or a plate rack. Consider, if possible, fitting a panel of glowing stained glass, perhaps in an internal door, copying one of Morris's botanical patterns or medieval themes. And one or two paintings hung on the walls can add to the atmosphere: prints of works by the Pre-Raphaelites (Dante Gabriel Rossetti and Edward Burne-Jones were friends of Morris) are perfect for this style.

FABRICS

These very evocative prints by William Morris are instantly recognizable and look as fresh today as they did more than a century ago. Their rhythmic patterns and natural images, in harmonious, muted colours, have a highly distinctive effect and would create a totally authentic and truly beautiful Arts and Crafts scheme.

ABOVE William Morris's company, Morris & Co., made traditional rush-seated chairs such as this. They were either left as bare wood, stained green or ebonized.

Furniture

The Arts and Crafts artisans were renowned for their finely made furniture, in which decoration was very much secondary to construction. In fact, the furniture's pegged joints were frequently left exposed in order to draw attention to the traditional methods with which it had been made. The wood itself, usually oak, was the star – this was furniture not just to be sat in, but also to be admired – remember: both 'useful' and 'beautiful'.

In 1868 the design writer Charles Eastlake published his book *Hints on Household Taste in Furniture, Upholstery and Other Details*, which was highly influential both in Britain and the United States. It advocated Arts and Crafts simplicity, with cheap, simple, rectangular furniture, made with pegged joints, panelling and boarding, no staining or French polishing, and little or no ornamentation. William Morris's company, formed as a direct result of his inability to find fittings that

he liked for his own house, made two types of furniture: massive, Gothic-style pieces in oak, sometimes with carving, inlays or hand-painted panels showing medieval scenes or motifs; and less expensive, rush-seated chairs and settees based on a traditional Sussex chair, left plain or occasionally stained green or ebonized. There was also an adjustable Morris chair, a simple fame with upholstered arm rests, seat and back. In the USA, Gustav Stickley's Arts and Crafts oak furniture was more block-shaped, emphasizing horizontals and verticals, though still leaving the wood unadorned and revealing the jointed construction method. This very popular style was often called Mission furniture, because it was believed to have been inspired by the furnishings of Spanish colonial churches.

With the exception of Morris's Sussex chairs, which sold in large numbers, original Arts and Crafts furnishings were mostly made as one-offs and are usually extremely expensive. There are, however, a few firms which make good reproductions, or you could simply choose country or medieval-style pieces, both of which directly inspired Morris and his fellow designers. Victorian furniture will do, too, if you pick it carefully for a lack of showy extravagance. Woven willow chairs and settees were recommended at the time, making an inexpensive alternative, especially for a conservatory or perhaps a kitchen. The main emphasis should be on an expressive use of beautiful materials, well-finished and preferably handmade, avoiding fussy, non-functional items. Curving lines and ornament are out; upright shapes and straight backs in, sometimes with cut-out motifs of spear-heads or hearts. Seating should be sturdy, with broad arms and a supportive seat and back; benches, settles and simply styled four-poster beds are a good choice, matched with sideboards, oak refectory dining tables, dressers, blanket boxes, ladderback chairs and simple chests. Larger pieces such as cupboards could, perhaps, feature a relief decoration in pewter, brass, ivory or leather, and over-sized hinges fitted to cupboard doors are very typical of this look.

Less crowded than the typical Victorian room, this Arts and Crafts setting demonstrates the basic tenet of William Morris's work: combining the useful with the beautiful.

Summing up the style

1 This nature-inspired wallpaper, light and unfussy, in subtle colours, is typical of Arts and Crafts designs.

2 An oriental carpet, again in subtle colours and with fairly restrained patterns, sets off the room beautifully.

3 The warm, earthy shades of this upholstery is typical of Arts and Crafts fabric and plain colours avoid the over-patterned look of many Victorian rooms.

4 Unlike mainstream Victorian furniture, which was frequently over-decorated and badly made, Arts and Crafts pieces were solid and attractively simple – like this wide chair with its padded armrests. The delicate tea table demonstrates the attention to detail that was common to the movement.

5 Beaten metal is one of the signatures of Arts and Crafts style, and this fender is a lovely example. The pokers are another nice finishing touch, as is the romantic portrait to the right of the fireplace.

Art Nouveau

The 'art of the new' first flowered (almost literally) in the homes of the rich European avant-garde in the mid 1880s, bringing a new, if short-lived, era that combined craftsmanship with fantasy and *fin-de-siècle* decadence. Never an organized movement, it was characterized by the spontaneity and eccentricity of a number of influential individuals, whose aim was to cast off convention and look ahead to a new century, while at the same time creating a fully integrated and expressive environment that made use of new forms, materials and techniques.

The style was inspired by a number of sources, including Arts and Crafts simplicity; Rococo curves; complex, interlacing Celtic patterning; the paintings of the Post-Impressionists, Symbolists and Pre-Raphaelites; the British Aesthetic movement and a vogue for exotic japonisme. Most of all, however, it was the organic shapes of nature that defined Art Nouveau's sinuous forms, asymmetrical shapes and dynamic whiplash lines. Dramatic flower forms recurred, as did insects, serpents and birds, especially swallows, herons and peacocks. The imagery was sensual, occasionally explicit, and female figures with long, flowing hair, sometimes nude, sometimes with floating robes, were another frequently employed motif.

Art Nouveau was also known as Yachting Style, Le Style Moderne, Stile Inglese, Youth Style and even Noodle Style, but the title by which it is generally described today arose from the name of a gallery opened in Paris in 1895 by Siegfried Bing, a furniture dealer and admirer of Far Eastern artefacts. The style originated in Belgium, with the work of the architect-designer Victor Horta, whose Tassel house of 1893 featured exposed cast-iron supports embellished with metal tendrils, their rhythmic curves echoed in wall paintings, floor mosaics and light fittings. This new approach

The nineteenth century's last great decorative style came in the form of Art Nouveau. Imaginative, sensuous and richly ornamented, it combined flowing shapes and glowing colours in a unique, exciting and totally unprecedented new way.

made a huge impact in France, particularly on the designer Hector Guimard, who created whole buildings in this new free-flowing style, and also the distinctive metalwork entrances to the Paris Metro stations.

Art Nouveau was widely practised in Germany, Italy and Austria, too. In Spain, Antoni Gaudí's incredible, fanciful structures defy categorization, but were an extension of the style's non-linear shapes and decorative tendencies. The American version of Art Nouveau was led by glassware designer Louis Comfort Tiffany, and by Louis Sullivan, who covered his buildings with colourful relief foliage. In Britain, meanwhile, Art Nouveau found favour only for textiles, wallpaper and metalwork. The work of Charles Rennie Mackintosh and the Glasgow School, however, was linked to Art Nouveau in its ideals of unified design and the search for a new style. Taking its stylized plant forms as a starting point, it counterpointed them with severe geometry, exaggerated verticals, minimal decorative details and delicate colour schemes that contrasted light and dark, producing a thrilling combination of sophistication and sparsity.

CREATING
THE LOOK

The general ambience of Art Nouveau can be achieved with a small selection of well-chosen pieces against a light and airy background. Aim for a simple, uncluttered elegance, with an emphasis on delicate, winding shapes and botanical imagery. Although European Art Nouveau furniture is extraordinarily costly, there are some good reproductions of Mackintosh-style pieces, while attractive replica lights, wallcoverings, fabrics and accessories should be relatively inexpensive and easy to find.

ABOVE The instantly recognizable signature of Charles Rennie Mackintosh can be seen in these strong horizontals and verticals, repeated squares and stylized cabbage roses.

Walls

In contrast to the naturalist designs in rich colours that covered Victorian rooms, Art Nouveau interiors were of a much quieter and calmer nature. Choose wallpapers in soft colours, with rhythmic, curving patterns of botanical forms such as birds, flowers, sea plants and peacock feathers. William Morris designs are also suitable, though later in the period patterns became more highly stylized and took on a more sensual, emotive nature.

If you prefer painted walls, choose white or a cool pastel colour and add a wallpaper border, or paint your own frieze using typical Art Nouveau motifs. Colourwashing was a paint effect found in more 'artistic' homes, and helps to break up the flat expanses of large areas. More daringly, whole walls would be painted with murals, like those of Mackintosh's Willow Tea Rooms, where slender

female figures were surrounded by twining plants. Wood panelling, painted white or cream, also works well as a backdrop to Art Nouveau furnishings – the emphasis should be on the vertical, with slim boards and the panelling reaching quite high. Porches, hallways, bathrooms and kitchens can be decorated with Art Nouveau-style glazed ceramic wall tiles, which are still mass-produced today and add an authentic splash of colour and pattern.

Floors

Some Art Nouveau flooring featured curving patterns in expensive mosaics or inlaid wood, but it would be equally appropriate if you decide on bare wooden boards or parquet, polished and perhaps stained. These provide an invaluable backdrop to carpets and rugs, which should be an essential part of your scheme. Look for faded oriental rugs, abstract floral designs or perhaps a ribbon-like pattern. Failing that, a completely plain rug in a pale, muted colour is equally good – or a Mackintosh-style one with very simple, square motifs around the edge. If you have a large expanse of wood around the outside of your rug, you could use floor paints to stencil on a curving whiplash border design in toning colours. Fitted carpets look best in plain, soft colours, topped with a suitable rug.

Lights

With electricity just beginning to make its mark at the turn of the century, this was one of the most creative periods in the history of domestic lighting. Most closely associated with Art Nouveau lighting are females and flowers – sometimes both at the same time! Look for sculpted figures with diaphanous dresses and flowing hair holding globes or torches, and flower-head shades in opaque, coloured glass, on a curving metal stem. Other botanical motifs to choose from include butterflies, stag beetles, dragonflies and the praying mantis, and table lamps shaped like a toadstool with glass shades in glowing colours. Not quite so over-the-top, but still in the right spirit, would be gilded wall sconces, bronze and crystal wall lights, and cut-glass ceiling lights. Originals are not terribly expensive, and reproductions are

widely available; if, however, you are on a very tight budget, choose a softly curved base with a plain fabric shade and paint on your own Art Nouveau motifs in a free-flowing style.

Another variation on the botanical theme, and also easily obtained in reproduction form, is the Tiffany-style lamp. First designed for use with oil, then later electricity, Louis Comfort Tiffany's beautiful hand-made lamps featured shades made of lead and stained glass in jewel-like patterns of plants, flowers and leaves. Much copied, but never improved on, they were, and still are, classics of their time.

ABOVE Tiffany lamps, with their botanical forms and jewel-coloured stained glass, are *the* classic Art Nouveau light, and will create an impression in any style of interior.

COLOURS

Art Nouveau colours are very distinctive and easy to use. The main ingredients are white, cream, grey and pastels – rose pink, pale yellow, lilac, pale blue and leafy green – as a calming background. Charles Rennie Mackintosh sometimes employed black for his distinctive furniture, and darker colours can be used sparingly to offset these soft tones, with gem-like touches of red, acid green, amber, turquoise and bright blue to add a typically surprising flash of contrast.

Soft furnishings

The sinuously curving lines, repeating botanical patterns and soft, sensual colours of Art Nouveau fabrics make them very distinctive. Because they create a huge impact in a room you can afford to be selective in your use of them, putting together a restrained look which accords with the turn-of-the-century dislike of abundant textiles in the Victorian manner. Plain fabrics with interesting textures, such as velvet or silk, are a good way of adding to the general ambience.

No Art Nouveau fabrics were more influential than the distinctive prints produced by Liberty of London. The first fabrics sold when the shop opened in 1875 were imported from Japan, but within a few years British designers, including Arthur Silver, Arthur Wilcock and Lindsay Butterfield, had developed a unique style featuring exuberant abstract animals and plants in pastels and brighter colours. By the 1890s the fabrics were at the height of European fashion, so much so that in Italy Art Nouveau was called Stile Liberty. Today a number of these fabrics, in upholstery-weight cotton and linen union, are still in production, as well as others designed later in similar style.

As well as prints, Art Nouveau motifs frequently featured on intricate hand-made embroidery and tapestries. Though often used as decorative wall-hangings, such needlework was also found on curtains, pillows, table runners and even tea cosies! As an inexpensive way of achieving this look, you could adorn plain fabric (a bedcover or tablecloth, for example) with Art Nouveau detailing, making it as simple and unobtrusive or complex and detailed as you wish – a row of lilac, pink and turquoise squares looks beautiful, or you could go wild with intertwining plants and flowers in a range of colours, with added beads, ribbons and metal thread.

When it comes to window treatments, however, opt for elegant simplicity, the aim being to draw

LEFT More cabbage roses in subdued colours make for elegant, softly draped curtains and a stylish seat cover for a high-backed Mackintosh chair.

attention to the window itself rather than how it is dressed. Pelmets should be flat and the curtains themselves just two lengths of unlined fabric, hung from a slender wooden or brass pole, without any drapes, swags or tie-backs. Mackintosh often used only a panel of muslin stretched across a window to filter light while retaining privacy; where more decoration was called for he sometimes used sheer white fabric with appliquéd motifs such as cabbage roses or pink squares on long 'stems', edged with a graphic black border.

Later in life, Mackintosh created a number of designs for commercially printed textiles, ranging from stylized roses, tulips and chrysanthemums to more abstract shapes, including lattices and teardrops. Rich and dynamic, they prefigured Art Deco by a number of years. Such vibrant and complicated patterns, by Mackintosh or one of the Liberty designers, can be used for upholstery, but if you are unable to find a suitable fabric, or if you prefer a less stylized look, simply choose a one-colour fabric – Mackintosh used canvas, linen, silk and velvet in rose, purple as well as unbleached naturals – and either leave it plain or add embroidered or stencilled Art Nouveau motifs.

Accessories

The organic shapes of Art Nouveau accessories, either originals or reproductions, are easy to find – small, decorative pieces such as gilded statuettes of nymphs, lightly clad women or mermaids; candlesticks; photo frames and dressing table sets. Look,

ABOVE This reproduction Art Nouveau fireplace features softly coloured figurative tile inserts and a metal hood with a typically sinuous design.

too, for silver tea services and pewterware, the latter sometimes inlaid with enamel or semi-precious stones or embellished with the surface decoration of foliage, flora and fauna so beloved of the Art Nouveau craftsmen. As with his furniture, it is possible to find modern reproductions of Mackintosh-style clocks, cutlery, vases, mirrors, mugs and table mats, all with the familiar geometric, tulip and cabbage-rose motifs.

FABRICS

Classic Liberty prints are extremely evocative of Art Nouveau, involving swirling designs and complex colours – either fresh and bright, or relatively muted. Lace is another suitable fabric to choose, particularly with a pattern like the one shown here. In addition, it is still possible to obtain fabrics (such as these grey, lilac and blue tulips, and the pink and white cabbage roses) by Charles Rennie Mackintosh, with their stylized, graphic look that characterizes his designs.

Prints of posters, paintings and drawings by contemporary artists such as Henri de Toulouse-Lautrec, Gustav Klimt, Pierre Bonnard and Alphonse Mucha strike the right note of sensual exoticism, with their simplified forms, vivid colours and complex, swirling lines.

Iridescent glass and lustreware pottery, too, is shimmering and mysteriously pretty, while the place to let your imagination really run riot is with Art Nouveau-style stained glass, if you can find a suitable place to install some. With sinuous curves of metal holding a kaleidoscope of colours, even a tiny interior window or door pane will really bring a room to life.

ABOVE This impressive bed, in the Victor Horta House Museum, Brussels, demonstrates the complex, organic shapes of Art Nouveau furniture.

Furniture

The Art Nouveau designers created a new idiom in furniture, abandoning the usual traditions of shape and decoration in favour of incredibly complex pieces that resembled plants and animals. A table, for example, could be a flowering bush, with its feet as the roots, the framework the trunk and branches, and the top the blossoms. Other items might be decorated with carvings of beetles, dragonflies and other insects, while the whole was shaped like melted wax in sweeping organic curves. Such works, by all accounts almost impossible to make up from the designers' sketches, were custom-produced for well-off clients, and little was ever manufactured in any great quantity.

Original Art Nouveau furniture, then, is for serious collectors only, while faithful reproductions are almost non-existent, so when creating this style your best option is to choose furniture that is relatively plain and simple in appearance. Look for pleasant curves and delicate scrolls rather than heavy, square outlines – perhaps quiet Edwardian pieces in oak or satinwood, waxed to show off the grain, with decoration, if any, in the form of sculpted finials, simple inlays and cut-out hearts. Painting Art Nouveau motifs on to wooden furniture is one way to achieve an impression of the look – curling tendrils up a chair back or around a table edge, for example – and a subtle touch would be to add drawer pulls in the shape of small insects, or sinuous etched patterns on the glass of cabinet doors.

An alternative to all these organic curves would be to opt for the highly individual style of Charles Rennie Mackintosh, which shared the origins of Art Nouveau though not all of its essential forms. It is for his uncompromisingly geometrical chairs that most of us know Mackintosh best – in natural wood, ebonized or painted with white enamel, with elongated backs that sometimes extend right down to the floor, they are frequently reproduced today, making a strong statement in any home, and working just as well alone as in an entire Mackintosh-style interior.

In the bathroom, the clean, generous lines of Edwardian fittings – reproduction or salvaged – are highly suitable, and you may be able to find a bath, basic, WC or cistern with Art Nouveau painted decoration (or even paint it on yourself). Colourful tiles by leading *fin de siècle* artist Alphonse Mucha – elegant women surrounded by delicate flowers, or featuring irises, roses, foxgloves, peonies and other flowers – were popular at the time, and create a beautiful impression whether in a modern bathroom or kitchen, or elsewhere in the house.

This is a typical Mackintosh room, where the whiplash lines and intense colours of Art Nouveau have been pared down and stylized into the distinctive style of the Glasgow School.

Summing up the style

1 Stylized floral murals and strong vertical lines are immediately recognizable as the Mackintosh style.

2 A neutral coloured carpet with a gridded design emphasizes the graphic elements in the rest of the room.

3 The square ceiling lamp again echoes the linear Mackintosh feel. Most often associated with Art Nouveau are Tiffany lamps or figurines holding globes.

4 Square shapes are typical of Mackintosh's furniture and this chair is no exception. Equally appropriate would be a ladderback chair with a very elongated back.

5 The square shape and etiolated numerals of this dramatic clock make a strong statement — it is the only accessory in the room and as such stands out even more. The gleaming squares of stained glass inset in the door are another wonderful way to evoke this style.

Edwardian

When Edward VII ascended the British throne in 1901 he took charge of a nation that was experiencing enormous and exciting changes. Advances in medicine, transport and public sanitation; the invention of the cinema, the telephone and lifts; the increased installation of electricity, central heating and running hot water; labour-saving devices such as vacuum cleaners and prototype washing machines: it all added up to a totally new way of life. Perhaps it is no surprise, then, that the Edwardians, while enjoying their modernity, also looked back to the security of bygone times for inspiration in home decorating. Coinciding with a revival of Empire style in France and with Biedermeier in Germany and Austria, Britain brought back Georgian neo-classicism, Tudor olde English and the domestic style known as Queen Anne.

Houses were generously sized, built in red brick, with half-timbered gable ends and bay windows. Decorative relief work on the facades, using a seventeenth-century incised-plaster technique, was common, and windows featured small leaded lights in the sixteenth-century fashion. Like the Victorians, the Edwardians chose to have porches, stained glass windows and tiled paths at their entrances; the difference was that they preferred white-painted woodwork, paths in muted black, white, grey and beige, and glass in softer colours.

Inside, too, it was a different story. Rooms were large, well-lit and used less formally, the old-fashioned drawing room just beginning its transformation to today's comfortable living room. With the commercialization of Arts and Crafts ideals from the artistic avant-garde to the general public, Victorian homes had come to be widely regarded as gloomy and uncomfortable, their clutter excessive and even vulgar. Edwardians reduced the amount of furniture and ornaments, decreased

The Edwardian era may have stretched only from the start of the twentieth century to the First World War, but its influence was wide-ranging and long-lasting and it is still a model for easy, elegant good living.

frills, flounces and draperies, used paler colours and generally aimed for a more spacious look – wealthy, successful, in charge of a far-flung British Empire and embarking on a new century, these people no longer needed to show off about their status in the world.

Thanks to a rise in the middle classes, better-educated and with secure jobs, Edwardian society had new aspirations. People were increasingly interested in the possibilities of interior decoration, and they wanted homes that were affordable, manageable (there being fewer domestic servants around than ever before) and away from inner city smog. 'Garden cities' and suburbs sprang up, appealing to the Edwardian obsession with sunlight and fresh air, while in city centres the mansion block was the newest and most convenient form of housing. But perhaps the high point of Edwardian achievement was the bathroom. Still rather spartan to our eyes, it was then the last word in comfort and performance. Hermann Muthesius (whose study of English homes and interiors, *Das Englische Haus*, was published in 1904) raved about the functionality of English bathrooms, helping to make the Edwardian style one that was admired and emulated all over Europe.

CREATING THE LOOK

These homes were lighter, brighter and more simple in style than their Victorian predecessors, combining practicality with pale prettiness and elegant furnishings. You can make this a very feminine style if you wish, including lots of flowers, lace and pastel colours, but there's no reason why you shouldn't introduce one or two stronger tones, drawing on the masculine domains of the very Edwardian billiards room, library and study.

Walls

Edwardian rooms feature generous skirting boards and, except in the most avant-garde of homes, a profusion of mouldings dividing walls into dado, infill and frieze. High-panelled dados, with the top marked by a plate rack, were extremely fashionable, and oak panelling below a dado was thought suitable for a dining room or hallway. Ceramic tiles were popular for kitchens, conservatories, hallways and bathrooms.

The easiest way, however, to emulate an Edwardian wall finish in your scheme would be by using wallpaper or paint. Pick out woodwork in white or cream and complement with a white or tinted distemper (or a modern paint with a matt, chalky surface). Alternatively, effects such as marbling, graining or rag rolling work well with this look.

ABOVE Delicate flowered wallpaper in pale, light shades typical of the era gives a pretty backdrop to this cosy, informal Edwardian kitchen.

Special wallpapers for friezes were featured prominently in the Edwardian home. They usually took the form of a highly decorative pattern, with the paper below more subtle and restrained. When choosing wallpapers today, look for airy, delicate patterns such as chintzes on a pale background – perhaps with ribbons and bows, trelliswork and baskets; stripes; fabric effects such as moiré and flock; imitation woodgrain, mosaic and marble; and classically inspired, Adamesque designs. An embossed wallpaper up to dado height in halls and stairways makes a hard-wearing surface in keeping with the style.

Floors

The Edwardians favoured boards or parquet made of oak, teak or pine, and then covered most of the floor with a loose carpet. The wood was varnished around the edges and the carpet was in a Middle Eastern, oriental or neo-Georgian design. Complementary borders were sewn around the edges and colours were muted, with patterns relatively restrained. You can achieve this look with a well-worn, faded oriental rug, thrown down on top of either boards or a pale, plain fitted carpet. In front of the hearth, choose something a little grander – this was the showpiece of the living room, and more expensive rugs, or sometimes animal skins, were common. Bedrooms, however, can be simpler, with a scattering of homely rag rugs on wooden boards or a neutral fitted carpet, while bathrooms could have small black and white tiles in geometric patterns or warmer (and cheaper) cork or linoleum. A stone floor in the kitchen is authentic, as are black and white squares of lino, while you could cover a hall floor in either red quarry tiles or an attractive geometric design in black, white, blue, brown or beige encaustic tiles.

Lights

Electricity had become fairly widespread in middle and upper class homes by the early 1900s, its clean brilliance hailed as convenient, hygienic and attractive. It was a major factor in the development of lighter, brighter domestic colour schemes. Light fittings, however, still looked remarkably similar to those designed for use with gas. The

ABOVE This green glass desk lamp epitomizes lighting from the Edwardian era. Originals are now highly collectable, but reproductions are easy to find.

opulence of the era was reflected in elaborate styles, which followed classical, Arts and Crafts or Art Nouveau models.

Brass and glass (which was blown, moulded, etched, coloured or hand-painted) were the most frequently used materials. Look for wall lights with swan-neck arms and shades shaped like bells, pineapples and acorns, chandeliers with three or five curving arms, and the very collectable desk lamps with a wide, heavy base, an adjustable, curved arm and a trough-shaped shade made of brass or green glass. Table lamps could be in the form of brass columns, or else china vase shapes or figurines, and standard lamps are tall and

COLOURS

This colour palette was soft and mellow, with white and cream the predominant shades, toning with gentle flower colours. Lilac was extremely popular, with pink, pale yellow and light green its perfect partners. A recommended scheme for living rooms combined grey, mauve and rose, while dull red, green or blue were thought best for setting off the oil paintings that were compulsory on the walls of dining rooms.

graceful, sometimes with an adjustable side arm for reading by. Rise-and-fall pendant lights were common, but the most typical of all Edwardian lights to look for is the cut crystal or alabaster bowl, set in a brass or bronze mount and suspended from the ceiling by a chain. As an alternative, shades could be in the form of a fabric skirt, while beading and silk fringing is suitable, though, like all other Edwardian ornamentations, these were noticeably less fancy than they had been in the previous century.

Soft furnishings

Inspired by the countryside and gardens, Edwardian fabrics featured rich floral patterns – rambling roses, hollyhocks, wisteria, laburnum, tulips and irises – balanced by pale colours. Fabrics were lighter in weight than in Victorian times, and were used far less extravagantly. Tablecloths, for example, were being replaced by hard mats, which

meant an end to constant washing, while screens rather than heavy *portières* were employed as draught excluders in doorways.

Swags, trimmings and tassels should be used only in moderation, but lace-edged cushions, tablecloths and bedlinen are immediately effective, especially when combined with floral prints in pretty pastel colours. Lace also makes a good window covering, stretched against the lower panes, or you might prefer frilled or plain muslin, as favoured by the more forward-looking Edwardians. The custom of layering fabric at the windows continued in this era, so above the sheer undercurtain you could fix a wooden Venetian blind or a roller blind made of plain, striped or patterned fabric – semi-glazed cotton is particularly appropriate. Then, from a simple brass pole, hang floor-length pairs of floral-patterned curtains in damask, cotton, wool, linen union or brocade; pelmets can be plain, pleated or frilled but not too sumptuously draped.

Bedrooms should be especially light and airy. Match chintz curtains with floral bedcovers, pillowcases and mantelshelf borders – you can create a medley of patterns as long as you feel they work well together. Plain fabric is fine for a less elaborate look, but a few appliquéd or embroidered flower details in the corners or along the border hints at the delicate, feminine feel of this period.

Upholstery, now more slimline and elegant than in the Victoria era, was much less extravagantly buttoned and fringed. Silks and brocades were widely used, with practical loose covers made of flowered chintz – today, pale-coloured floral patterns in a relatively lightweight fabric will look the

FABRICS

Delicate patterns and pastel colours are characteristic of the Edwardian era. Floral lace and pale pink silk work well with glazed or unglazed cotton featuring tiny flowers, sprigs or pretty brocade in shiny but subtle colourways. An old rose chintz completes the effect. The fabrics shown here would be most suitable for, say, a bedroom, though deeper colours could be used for a less feminine look.

part. Cover small, round tables with floor-length cloths, and add lace antimacassars to chair backs and a few lace-trimmed cushions in different sizes and shapes. Although it may be tempting, however, do avoid going over the top, instead aiming for a simple prettiness that is both comfortable and abundantly attractive.

Accessories

Accessories and *objets d'art* can be chosen to complement the revivalist nature of Edwardian furnishings – clocks and barometers with classical details, Georgian-style mirrors and candlesticks and displays of plates, bowls, tankards and vases in pewter or copper. You could also add decorative enamelware, scent bottles with a filigree silver overlay or photographs and prints in frames made of silver, walnut or bird's eye maple. Desk sets (pen tray, blotter, letter rack, paper knife and inkstand) and dressing table sets – a silver-mounted hairbrush and comb, clothes brush, hand mirror, jewellery box, glove stretchers, button hook and powder puff – are equally appropriate, as are collections of children's toys. Accessories with an Arts and Crafts or Art Nouveau flavour would also work well with this look.

Furniture

Despite the reduction in clutter as compared to the overcrowded rooms of Victorian times, minimalism was still a long way off at the turn of the century, and the Edwardians owned a wide array of furniture. Their rooms boasted chairs, settees (the buttoned-leather chesterfield sofa is a classic of the time), chaise longues, music cabinets, display cases, side tables, desks, sideboards, bookcases, hall benches, coat stands, jardinières, card tables, umbrella stands, dinner gongs, even portable cake stands – and, of course, no home was complete without its very own piano, while a few possessed unwieldy phonographs.

The Edwardians also had a liking for reproduction antiques. To recreate the most popular look of the time – the Georgian style in the manner of Sheraton, Chippendale or Hepplewhite – look for pieces that are classical in appearance, made of satinwood, oak, walnut, birch and sycamore. This furniture is delicate, light and upright but, although it was based on eighteenth-century models, you can be grateful that Edwardian seating was made infinitely more comfortable with the addition of large, padded cushions.

ABOVE This fitted kitchen is utterly modern, yet its cream paintwork and the plain cupboard doors with their bun-shaped handles add up to a thoroughly Edwardian style.

Another revival style to look out for is a sort of Tudorbethan olde English, which included oak dining chairs with rush- or hide-covered seats, Charles I tables with bulbous turned legs and anything with a dark, heavy, sixteenth-century appearance. This was a fashion not just in Britain, but all over Europe and in the United States, too, again made in a more comfortable form to suit twentieth-century expectations.

The Arts and Crafts ethos was, by this time, gaining popular ground, disseminated via the designs of pioneering shops such as Waring and Gillow, Heal's and Liberty. Their functional pieces, with the minimum of detailing, would work well in a modern home. All the rage, too, were wickerwork chairs and settees, built-in furniture – convenient and space-saving for owners of town-centre apartments – and suites sold in matching sets: not just settees and chairs, but also cabinets, mirrors and side tables for the living room, and a wide range of items for the bedroom. To emulate a truly stylish Edwardian house, you should paint all bedroom furniture white. The exception would be a metal bed, made of iron and brass in a classical, geometric style, that could be left unadorned or enamelled in an 'art colour' such as apple green, light brown or sparrow egg blue.

In the kitchen, Edwardian-style fitted units are an attractive solution to the problem of creating a period look in a way that is practical and easy to use. Simple panelled or glazed cupboards with round knob handles and an open dresser, painted in soft shades of green and cream, will satisfy today's technological requirements while being highly evocative of the era. A similar effect can be created in the bathroom, using salvaged or reproduction Edwardian ceramics, both of which can be obtained relatively easily. Here, unadorned fittings, in white or off-white, could include a roll-top bath on ball-and-claw feet, a large, marble-topped washstand on legs, a huge shower rose, an etched-glass shower screen, free-standing metal towel rails and gleaming taps made of nickel or silver-plated bronze, resulting in a room that is distinctive to look at, easy to clean and pleasurable to use.

A delicate and airy look such as this is typical of the early twentieth century, its comfort and practicality evident at first glance.

Summing up the style

1 Delicate, trailing floral patterns on a pale background are the perfect option for an Edwardian-style wallpaper.

2 A pretty rug in front of the hearth was often the Edwardian choice, placed on top of neutral-coloured carpets or wooden flooring.

3 The classic lines of this table lamp fit very well into a scheme of this nature. In general, rooms were lit more brightly than they had ever been before, showing off their decoration to good advantage.

4 Patterned silks in pale colours are just right for upholstery, if not very hard-wearing. And cushions with embroidered or needlepoint flowers add just the right touch – a little lace here and there would not go amiss, either.

5 The Edwardians owned a wide variety of furniture, and these pieces show the influence of Victorian, Arts and Crafts and Georgian-revival styles.

6 An old-fashioned wall clock and an informal grouping of prints are not showy, but do add to the overall authenticity of this look.

Art Deco

Art Deco, also known as Art Moderne, Jazz Moderne or simply Deco, had its roots in the work of leading French designers before the First World War, but only became widely recognized after the 1925 Paris Exposition Internationale des Arts Décoratifs et Industriels Modernes – from which it derived its name. The aim of the exhibition was to modernize French interior design, and although other nations participated it was French fabrics, furniture, interior decoration, fashion and architecture that made the greatest impact.

French design had moved into a new era. Though still employing classical features and the most exclusive and rare materials, it added contemporary influences to produce a style that perfectly expressed the excitement of the time. The geometry of the Cubist artists, the shocking colours of the Fauvist painters, the exoticism of Serge Diaghilev's Ballets Russes, a craze for all things Egyptian (the tomb of Tutankhamun had been discovered in 1922), and a taste for the art and artefacts of the Middle East, Africa, native America, Mexico and ancient Babylonia – they all added up to a heady and irresistible mix. As the style took hold, later designers used new developments in technology to their advantage, so stainless steel, chrome and Bakelite plastic were added to the Art Deco repertoire of expensive hardwoods, lacquer, mother of pearl, shark skin, tortoiseshell and leather.

American delegates to the Exposition were particularly impressed by this innovative look. Deco's dashing, up-to-date effect was just right for a thrusting young nation, and it soon travelled across the Atlantic to be used for the interiors of buildings, especially hotels and skyscrapers, from Miami to New York. However, American designers did more than just import and embrace Art

Glamorous, modern and dramatic, the Art Deco style dominated the Twenties and Thirties. Its clean lines and bright colours were enthusiastically adopted for every aspect of design and decoration from skyscrapers to suburban homes, cinemas to cruise ships.

Deco – they gave it a new twist. Inspired by the latest fascination for speed and the aerodynamic detailing of cars, planes and trains, they overlaid a streamlined effect that was both sleek and chic. The look beautifully complemented the smooth, reflective surfaces and simple shapes of European Deco, and came to be known as Streamlining.

In Britain, Art Deco began to make its mark in the early Thirties. Thousands of suburban homes were built with Deco features such as metal-framed, rounded bay windows, doorways with stepped surrounds and garden gates featuring the sunrise motif. Bakelite was used for locks, handles and fingerplates, while exterior doors were sometimes clad with sheet metal, complementing the metallic finishes inside. Brightly coloured zigzags, chevrons, ziggurats, exotic animals and stylized flowers could be found on furnishings, accessories and practically any type of homeware to which the Art Deco vocabulary could be applied; indeed, the style became so commercial it was occasionally kitsch. What was once a luxurious style available only to the few had now become a popular domestic style.

CREATING THE LOOK

The widespread availability of Art Deco objects makes this one of the easiest styles to put together. Original furniture and furnishings can be found at all price levels and in many different outlets, from junk shops to the grandest auction houses, and there's a thriving industry producing reproductions of many kinds. What's more, whether you want just a touch of Deco decadence or the all-over authentic appearance, the look's clean lines and splashes of colour fit really well into a modern home.

Walls

It's fortunate that the most fashionable of Art Deco wall treatments – white, off-white or beige paint – is also the simplest to accomplish. Whether plain, rag-rolled, stippled or marbled, this restrained look makes an excellent backdrop to boldly coloured fabric and accessories. If you prefer a slightly more decorative effect, add stencilled or papered borders and corners which echo contemporary motifs such as sunrays or ziggurats. Wallpaper, which was a popular choice in suburban homes, frequently featured geometric patterns and stylized botanical themes. Though dramatic, the effect today may be overwhelming, and a good alternative would be embossed or wood-effect paper. At the opposite end of the scale, it was the height of luxury for walls to be panelled in lacquer or wood (stripped and waxed, or perhaps stained), or embellished with painted mouldings. Mural painting was enjoying a revival in this period, and some Deco houses featured trompe-l'oeil or abstract designs by professional artists. To create a similar effect you could cut out a section from a suitably patterned roll of wallpaper and paste it up – or you may feel brave enough to paint your own. Only for the very bold, though, are two eye-catching treatments that became popular at the end of the Twenties: the all-over metallic look, and whole walls covered with mirror tiles. Try them if you dare!

Floors

The favoured flooring for an Art Deco living area was pale wood, in the form of boards, block or various patterns of parquet. Wall-to-wall carpet, although not usual at the time, has the right streamlined look to it if you stick to pale colours such as cream or taupe. Throw down a selection of rugs – fake animal skin is suitably decadent, while graphic geometric patterns in vivid colours also fit the bill. In other rooms, especially halls, kitchens and bathrooms, this was the heyday of linoleum, a natural material which is now seen as thoroughly fashionable once more. Lino tiles are the simplest to use, and look wonderful arranged in checks of two or

LEFT Beige walls are enlivened by a sunrise-motif stencil, while an animal-skin rug is an exotic addition to the plain floor. The marbled glass pendant, column-shaped uplighter and table lamp with dancing figure are all very typical.

RIGHT Chrome and glass were often used by Art Deco lighting designers, and this stepped ziggurat shape was very popular.

three colours. Alternatively, you could cover an area with a solid block of colour – green, beige or brown would be appropriate. Or take advantage of the ease with which lino can be cut in any pattern, and have it laid to your own design in wild Deco motifs.

COLOURS

Pale colours are predominant in the Art Deco look, cream, beige and eau de nil providing a cool, calm background for the hotter accent colours. Inspired by contemporary art and, in particular, the fashionable Ballets Russes, these include orange, lime green, mauve, crimson and yellow. Black and the shiny, reflective surfaces of glass, mirror and metals are the perfect foil for this dramatic combination.

Lights

As the use of electricity became increasingly widespread throughout the Twenties, more attention than ever before was paid to the function and appearance of domestic lighting. Art Deco designers made use of the many new materials available, such as aluminium, tubular steel, plastics, pressed glass and plywood, to produce a wide variety of fittings with the aim of producing a soft, diffused glow.

One typical style to look out for is a pendant light in the form of an inverted bowl in marbled glass, hung from three chains. Though usually round, these were sometimes hexagonal, stepped or cone-shaped, and occasionally featured patterns of animals, flowers, fruit or geometric designs. You could also choose wall lights made of glass and chrome, in the shape of a ziggurat, shell or fan, and table lamps in streamlined styles, often with columnar bases. These were often adorned with Art Deco motifs such as the sunray, leaping gazelles or borzoi dogs. Materials used were chrome, acrylic, Bakelite or pale, grained wood, while shades were in moulded glass, parchment, plastic and silk. If you have some plain lamps to which you'd like to give the Deco treatment, adding deep fringing (think of flappers' dresses) or stencilled motifs to a fabric shade is both easy and instant. The archetypical Art Deco light, however, is the figure lamp – a stylized female in graceful pose, holding an illuminated globe. They were produced in vast quantities, mostly in Paris and Vienna, and are still widely available in reproduction form, adding an elegant touch to any interior.

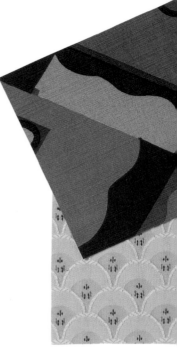

Soft furnishings

Up-market Art Deco interiors used sumptuous soft furnishings in silk, satin, velvet and leather, but as the look gained wide appeal it was cotton, moquette and chenille that appeared in the homes of ordinary people. And, as designs were mass produced, their colours and patterns tended to become more garish and crude, so that the suburban living room of a middle-class British couple bore no more than a passing resemblance to the hand-crafted apartment of a chic Parisian.

The most frequently used Art Deco textiles featured graphic patterns, either in black on a grey, white or beige background or in a clashing palette of bold hues. Batik (see page 184) was especially popular in Europe and the USA in the Twenties, due to its rich colours and associations with the Far East, while prints often featured African-inspired motifs, such as exotic animals or lush vegetation.

For upholstery, choose leather (expensive but hard-wearing), chenille, velveteen or moquette, which comes in a velvety, cut pile or an uncut, loopy pile. Plain, neutral colours are easy to co-ordinate, or you could make more of an impact with strong geometrics in brighter shades. Patterns can be based on the familiar Art Deco vocabulary of zigzags, chevrons, lightning flashes, shells, sunrays, fans and stylized flowers.

Window treatments took a back seat in the Art Deco room. Wide-slatted Venetian blinds were

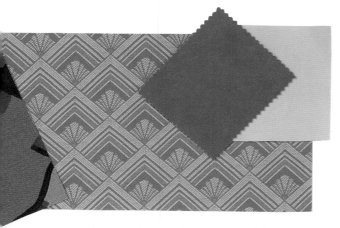

FABRICS

Suede and leather (real or imitation) can be used in natural or artificial colours – this mid-green Alcantara suede is particularly typical of the era. The motifs of the other fabrics – shells, sunrises, diamonds and strong abstracts – also have a uniquely jazz-age appearance, as well as interesting textures. Chenille, velveteen or moquette would make equally suitable choices.

popular, in metal or pale wood, while curtains were very often made from plain fabrics and hung in simple, floor-length pairs. If you wish, however, you could border the fabric with a pattern that co-ordinates with your upholstery, or even block-print it yourself using stencils and fabric paints – a simple design can be highly effective. An Art Deco pelmet would be made of wood, painted or covered with stretched fabric, and in simple shapes such as a rectangle with stepped detailing. Alternatively, dispense with a pelmet altogether and hang your curtains from a showy chrome pole.

It's best to keep bedlinen fairly simple – all-over white or a pastel shade won't detract from the jazzier elements in the room, though satin sheets would add an air of Hollywood extravagance. Where you can go to town is with accessories: fake fur throws and tasselled shawls casually flung over a bed, sofa or chair are suitably louche and can be used to provide accent colour, and large velvet- or silk-covered cushions with lots of fringing add an indispensable hint of the exotic east.

Accessories

Give yourself free rein with exciting accessories and ornaments to sum up every aspect of the Art Deco look. With its bright colours and vivacious, energetic patterns, Deco pottery, for example, adds an instant lift to a room – the work of Clarice Cliff is always the first to spring to mind. Her very collectable 'Bizarre' range, for example, is splashy and bold in bright reds, oranges, yellows, greens and black for a graphic effect. Glassware was very much used, in the shape of anything from vases to fruit bowls, perfume bottles to

lamp bases, and you could choose either expensive crystal featuring Lalique-inspired curves or cheaper, opaque pressed glass, depending on your pocket. Sit graceful bronze ornaments beside a chrome clock and a Bakelite radio (which should incorporate a sunrise motif), and on the wall hang mirrors, either circular or with a ziggurat-shaped top, and plaques in the form of faces, baskets, garlands of flowers, fans and feathers. Add glamour with shiny cocktail accessories and silver dressing table sets, and a hint of the exotic with lacquer boxes or trays and collections of African or South American artefacts – hanging a row of tribal masks, for example, is highly effective. Finally, add several large palms and decorate anything you can think of – lampshades, drawer pulls, cushions and seat backs – with silky tassels and fringing for the required touch of glamour and luxury.

ABOVE This crockery is by Clarice Cliff, probably the best-known Deco designer today. With graphic shapes and bold colours, her work is prized by collectors all over the world.

Furniture

The pioneers of Art Deco furniture design tended to favour materials that were rare, luxurious and extremely expensive. Popular Art Deco, however, employed a more down-to-earth approach, and furniture was robust, crafted from ordinary woods and forgoing extravagant veneering and inlaid decoration. Overall, styles became lower and more upright, the detailing less ornate and the colours paler.

Furniture made from the most luxurious of Art Deco materials is expensive and hard to find so, unless you wish to invest heavily in one or two very special pieces, you will want to concentrate more on shape, colour and texture. Geometric outlines and rounded corners are characteristic, and sofas and armchairs – the three-piece suite was a recent addition to the middle-class home – should be rectangular or have simply rounded back and sides. Square, glass-fronted sideboards were popular for displaying china, and two completely new types of furniture had recently been invented: the coffee table and the cocktail cabinet. Smooth, shiny and reflective surfaces were part of the look, so try to find pieces in pale woods such as light oak, walnut, ash or sycamore, or else chrome, aluminium, steel, glass and mirror. A chrome and glass drinks trolley with circular sides is typical, as are round side tables and mirrored dressing tables.

In the move to simplify and streamline domestic items, fitted furniture became more common during this period, and one room in which this was more obvious than any other was the kitchen. A modern fitted kitchen, if relatively plain, is not remarkably dissimilar from one of this period, though a deep, square butler's sink and wooden draining board would add authenticity, and you could emphasize the Art Deco effect by stencilling corner motifs on to your units.

Bathrooms in an Art Deco style are extremely popular; the attraction lies in their solid yet elegant shapes and their glamorous looks. Fortunately, this type of sanitaryware is readily available, reproduced by many of the major manufacturers or, if you want to hunt for an original, from salvage yards and antiques dealers. Colours are black, white and pastels, or a minty or bottle green, combined with plenty of chrome and mirrored surfaces. By the Thirties baths were beginning to be boxed in, but until then cast iron baths on legs were still the norm. WCs had a separate cistern with a chain flush, and basins were on chrome legs, with a handy rail underneath for towels. Even without an Art Deco suite, however, you can create the effect by combining chrome towel rails with checkerboard tiles, hexagonal taps and mirrors with bevelled edges.

LEFT Mint green combined with black and white were favourite Art Deco colours. The chunky shapes and stepped outlines of this bathroom suite, too, give it an entirely Thirties feel.

The sunrise motif in the stained-glass windows was an obvious pointer towards choosing an Art Deco style for this sitting room.

Summing up the style

1 Cream-painted walls give the right clean, neutral background for an Art Deco scheme. For more interest, you could add stencilled or paper borders in Art Deco motifs.

2 Pale floors are more typical of the era, but the darker colour of these wooden floorboards beautifully offsets the lighter colours used elsewhere. An ivory-coloured shag pile rug adds comfort and just a hint of glamour.

3 Upholstered furniture of the Twenties and Thirties often featured colourful fabrics with distinctive geometric designs. Here, however, restraint has been exercised with the use of beige leather and contrasting cream piping to emphasize the very Twenties shape. The understated curtains are beautifully complementary.

4 Glass-fronted wooden sideboards, used to display china, were found in many an Art Deco home. The shape of this piece nicely echoes the dramatic curves of the sofa and chair. The circular side table, with its chromed legs, is very authentic.

5 Art Deco crockery is very collectable and can be used all around the home. Here its bright geometric patterns bring a dash of colour to the window sill.

Modernist

The Modern movement had its roots in the work of design reformers of the late nineteenth century, who saw themselves as the creators of a modern machine age. As Europe rapidly became more urban and industrial, the early Modernists explored the forms and materials of mass production, rejecting the ornamentation of Art Nouveau and the hand-made nature of Arts and Crafts, but retaining the latter's belief in the necessity of honesty and social purpose in design.

Two names are inextricably linked with Modernism – the German Bauhaus design school and the French architect Le Corbusier. Founded in 1919, the Bauhaus was associated with many of the movement's major names, including Walter Gropius, Ludwig Mies van der Rohe, László Moholy-Nagy, Marcel Breuer and Wassily Kandinsky. Using geometric forms and primary colours, and aiming to ally art, craft and industry, by the mid Twenties the school was a leading light in the creation of functional architecture, interiors and objects. Le Corbusier, who exhibited his Pavillon de l'Esprit Nouveau at the predominantly Art Deco Paris Exposition in 1925, is now seen as the century's most influential architect. He promoted a pure design vocabulary in which clean lines, bare walls and economic furnishings in open-plan rooms were accompanied by the extensive use of glass, metal and concrete. Groups in other countries, including the Dutch De Stijl and the Russian Constructivists, were working along similar lines, although Britain was resistant, preferring Arts and Crafts, Art Deco or mock Tudor to such a radical departure from national heritage.

The next step was for the style to cross the Atlantic. As European designers fled the Second World War, their Modernist principles were eagerly adopted in the USA and, re-named International Style, became synonymous with cutting-

It has been the dominant look of the twentieth century, and though Modernism's essential elements – concrete and glass, open-plan living, modular furniture, geometric shapes and primary colours – provide no room for unnecessary decorative effects, there is still plenty of space for stylish living.

edge American architecture. For several decades, America's most important designers worked closely within Modernist idioms, building deceptively simple concrete-and-steel houses with flat roofs and expanses of glass and plain surfaces.

But it was not to last. As quality was sacrificed for quantity, the crude tower blocks built during the Sixties in the name of Modernism brought widespread condemnation of the movement as narrow-minded and unemotional. Le Corbusier's description of a house as 'a machine for living in' was much criticized – though it was often forgotten that his quotation ended: 'But it should also be a place conducive to meditation, and lastly, a beautiful place.' Perhaps it is only from a suitable distance that we have been able to re-evaluate the contribution that Modernism has made to contemporary design. Recent years have seen a renewed interest in the movement's ideals, and now – a century on from its origins – Modernist houses in Europe and the USA have become, for many, icons of our time.

CREATING THE LOOK

Understated and sophisticated, this is a look that's both of the moment and timelessly classic. Seek out designer furniture in the many new shops that specialize in twentieth-century antiques (although such purchases can be expensive, it's likely that they will accumulate in value), and co-ordinate with light, spare and attractive modern pieces inspired by Le Corbusier and his allies. Overall, the feeling should be bright and airy, emphasizing space, horizontal and vertical lines and the flow of movement from one room to another.

ABOVE A vast expanse of white walls, plus smooth wooden flooring and a graphic light, all conform to the Modernist ethos, here setting off a table and chairs in minimal style.

Walls

Modernist homes are precise and logical, and are, therefore, inevitably associated with plain white walls, across which the play of sunlight through large windows can make interesting, abstract patterns. Vast expanses of smooth, flat plaster are best, without any pattern or texture, though if you have decorative details such as cornices, skirtings, ceiling roses or other mouldings, don't rip them out but simply paint them in plain white to minimize their impact. One plane of a bright colour is allowed – you may decide to paint just one wall of a room in a seasonal 'fashion' colour – and simple white tiles can substitute for plaster in kitchens and bathrooms. Plywood was sometimes used to line the dining rooms and studies of Modernist houses,

and these days MDF (medium density fibreboard, or particleboard) is a cheap and easy-to-use contemporary solution. It has no grain, is available in different thicknesses and, though usually painted, also has a minimalist appeal when covered with a clear varnish.

Strangely enough, one of the most popular Bauhaus products was wallpaper, which came in vivid colours such as orange, mustard and sharp green, featuring splattered dots, narrow stripes and checks. For an unconventional Modernist look, you could try adding a splash of colour by using a bright wallpaper in a similar design, though you'll need to exercise care for it not to look out of place. If any building works are to be done, try to include glass bricks where possible (they look marvellous as shower walls), to give just the right feeling of open space, transparency and fluidity.

Floors

In a similar vein, flooring, whether wood, carpet, stone or other, should also be rather plain. Lay dark hardwood – reclaimed wood is environmentally friendly – as boards or parquet, and polish for a refined elegance. Unglazed quarry tiles are functional and attractive in kitchens and halls, while cork or lino are ideal for bathrooms. The industrial flatness of lino or vinyl, perhaps divided into blocks of different colours for interest is, in fact, perfect for any room in the house, while rubber or polished concrete would fit well with this look if you want a surface that's dramatically different.

Flat-weave rugs, in bold, abstract patterns, soften the effect of these tough, hard-working floors, and fitted carpets in neutral colours, or robust natural mattings, such as sisal or coir, are a good substitute for hard flooring. Do, however, avoid oriental styles, florals, or anything too soft and pretty, as they are simply not in keeping.

Lights

The industrial styling of Modernism can really come to the fore in your use of lighting. The architect Richard Neutra, for example, adapted a

RIGHT The Anglepoise lamp first appeared in 1932 and has been immensely popular ever since, its good looks combining with maximum adaptability.

Model T Ford headlight for use as a wall lamp in his famous Lovell House of 1929, and anything of a similarly functional nature that you can find will create the correct effect. It's hard to beat the metal Anglepoise, invented in 1932 by automobile engineer George Carwardine, for its ultra-efficient, usable shape, while the good-looking Bestlite, which comes in the form of table, floor, desk and wall lamps, is another classic design. Fluorescent tubes were first developed in 1939 and are bright and economical for bathrooms and kitchens, and halogen spotlights work extremely well in any room. Cube-shaped or hemispherical pendant lights, and cone-shaped coolie shades, are all typical of the restrained Modernist styling, and should be made of glass, chrome or plastic; integrated systems, as used by Le Corbusier, increase the sense of space, and there are plenty of contemporary designs around which capture the right sort of clean-lined, undecorated look.

COLOURS

White should be the predominant shade in any Modernist-style house – it is bright and reflective, emphasizing spaciousness, hygiene, and the open nature of the architecture. As an antithesis, black was often favoured for the leather upholstery of Modernist furniture, although some designers, especially the Scandinavians, favoured bare, blond wood. Grey, taupe and chrome can be added to this sparsity, while primaries will give a touch of colour.

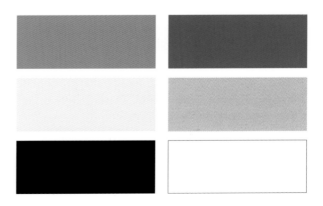

Soft furnishings

What with plain walls, plain floors and pared-down styles of furniture, fabric often provided the only colour or decorative feature in the Modernist house. Soft furnishings at the time were inspired by abstract art, the Fauves and Cubists in particular, and could be surprisingly bold and rich. They might feature squares, diamonds, wave-like curves, stripes, zigzags and chevrons, all combined at once and executed in a multitude of vivid colours. Weaving, for example, was an important discipline at the Bauhaus, and fabrics tended to feature geometric shapes, such as checks, stripes and small repeat motifs, in bright shades. Similarly, the prominent Modernist fabric designer Sonia Delaunay worked with rhythmic geometry, combining many colours at once, while Marion Dorn's celebrated abstract designs employed confident colourways and bold forms. The avant-garde Edinburgh Weavers company was well-known for its Modernist fabrics, and

ABOVE Modular seating has the streamlined look so beloved of Modernist designers. This upholstery is sophisticated and sharply tailored, yet comfortable enough for everyday use.

its 1937 Constructivist collection was designed by the sculptor Barbara Hepworth and painters Ben Nicholson and Duncan Grant.

You can have too much of a good thing, however, and such complex, polychromatic textiles should never be allowed to dominate a Modernist-style interior. The impact is greater if used sparingly, and one element of such colour and pattern in any room is easily enough – Modernist homes tended to use such pieces as single wall-hangings, a bright focus for the eye in what was otherwise an oasis of calm. Upholstery is best limited to plain fabrics – black, white, grey or brown leather is best, though quiet colours in other fabrics are fine; texture is important, and rough canvas is equally as suitable as the finest silk. You can add interest with cushions or throws in graphic zebra stripes or 'cow hide', or in hot colours such as orange, yellow and red. The same goes for other soft furnishings such as bedlinen and tablecloths – if in doubt, play safe and simply stick to white or a solid colour.

At the windows, it's time to forget about any sort of elaborate treatment. Don't do anything more decorative than a plain-coloured fabric (preferably white or unbleached cotton or linen) hung in simple gathers on a metal or plastic track – with no pelmet or fussy swags, drapes or tie-backs. Better still would be roller blinds, again kept extremely plain and simple, or Venetian blinds in wood or plastic, which can be adjusted to filter in the required amount of sunlight. Best of all, however, is nothing at all, the Modernist aim being to keep spaces open and functional, exposing their structure to the world. Bearing in mind the expanse of glass found in many Modernist homes, this is often a very brave move, a little like living in a fish bowl, but for extroverts or those who don't have nosy neighbours it is the ultimate expression of that famous Modernist maxim: 'Less is more'.

Accessories

Modernist homes can be defined more by their absence of 'things' than by any decorative themes, collections or accessories. The look is cool, clean and uncluttered, and careful placing of just one or two special objects makes more of a statement than a crowded room filled with mismatching pieces. Slim vases in bright colours, undulating, translucent glassware (Alvar Aalto's Savoy vase of 1937 is highly desirable) and plain, geometrically shaped crockery could form the basis of a minimal display, while abstract paintings and sculptures add to the cool, restrained feel. Try, if you can, to find prints of works by prominent artists of the era – Piet Mondrian was an influential member of the De Stijl group, producing black, white and primary coloured, grid-like paintings, and the designer Cassandre created wonderful posters for French Railways and the London Underground in the Twenties and Thirties. This is a style where quality of detail can make all the difference, so concentrate on elements such as elegant stainless steel door handles and light switches, perfect paint finishes, and rigorous tidiness.

FABRICS

The Modernist scheme is a clever combination of the restrained and the striking, in fabrics just as much as everywhere else. Suede and canvas in natural tones or vivid primaries can provide a uniform backdrop, while busier, brighter abstract designs in a variety of strong hues are perfectly suited to a room which has pared-down furniture and white walls.

Furniture

A key Modernist concept is 'form follows function', and the movement's furniture was influenced not only by technological developments and industrial materials, but also by new concepts in efficiency and space-saving. Emulating the interiors of ships and trains, convenience and ease of use was the goal, and any type of decoration was thought unnecessary and impure. The forms that arose were light, durable and, of course, eminently functional.

simple, squared-off shapes are particularly suitable. Also appropriate are modular furniture ranges, sideboards with sliding doors and storage systems used as room dividers. Built-in furniture is a good way to use your space efficiently, and this could include anything from wardrobes, bookshelves and beds to sound systems and cocktail cabinets.

This emphasis on efficiency had a significant effect on the appearance of kitchens and bathrooms. Now that cooking and cleaning were no

LEFT Ludwig Mies van der Rohe was the last director of the Bauhaus school of design. He designed the classic Barcelona chair and chaise seen here, in 1930; both are still being produced.

So much so, in fact, that you are more likely to see these pieces used in offices than a domestic setting.

Many of the designs created by the Modernist masters have now become classics. The big names include Alvar Aalto's tables, chairs and stools, Le Corbusier and Charlotte Perriand's chaise longue and Confort armchairs, Mies van der Rohe's Barcelona chair and Eileen Gray's adjustable side table and Bibendum chair. All are still in production today, while older pieces can occasionally be tracked down in specialist shops and auctions.

Those looking for a less expensive option can, however, find plenty of pieces of the same idiom in high-street shops. Clear away the clutter and add specially chosen pieces in chrome, glass, plywood, leather and tubular steel. Cantilevered chairs, circular bent-ply stools and sofas and chairs in

longer the exclusive preserve of servants, housewives demanded labour-saving devices and practical, attractive kitchens in which to use them. In fact a modern fitted kitchen is not too far from the Modernist look – built-in wall and floor cupboards, laminated worksurfaces and rows of uniform storage jars having been introduced by the Bauhaus as far back as the Twenties.

Nor is a modern bathroom too dissimilar from a Modernist one, with boxed-in plumbing and bath, low-level cistern and heated towel rail. To achieve this look, a plain white suite is a good starting point, with glass shelves on chrome brackets, plus taps and fittings in a functional style. Stainless steel cabinets or a row of matching pots, will conceal bathroom gear and give the clean (even slightly hospital-like) effect you require.

You will probably either love or hate this Corbusier living room. The open-plan space is highly dramatic, and each piece of furniture makes a big statement.

Summing up the style

1 Solid walls are banished in favour of the extensive use of glass, making for wonderful light and beautiful views.

2 An expanse of pale, polished timber flooring is chic and sophisticated. Rugs featuring splashes of vivid colour and abstract design can create extra interest if needed.

3 Adjustable lighting such as this came into its own in the Thirties, in graphically simple, streamlined shapes. Concealed lighting, too, is an integral part of the Modernist ethos.

4 These long curtains are essential for both insulation and privacy, but have been kept as minimal in style as possible. Pelmets, swags and tie-backs were anathema to the Modernists.

5 A Le Corbusier chaise longue is the ideal resting place from which to admire the scenery outside, its minimal, flowing lines a perfect example of the 'form follows function' aesthetic. On the left is a leather 'Lounge' chair and ottoman by Charles and Ray Eames.

6 A striking piece of sculpture in the right style creates huge impact.

Fifties

The Fifties were a time of unprecedented social change. The war had broadened cultural contacts, brought new roles for women and developed a sense of common purpose and working together. Afterwards, state-provided health and welfare schemes were set up in many countries, and massive housing schemes replaced bomb damage and swept away the slums. As science and technology advanced with great rapidity, anything seemed possible, from nuclear energy to space exploration, while Melamine, Formica, Terylene and Perspex found their way into domestic settings. A desire for home improvement combined with little money and a make-do-and-mend approach meant that by the end of the decade DIY had become big business, with everything from making a lampshade to converting an attic promoted as both practical and enjoyable.

The 1951 Festival of Britain, a morale-boosting celebration of British achievements, attracted 8.5 million visitors and brought far-reaching changes to the British attitude to home furnishing. Room sets and designs on show attempted to demonstrate 'good design' that was accessible to all. Pale, lightweight and informal, this Contemporary Style was a revelation, and soon its sculptural yet practical shapes and distinctive use of pattern and colour were widely featured in magazines and could be found in all the most fashionable homes.

No British house was complete without at least one item of Scandinavian furniture, glass, ceramics or fabric. Usable and beautiful, the Scandinavian version of Modernism dominated the Fifties, blending mass production with hand craftsmanship, quality with democratic ideals and tradition with an exploration of the new organic forms. It was the United States, however, that gave the Fifties their most potent symbols. From the post-war economic boom that had begun in the USA

The war was over, and in a reaction to those dark days of fear and deprivation, a new tomorrow dawned with an explosion of bright colour and exciting patterns. By the 1950s a distinctive look had emerged, symbolizing the unquenchable optimism of the era.

sprang a new consumer culture, embodied in the highly desirable American Look. Fanciful, larger-than-life and up-to-the-minute, it could be seen in showy tail-fin Cadillacs, labour-saving devices, the first-ever shopping malls, drive-in cinemas, vivid neon signs and huge corporations such as Coca-Cola and McDonald's.

Hand in hand with the 'you've never had it so good' culture went a confident vision of the future, largely spurred on by scientific discoveries that caught the public imagination. The neutron had been discovered and DNA identified, the Space Race took off in earnest with the launch of Sputnik in 1957, and popular images connected with science and space could be found on furniture and fabrics – Hoover even brought out a Constellation vacuum cleaner, while the 1956 Frigidaire Kitchen of Tomorrow featured an ultrasonic dishwasher, a domed oven and an electro-recipe file which automatically activated an ingredients dispenser. The future, it seemed, had arrived, and it was a pretty good place to be.

CREATING THE LOOK

Fifties pieces have recently become collectable, and high prices are paid in auction houses for designer names associated with the era. However, kitsch, mass-produced items can be purchased for next to nothing in junk shops and flea markets, so it is eminently possible to achieve a fabulous Fifties style on a shoestring. Select light, organic shapes and bright, abstract patterns, juxtaposing them with cheery, innocent confidence.

Walls

Rather than any plethora of dados, picture rails and cornices, the Fifties wall was rather plain, often with just a small skirting as the only form of applied moulding. Their bold colours and patterns, however, made a huge impact. To achieve this look, you could paint your walls in different planes of bright colour, varying the shades so that they give an exciting clashing effect, but with an overall feel that is light and airy. Or choose a wallpaper in one of the many cheerful, Contemporary Style patterns that were available then at all prices. Sources include geometric designs, wood- or stone-effect, marble, trellis and scientific atoms or space motifs. Fruit and veg or crockery patterns were often used for kitchens, while everywhere the new washable wallpapers were extremely popular. In the late Fifties, especially, different patterns were put together in an unrestrained and unaffected way, a style which can be recreated with flamboyant patterns or perhaps a more tasteful combination of polka dots and stripes.

Floors

If all this colour and pattern is too much for you, a single-colour fitted carpet may be the answer, a perfect foil for bright textiles and furniture. That said, carpets featuring typical contemporary motifs, or with abstract patterns in two or three tones, would also be very suitable. Carpet tiles, too, came in strong colours and often featured dramatic contrasts – black, white and another bold shade would be a good choice for this look. Natural matting is also appropriate – at the time it was recommended for hallways, in particular.

Another type of floor covering you may wish to consider is fake animal skin, which was one element of the glamorous American style. Lino and vinyl (the latter a new product in the Fifties) were easy-to-clean, hygenic floorcoverings advocated for use in kitchens, bathrooms and children's rooms. Today they come in sheet or tile form and can be used as solid colours, bold checks or cut out (by a professional) to produce a unique design in any colours you like.

LEFT A boldly patterned rug makes the ideal floorcovering for a room that is furnished in authentic Fifties style. Pendant lamps such as this can still be found in many secondhand shops today.

RIGHT Intense colours can create a vivid Fifties look. These angular lights reflect the quirky styling of the era, and work well with the slightly kitsch furniture.

Lights

By now, lighting was seen to be as much a science as it was an art, with fittings designed primarily for function rather than just to look attractive. Uplighters which give overall illumination without harsh shadows were used more and more, while task lighting, for reading or sewing, for example, was being taken into consideration, in the form of free-standing, movable and adjustable table lamps. Look for bases made of teak or wrought iron, with shades of plastic, waxed paper, aluminium, raffia, wicker or pleated fabric. Shapes are generally fairly simple, although elegant, occasionally idiosyncratic and – especially in the hands of Italian designers – a form of domestic sculpture. The simplest styles to look for, all of them very evocative of the era, are cones, bubbles, pear shapes, hour glasses and outlines which echo the appearance of contemporary hats such as the coolie and the cloche. Then there are the hanging lights

COLOURS

The Fifties colour palette is instantly recognizable. Though graphic black and white play a part, on the whole it is an insouciant combination of breezy, vibrant shades that makes this look so attractive. Choose sherbet pink, sunshine yellow, vivid blue, sizzling tangerine, searing crimson, dazzling turquoise and acid green, and don't hold back from combining them in fresh and exciting ways – the result should be full of impact.

ABOVE Fifties fabric could sometimes be wild and wacky – here, the upholstery matches not only the wall panel and the light fitting, but the telephone, too!

which emulate the spindly, multicoloured mobile sculptures of Alexander Calder. And finally, and perhaps most importantly, don't forget lights which evoke the dramatic, futuristic, sci-fi forms of space exploration – a whole genre of lamps that look like hovering flying saucers, space rockets and even the Skylon, the Festival of Britain's sky-scraping metal structure that spawned a thousand standard lamps.

Soft furnishings

Fifties fabrics are renowned for their use of vivid, contrasting colours and daring, often intricate patterns. After the dull hardships of war, such bright soft furnishings gave an instant lift to any home, and although the self-appointed arbiters of 'good taste' advocated not mixing too many patterns together at any one time, most people simply ignored them and enjoyed the riot of colour that was at last available to them. Progressive designers were employed by high-street firms, and such pioneering textiles can be found in auction houses

and junk shops, priced according to the importance of the designer and the quality of the fabric.

A major influence on Fifties fabrics was the first-time domestic use of a wide range of man-made fibres, developed during the war when the import of raw materials for textile manufacturers came almost to a complete standstill. Easy-care, washable and wipe-clean, these new fabrics included rayon, nylon and Terylene, used alongside cotton, wool, linen and other affordable materials. Today, choose, for example, plain, unfussy bed- and table linen (but perhaps with a bright bed cover), and neat and tailored upholstery, with barely-there, flat cushions. Simple, gathered curtains should be window-length, hung from a track disguised by a short fabric pelmet and with lacy nets underneath.

Exciting pattern is predominant in Fifties fabrics and one of the most important themes began with the 1951 Festival of Britain, when the Festival Pattern Group attempted to bring decoration up to date by harnessing science as a basis for new designs. Using blueprints of crystal structures, the designers produced abstract patterns which were to prove highly influential. Aim for a Fifties look by seeking out fabrics that incorporate the long, thin chains, hour-glass shapes and small blobs that were inspired by the scientific discoveries that had recently taken place.

Not all patterns were based on molecules and crystals, however, and a typical Fifties home may have incorporated soft furnishings featuring trellises and lattices, cowboys (from the popular American TV shows), food and drink (especially in kitchens and dining rooms), African motifs, round-cornered squares, skeletal abstract outlines and surreal images taken from works by artists such as Salvador Dalí. Using these fabrics is a bold move, but will appeal to lovers of the colourful and the kitsch, and is bound to be distinctive. You might, for example, line an oval basket with them to create a typically Fifties magazine rack, or cover boxes and files with them to work with in a funky study, or use them to cover hat boxes of different sizes for handy storage in a bedroom.

For an interior that tends more towards the cool and elegant Fifties version of Modernism, follow the trend that was in direct opposition to all these artificial brights – the hand-woven, natural-dyed look, predominantly influenced by Scandinavian designers. Their work, though simple, was warm and of very high quality, using dark, saturated colours and sometimes unusual materials such as paper and birch bark. Today, this look is very much in vogue once more, and it is easy to find tactile fibres with a hand-crafted appearance in natural colours and with interesting textures, to use for curtains, upholstery and cushion covers.

Accessories

Fun and fantasy are the two themes which should be predominant in assembling Fifties-style accessories. This was the era of 'You've never had it so good', and the average home possessed far more in the way of knick-knacks than in previous years, much of it unutterably kitsch – and all the more enjoyable for being so. Flying ducks and nodding dogs are number one in the bad-but-great taste stakes, with the green 'Chinese Girl' painting a close second, followed by the iconic pineapple-shaped plastic ice bucket. Coloured glass ornaments, especially in the form of fish and clowns, are ubiquitous, while the famous 'handkerchief' glass is either wonderful or horrible, depending on your point of view. You could add multicoloured drinks tumblers, bright Melamine mix 'n' match tableware, and plastic telephones and 'trannies' – portable transistor radios.

In better taste – albeit an acquired one – are ceramics by the likes of Midwinter and Poole potteries, which turned tableware into a fashion item. Their novel shapes are adorned with 'artistic' surface patterns, ranging from checks, spots and zebra stripes to playing cards, poodles, street scenes, the ballet, stylized plants and even – in the ultimate celebration of consumer culture – objects such as jugs, teapots and cups themselves.

FABRICS

Kitsch cottons are the basis for fab Fifties fabrics, especially pink cabbage roses and small floral motifs combined with stripes or polka dots. The scarlet, yellow and black of these stylized apples are typical colours, as are the black, white and mustard of the 'poodle' fabric – another light-hearted Fifties motif. The cute, bubble-blowing children on baby-blue silk are also a lot of fun.

ABOVE A fibreglass chair and multicoloured storage unit, designed in the early 1950s by Americans Charles and Ray Eames, are examples of upmarket furniture from the decade.

Furniture

The designers and makers of Fifties furniture were among the beneficiaries of new materials and techniques that had been developed during the war. The use of laminated woods, fibreglass and moulded plastics, in particular, allowed them to bend and sculpt their creations into shapes that were previously unthinkable, while Formica – colourful and easy to keep clean, vinyl (which could imitate the appearance of wood), rubber, plastic and acrylic all came into use. Some designs from this era are scarce, desirable and will cost thousands today, but there are still many mass-produced pieces to be had for a bargain in ordinary second-hand shops.

New, smaller houses meant that built-in furniture was both fashionable and practical, while free-standing pieces were compact, slimline, light and movable: Harry Bertoia's much-copied wire chair, for example, consisted of more air than chair, though it was (and still is) pretty uncomfortable without the addition of a padded cushion. In Britain the era began with the rejection of Utility furniture, manufactured to government specifications during the war and widely disliked, in favour of Contemporary furniture, as promoted by the Council of Industrial Design at the Festival of Britain. These pieces were simple and practical, with little or no surface decoration, and in pale timbers or natural materials such as cane, wicker and bamboo. The bulky three-piece suite was banished, replaced by carefully mismatching armchairs and sofas with minimal upholstery.

These sleek lines are what distinguishes British furniture of the Fifties, and to create this look seek out long, lean and low pieces with the familiar spindly, splayed legs ending in molecule-like bobble feet. A wire magazine rack would be very typical, as would box-like sideboards on legs, coffee tables shaped like artist's palettes, kidneys or boomerangs, coat racks with coloured plastic bobbles on the arms, Formica-topped kitchen tables and semi-circular cocktail bars.

An alternative look would depend more on American and Scandinavian pieces, which place their emphasis on sculptural form. Often shaped like vessels or amoebas, even the names of chairs by Arne Jacobsen, Eero Saarinen and Verner Panton – Swan, Egg, Ant, Tulip, Womb and S – evoke their organic form. When selecting furniture, remember that Scandinavian designers tended to concentrate on fine craftsmanship and subtle good looks, while the Americans were more colourful and employed fibreglass and plastic to full advantage, though both nations emphasized simplicity and lightness, so the look is one where pieces almost seem to float in mid air.

It was in America, too, that the notion of the 'dream kitchen' originated. Tied in with ideas of glamour, streamlining, labour-saving, automation and efficiency, the aim was for the room to be large and cheery, with patterned laminates on surfaces and cupboard doors, and filled with new gadgets such as toasters, kettles, food mixers and enormous fridges. Fortunately for the Fifties addict, this look has come round full circle, and all the necessary ingredients – from chrome blenders and industrial toasters to pastel-coloured units with sliding glass doors – are all available in the shops today.

This living room is a good example of the restrained Contemporary Style look that was found in the most fashion-conscious of Fifties homes.

Summing up the style

1 Plain white walls, with no architectural detailing, are the very opposite of some flamboyant Fifties wallpaper patterns. However, they work extremely well in this room, which is stylish rather than kitsch.

2 The lively, abstract pattern of this colourful rug offsets the restrained floorboards and adds a touch of light-hearted Fifties fun.

3 The shapes of Fifties lights were often, as here, quite simple, like a form of domestic sculpture.

4 This upholstery is in very subtle taste, with colour and fabric that are typical of the era.

5 The unconventional, asymmetrical shape of this coffee table is typically Fifties, as are its slender, splayed legs – echoed by those of the chairs. The chunky, square sideboard is another item which is totally authentic in appearance.

6 These understated ceramics are timeless in appeal, although their shapes – tall and thin, squat and bulbous – are highly evocative of this particular decade.

Sixties

The advent of the Sixties meant a definite end to post-war austerity. The world economy was thriving and consumers had more choice than ever before. The new notion of 'lifestyle' was keenly promoted in magazines and on TV and suddenly people – especially young people – had the opportunity to show off their taste in everything from clothing to home furnishings. With money in their pockets and increased leisure time, teenagers dominated this new market, developing a style which challenged convention and emphasized the 'generation gap'. Though the Italian styling of sharp suits, Vespa bikes and gleaming espresso machines in the coffee bars was important, London was the world centre of new design trends in everything from fashion and film to music and photography.

This new 'Popular' culture excelled in the ephemeral, the frivolous, the zany; colours were bright and patterns bold, inspired by comics, adverts, films, music, television and everyday objects from flags to domestic appliances. It was bright, fun, instant and disposable, mingling mass culture and high art with supreme confidence. Like it or loathe it, the result was nothing if not memorable.

Sixties style was open to many trends. The swirling geometric patterns of Op Art aimed to deceive the eye, while technological advances brought synthetics to the fore, allied with the idea of human ergonomics – TVs were placed in globe-shaped podules, and moulded furniture came in unexpected, fluid shapes. Space was, of course, the final frontier, and whole interiors in chrome, white and silver echoed the adventure of the space race. At the other end of the spectrum, styles from the past were plundered and plagiarized to create a theatrical melange. Victorian, Art Deco and Art Nouveau were thrown together, with nineteenth-

The Sixties 'pad' was fab, fun and funky – the style was all about rebellion, youth and attitude, and encompassed everything that was new and exciting, from eye-catching colours and curving plastics to space-age silver and hippy, trippy naturals.

century brass bedsteads considered especially cool.

Towards the end of the decade homes also began to reflect styles from around the world. African pots, Indian rugs, rattan and bamboo furniture and floor cushions were all part of this cultural trade, and Habitat, which opened its first shop in 1964, provided affordable design to suit this new mood; its motto: 'A swinging shop for switched-on people'. The natural look was part of an increased interest in alternative lifestyles; it went hand in hand with a new political awareness that eventually led to peace protests, race riots, student sit-ins and a radical, anti-establishment movement.

By the close of the Sixties there had been a certain loss of innocence and glamorous Pop was replaced by the surreal fantasy of Psychedelia, which arose largely from the Californian hippy movement. Influenced by Art Nouveau, free love, eastern religions and drug culture, it featured amoeba-like patterns and clashing acid colours, making for disorientating environments and sometimes sinister images. The fun was over – but what a great decade it had been!

CREATING THE LOOK

It takes courage to go for an all-over Sixties style — the colours are loud, the shapes unusual and the overall effect can be somewhat extreme — but the fainter hearted will find that a few well-chosen pieces can sum up the style and add wit and humour to any home. Key items include a funky lamp, shag-pile rug and anything made of bright plastic for a fantastic, 'far-out' look.

Walls

If you like the Sixties look then you've already proved that your taste is bold and brave rather than pretty and pastel-coloured. So why not be daring and go for wacky walls, covered in stripes of various primary colours and giant, computer-style lettering? Or huge murals of Sixties motifs such as Mary Quant daisies, bullseyes, union jacks and swirling black-and-white Op Art patterns? Continue the painted patterns all over the ceiling for maximum effect. Or, if you wish, use just one, all-enveloping colour scheme in which to create your very own 'happening'. Brilliant white paint, made synthetically for the first time in the Sixties, is a wonderful backdrop for brightly coloured furniture and accessories, while metal cladding or — easier and less expensive — silver spray paint can produce an effect like the inside of a space ship. Finally, posters were very much a part of the Sixties scene, and you can create your very own wall coverings by pinning up prints of works by Pop artists such as Roy Lichtenstein, Andy Warhol (remember his Campbell's soup cans?), Peter Blake and David Hockney, or else music posters and record covers featuring flowers, rainbows and bubble-lettering in strong, contrasting colours.

Floors

When living with Sixties style you can afford to play safe with flooring, as the other elements are so eye-catching. All you really need is a neutral carpet or vinyl floorcovering, plain wooden boards or natural stone; for Sixties die-hards, however, nothing will do but to go the whole hog:

carpet in bright day-glo hues (maybe matching the colour of the walls – or carried on *up* the walls – to create a total environment), or with a black-and-white, graphic Op Art effect. If a fitted carpet is too much, just use a small rug, shag pile perhaps, or with a Union Jack or stars and stripes motif, or in a mix-and-match design with various vivid

LEFT This is a fairly sophisticated look, with plain white walls and a warm wooden ceiling, though some elements are unmistakably Sixties – the shag-pile rug, the vivid wall hanging and the bulbous, metallic floor lamp.

RIGHT The bright colours and fascinating amorphic forms of this Astro lamp provide a fun way to add some Sixties styling to a living room or bedroom.

colourways. For the more earthy look, suitable for a hallway, kitchen or conservatory, brown quarry tiles were made popular by Habitat, and for that Barbarella-style space-capsule home, silver floor tiles are really 'swinging'. Minimalists may desire

COLOURS

Sixties colours were, on the whole, bright, bright, bright. Brilliant white had been created for the first time, mixed with silver for a space-age look, while red, white and blue were the classic Pop colours and day-glo orange, green, purple and yellow made for fantastic plastics. Psychedelia had a slightly more complex palette, with pink, turquoise and 'trippy' colours, while there was also a natural backlash which included mid-brown, sludge green, charcoal and black.

a pure white carpet to go with their pure white walls – but this is one look that definitely does not work if you have children or pets, or are ever the slightest bit careless with food or drink!

Lights

Sixties lighting is extremely theatrical, with an emphasis on the use of spotlights (as sold by the early Habitat shops), for directional effect. Sometimes, even, lights were planned as the dominant feature of a room. In general, you should look out for styles that are over-sized, dramatically shaped and in man-made materials. Flashing neon signs, though not particularly useful as a means of illumination, wonderfully evoke the ethos of conspicuous consumption, while flexible tube lights are more practical and can be twisted wherever required. In common with other space-age themes, lamps may be shaped like moons, globes or flying saucers, or you could choose giant floor lamps with big curving arms. Simple drum and cylinder shapes were also common, and the Art Nouveau revival brought back Tiffany-style, stained-glass lampshades. For a natural look, it's very easy indeed to copy the paper lanterns designed by Isamu Noguchi – they're inexpensive, easily available and look great either used singly or hung in groups. The epitome of Sixties lighting is, of course, the Lava Lamp (Lava Lite in the USA), which came in various colours and shapes and goes with fibre-optic lights as the ultimate in kitsch. You can pick them up in second-hand shops today, while new ones are still being manufactured.

LEFT The soft furnishings in this room come in an array of bright and mismatching colours that are very Sixties in feel. Even the purple sofa is piped in a contrasting shocking pink.

Soft furnishings

For a Sixties look, it's best to use fabrics in a daring and innovative way, experimenting with texture, colour and pattern. Subtlety is not a priority, so there's no holding back – the brightest shades and boldest designs will make textiles really stand out. With all this instant impact there is no need for any fussy details – window treatments are extremely plain, just a pair of gathered curtains on a simple track with no pelmet, edging or tie-backs. Upholstery is tailored and, again, plain, without piping, frills or buttoning, and bedlinen should be strong and sexy but not at all fancy.

As young people gained increasing control over how their environments were decorated – either in a teenage bedroom or their own bedsit or flat – a new look emerged that relied on large, graphic images and vivid colours. Used for all sorts of soft furnishings, this was an inexpensive and instant way of achieving the Pop look. Typical motifs included the Mary Quant daisy, union jacks, stars and stripes, bullseyes and images from mass culture such as comics, seaside postcards, food packaging and advertisements. Abstract geometric shapes and polka dots were also popular, while – in tune with the craze for space technology – some fabrics literally depicted astronauts, rockets and views of the earth from the moon.

This Pop look is easy enough to achieve if you can find fabrics with suitable images; if not, look for plains in dazzling primary colours and use a variety of shades all at once for eye-catching effect. You might, for example, want to combine a duvet cover with clashing pillowcases, roller blinds and bright upholstery. Alternatively, the one-colour environment can look stunning, in a primary, white or even space-rocket silver. The latter option gives you the opportunity to try out unusual fabrics such as mesh and gauze – although these are especially suitable for curtains and cushion covers, feel free to adapt them to wherever you think they will work.

Synthetic fabrics were the big story of the decade, and the invention of nylon, in particular, revolutionized upholstery. Texture is important here, and the man-made look, though it might seem a subtle detail, helps to add to the overall atmosphere. Choose textiles that are shiny, stretchy, rubbery or plasticized, rather than matt cottons and wools.

The exception to this is if your 'pad' has a late Sixties-style ethnic, hippy look, in which case natural, muddy colours and hand-crafted fabrics are a prerequisite. Ranging from thick felt and coarse hessian to soft wool and loosely woven linen, these are easy to find in the shops today and very pleasurable to live with.

In addition to Pop, the Op Art movement had an impact on soft furnishings, and Sixties fabrics came in dramatically swirling, movement-filled designs that sometimes had a visually disturbing effect. Black-and-white prints of this nature are very effective for bedcovers, wall-hangings or roller blinds. And at the end of the decade Psychedelic fabrics featured prints with dense collages of round-petalled flowers, faces and rainbows – a highly distinctive look that may not be to everyone's taste, but is all the more exciting for those who dare to be different.

Accessories

Details can make all the difference when recreating Sixties style. Confident consumerism meant that homes were filled with accessories in bold shapes and even bolder colours – so there are no half-measures if you choose this look. You can guarantee, however, that the end result will be eye-catching, good-looking and unusual.

FABRICS

Sixties rooms can be quite wild in style, and this feeling is matched by fabrics of all varieties. Multicoloured stripes, spots and abstract designs make obvious Pop choices, while lime green PVC and orange felt add interesting textures and colours. Finally, silver fabric has a shimmering, space-age quality that would help to create a highly unusual and evocative scheme.

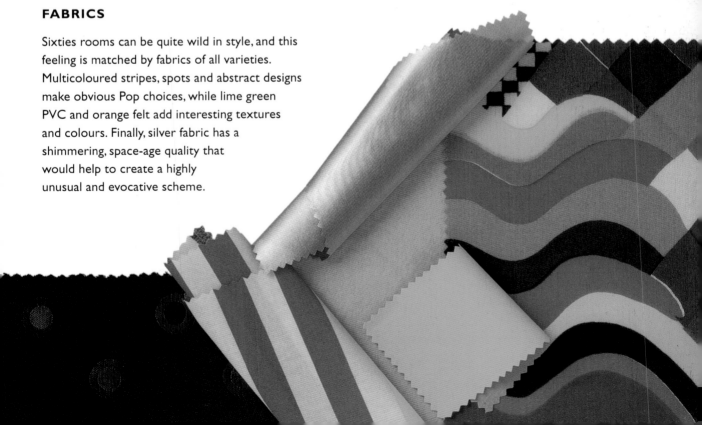

Spherical shapes were very prominent in this era, not just in lighting and furniture but also for clocks, radios, record players and TVs. Their casings, made of plastic, should be in vivid colours such as yellow, orange, red and green. Substituting your modern telephone for a Sixties-style plastic version will add to the authentic effect, and plastic dinner services in a variety of colours are also suitable, used with drinking glasses in bulbous shapes. Alternatively, rustic ceramics will make a good impression, with their thick, mottled glazes and muddy colours. Coloured glass vases, too, can

ABOVE Fibre optic lights, invented in the Sixties, have a suitably space-age look, and their gently waving fibres are strangely hypnotic.

form an attractive display – choose styles with elongated necks and bright, saturated hues. All that remains is to dot around some posters in Pop or Psychedelic style and light a couple of joss sticks because, like they said, it's time to turn on, tune in and drop out.

Furniture

With a self-assured liking for the instant, the mass-produced, the expendable, Pop culture brought about a backlash against the classic styles of furniture that were costly and expected to last forever. It was goodbye to old-fashioned, robust solidity, and hello to flexible, low-cost, innovative pieces.

Generally, furniture in a Sixties-style room should emphasize informality and dramatically sculptural outlines, with pieces made of nylon and plastic in bold, solid colours. Try to create an impression of laid-back relaxation, with low, curving seating or even just a selection of large floor cushions on which you can loll around in comfort. Some Sixties homes took this idea to its extreme and instead of living room furniture featured a 'conversation pit', which consisted of a lowered area covered with nothing but cushions.

As designers explored ways of making furniture to suit the spirit of the time, they came up with a number of solutions that ranged from the logical to the bizarre. Taking instant at face-value, in 1964 Peter Murdoch produced a bucket-shaped chair made of five layers of laminated paper. It was the ultimate in disposability, being expected to last just three to six months. The idea didn't really catch on, and neither did the radical anti-design pieces, such as seats shaped like giant blades of grass or a baseball glove, that were outrageously challenging one-offs rather than serious attempts to satisfy consumer demand.

Other innovations, however, were more practical: in the early Sixties Habitat helped popularize the now-ubiquitous flat-pack furniture, while beanbags were first seen in the form of the Sacco, a chair filled with millions of small polystyrene balls produced in 1969 for Zanotta of Milan. The same team also came up with the Blow inflatable armchair, a fun product that had a disconcerting tendency to deflate beneath its occupant. In 1968, the designer Quasar Khanh came up with a whole inflatable apartment. We haven't yet reached that stage, but it is now possible to buy blow-up chairs, fruit bowls, egg cups and even light fittings.

Much Sixties furniture is immediately recognizable for its curved shape, sometimes womb-like, sometimes with its structure on the outside rather than hidden within the upholstery. Look out for typical pieces in bio-morphic forms, made of a steel frame covered in foam and stretch jersey or nylon in bright colours. Stacking chairs in vivid colours became commonplace in this decade, too, while for a more hippy look, 'ethnic' furniture in bamboo or rattan was the in thing.

Eye-catching and exciting, this room has been recreated as a typical 'pad' from the Sixties without being so over-the-top that it would be difficult to live with.

Summing up the style

1 Vivid green walls make a strong statement in this room, together with a colourful banner hanging. Bright murals would add to the effect.

2 A sexy shag-pile rug was all the rage in this swinging decade – pure white might not be very practical, but is the ultimate in glamour.

3 A theatrical light in an unusual fan shape contributes to the look. Many modern light designs have the right sort of colourful, fun look.

4 The vivid colours of these silk and velvet cushions are really flamboyant.

Sixties soft furnishings were often daring in colour and pattern, though relatively plain in style – so ruching and bows should be avoided.

5 Bright-green plastic pod-shaped seating (designed by Eero Aarnio in 1968) demonstrates the experimental nature of much Sixties furniture. The 'conversation pit' in the background is another typical feature – the aim was to escape from the conventional and create an atmosphere of spirited informality.

6 These huge potted houseplants prove that a dramatic atmosphere can be created with the use of almost any accessories.

Contemporary

The style of the homes in which we live tends, very often, to reflect the current attitudes of our society. The Eighties. a 'me' decade that was hard-working, power-hungry, money-oriented, harsh and brash, produced a style where labels meant everything, matt black and chrome were everywhere, designer names became iconic and technology was the superstar. But then came the Nineties, bringing New Age ideals, 'downshifting' and a softer, more inclusive atmosphere; gradually, values have changed and a calmer, more subtle look has taken over.

Right now there is a sense of 'anything goes'. We're taking inspiration from any number of historical looks – freely adapting them to suit our lifestyles – while also placing increasing emphasis on the work of young, forward-looking designers; in line with this way of thinking, contemporary developments show a strong trend towards simplification, function and versatility.

Open-plan interiors have, once again, become desirable, and modern domestic architecture seeks to emphasize space and light above almost everything else. The standard palette of today's architect-designed house includes white walls, blond woods, fresh colours, plenty of glass and steel, large windows and double-height living areas. Such homes are clean-lined and uncluttered, furnished with carefully chosen pieces and sensual textiles that reinforce the idea of the home as a comfortable, pleasurable retreat. Minimalism has played a part in creating this look, but it is rarely taken to its utmost extreme.

The open-plan aesthetic is also a solution to some of the demands of modern life. The flexibility of movable screens as opposed to solid walls allows us, if the need arises, to work or study at home, install a gym or a children's playroom, or care for an elderly or disabled relative.

Contemporary homes are light, bright and airy, with fresh colours, clean-lined furniture and tactile fabrics. An emphasis on informality, practicality and good looks results in a style that is easy-going, easy to live with and exceptionally attractive.

Another huge influence on contemporary interiors is the ethnic look, but an east-meets-west sophistication with a considered approach that differs absolutely from the hippy clutter of the Seventies. Instead, good quality, genuine artefacts are employed to impart a certain personality, even spirituality, to a home, their honest good looks working in harmony with other pieces even though their origins are totally dissimilar.

And another trend is beginning to affect interior design, just as it affects every aspect of our day-to-day lives. 'Green' themes are just starting to make themselves felt, but are bound to play an ever-more important role as we become more aware of the scarcity of certain natural resources and the damage done by some manufacturing processes. Solar panels, water butts and ozone-friendly fridges are just one aspect of this movement; furniture made from recycled materials, the growth in popularity of salvaged architectural antiques, the ability to re-use the components of worn-out items ... all of these are manifestations of a desire to live in a way that is not just pleasant for us, but also kind to the planet.

CREATING THE LOOK

There are few rules to contemporary style – a hi-tech look might comprise coloured plastics, stainless steel, rubber and inflatables, while a more elemental approach would involve natural wood, stone, raffia and fleece. Whatever you choose, the aim is simplicity, streamlining and subtle sophistication. Remember the importance of texture, of pared-down shapes and of emphasizing space, creating a sense of pleasurable modern living.

Walls

There used to be a time when having all-white walls was the only way to express one's modernity. Now, however, colour has made a comeback as a contemporary option, and the choices are practically limitless. You could play safe with a subtle, smooth finish, or try out one of the range of increasingly popular paint effects which give added depth and interest to walls. Rag-rolling, colourwashing, stippling and sponging are all typical of the current look and are very easy for amateurs to carry out.

If you don't fancy doing it yourself, however, there are wallpapers that can create a very similar look to that of the different paint techniques. Papered walls, on the whole, should express the keep-it-simple attitude that is so important nowa-

ABOVE Smooth walls are clad in warm plywood or painted in citrus colours in this newly built, light-filled Nineties house. The timber flooring is understated but effective.

days – so fussy, busy, elaborate patterns should be avoided. Better still, why not leave brickwork or plaster bare, gaining an unsophisticated, natural look that fits in really well with this aesthetic? In kitchens and bathrooms, colourful tiles make beautiful splashbacks; mosaic, in particular, is fast becoming an essential in a contemporary home. Use intense colours and tiny, glittering mirrors for a sense of charming sophistication; as a weekend task, it is both easy and enjoyable, but don't just work in straightforward rectangles – a much more interesting effect can be achieved by creating sweeping curves or unusual geometric shapes.

Floors

The big story in contemporary floorcoverings has to be the rise and rise of natural mattings. Coir, sisal, rush and jute can be woven in a number of styles and colours, and offer a combination of good looks and value for money. With traditional carpets, sum up contemporary style by using pale, natural colours and, perhaps, contrast borders. Very much in the current vogue are blond wood floors – choose from solid boards, laminate or a vinyl lookalike. Reclaimed boards are equally attractive, with a ready-made character and patina of age, and they very much fit in with the current 'green' theme. As an alternative, you could seek out reclaimed bricks or terracotta tiles.

And then there are a range of slightly less usual floorings which would give your scheme enormous individuality. Rubber, for example, is flexible and durable, and comes in a surprisingly wide range of colours and textures. Concrete is suitably simple and can be minimalist-plain, or else waxed, stained, textured with glass or coloured with pigments. Metal, meanwhile – sheets of aluminium, zinc or steel – is tough and hard-wearing, with industrial overtones. To avoid tinny echoes, laminate the sheets on to a plywood base.

Lights

You can really have a lot of fun with lights in this style: there are endless possibilities for variety in form, colour and fabric, while the range of fittings available today means that it is easy to create a highly functional scheme that also looks fantastic.

COLOURS

Nineties colours are fresh and warm, sensuous and relaxing – with acid brights used for striking emphasis. As homes become more and more tactile, there's an elemental, natural feel – midnight blue, heather, gorse yellow, bark brown and pebble grey – mixed with oriental tones such as bamboo, Chinese red and the deep black/brown of wenge wood. Neutrals are important, too, in all shades from white, ivory and cream to taupe, sand and eau de nil.

RIGHT Adaptable and efficient, this spotlight in brushed stainless steel is also attractive to look at. It could be put to use more or less anywhere in a modern home.

Many modern lighting designers favour tiny, low-voltage halogen spotlights, which can be as unobtrusive as you want them to be and give out a clear, white light. Also in this slightly hi-tech style would be gleaming stainless steel wall and table lamps – a look that is up-front, businesslike and hard-working, ideal for a home office. For a softer feel, look for coloured, frosted glass or polypropylene shades on pendants and table lamps, which add a gentle glow to any room. Natural materials, such as paper, rattan, raffia, wood and stone, add interesting textures and create an earthy, understated atmosphere, blending easily with most schemes. In general, the ideal outlines to choose would be pared-down and very simple – cubes, drums, squares, cones and spheres, with perhaps the odd squiggly spiral or Henry Moore-like hollowed forms for a touch of wit and variety.

Soft furnishings

There are two clear directions to follow when choosing modern fabrics: either the tactile, natural look, in which the textiles give pleasure through their sensual feel, or the hi-tech, scientific approach in which fabric is made to perform to its utmost limits, and is sometimes combined with unusual materials, such as metal or plastic.

Touchy-feely fabrics have always been around, but they are now one of the main focuses in furnishing trends, appealing to the emotions in a direct and appealing way. The look is widely available, and is straightforward to put together: choose voile, muslin, lace, lightweight silk, satin, chiffon, organza and mesh-like fabrics for summer; and leather, suede, moleskin, corduroy, tweed, mohair, flannel, fleece, wool and cashmere for winter. Incidentally, knitting and crocheting have come out of granny's closet and are big in the modern interior: use them for cushion covers, bedspreads, throws or even blinds.

At the other end of the spectrum, the newest fabrics for domestic interiors are innovative and revolutionary. Using such fabrics will put your scheme right at the cutting edge and give your home an avant-garde and utterly individual look. You will need to approach specialists, or maybe even commission your own designer, but the extra effort may well be worthwhile: keep an eye out for such unusual fabrics as 'solar' cloth coated with powdered aluminium to reflect heat and light and maintain warmth in winter (perfect for curtains or blinds); polypropylene seat-belt upholstery (which doesn't stain and can be washed down); nylon coated with neoprene (water-, fire- and knife-proof); Teflon-coated fibres (breathes like fleece and is waterproof); scent-impregnated cloth and – most unusual of all – fibre-optic or fluorescent fabrics which, literally, glow in the dark.

Overall, you should use textiles in a clean-cut and unfussy way. Attention to detail is important, so give pillowcases or cushion covers, for example, interesting fastenings such as envelope-shapes or contrasting ties. Aim for bedlinen, generally, to be plain and simple, with the concentration on colour and texture rather than the addition of elaborate embroidery or folksy ornamentation; the same goes for throws, table linen and fabrics elsewhere in the house.

Keep window treatments, too, along minimal lines. Pelmets are not at all essential, and if they do exist should be restrained in style. Simple blinds are a good choice, but otherwise use curtains hung from wood or metal poles and add clever touches such as coloured finials or unusual fastenings – string, ribbon or raffia, maybe, or else a minimal metal wire with sheer fabric hung from bulldog clips, metal rings or shackles.

RIGHT These stone holders have an eastern quality to them. The contemporary look is all about natural materials and simple forms.

Accessories

There is a definite need to avoid clutter when creating a Nineties look; there are, however, a number of finishing touches that will help to complete your scheme in a most attractive and appealing way. The usual rules apply, such as sticking to clean lines, simple shapes and clear colours. Then, bear in mind that the way in which you arrange accessories has a huge impact – you could, for example, prop pictures on the floor rather than hanging them, or else cluster them together, covering a whole wall with different shapes, sizes and colours of frame and image. When it comes to vases, ornaments or collections, display by spacing them out in orderly rows. Or you can make less formal displays of art and artefacts picked up on travels to foreign countries. In general, vivid splashes of colour help create a sense of warmth and drama: perhaps glass vases, frosted plastic bathroom accessories, cardboard storage boxes or painted

FABRICS

Modern fabrics emphasize interesting textures, unusual weaves and spare, stylized designs. There are times when subtlety is called for (as with the understated sun motifs on the taupe fabric here) but, equally, some fabrics can be quite bright and even daring, featuring large stylized flowers and metallic inks that are full of impact. Anything goes as far as the type of fabric is concerned, from simple naturals to the newly developed, hi-tech artificials.

LEFT Working from home is a very contemporary phenomenon, and these days more and more designers are producing furnishings that work well in home offices but are also attractive enough not to be hidden away at the end of the day.

ceramics, as well as dramatic, sculptural, fresh flowers. Contrast the mellow tones of wood with shiny stainless steel, pewter, chrome and silver, adding, if you like, some items made of leather, stone or wicker for a natural look. In the kitchen, the retro styling of certain pieces of equipment – such as toasters, mixers and juicers – is making a big comeback, and though relatively expensive, these sturdy objects should last a lifetime. If your taste is, however, more forward- than backward-looking, you may gain a great deal of pleasure (and encourage new talent) by buying some beautiful craft pieces – ceramics, wood, basketry, fabric and the like – by a contemporary maker.

Furniture

Much modern furniture is very restrained in style, making its presence known more by an absence of adornment than any obvious flourishes and fancies. For a Nineties scheme, then, you should look for pieces that are slim, light and minimal. Bent-ply makes a good choice: its typically organic, flowing shapes fit well with the modern look, while MDF (medium density fibreboard), has a smooth surface and functional appearance which is ideal for the modern home. The pale gold of birch and beech, too, will create the right effect, or you may prefer reclaimed pine, which has a solidity and attractive colour that is simply not matched by brand-new pine. Instead of wood, you

may want to pick out some plastic furniture, which makes for an even more up-to-the-minute impact. Coloured plastic chairs, side tables and trolleys are fun and funky, working well with glass and steel, another major element in this type of scheme.

The predominance of light, spare furniture is not just due to its attractive appearance – flexibility is an absolute necessity in the contemporary home, and furniture must be easily cleanable, movable from one room to another and usable in a variety of ways. Make adaptability your priority, then, and buy pieces that, for example, work as both office storage and room dividers, as stools and side tables, or as seats and beds. Modular furniture is perfect; look out, too, for anything that folds, stacks, is very mobile, transforms or saves space in any way.

Finally, environmental themes are uppermost in everyone's minds today, and are sure to impinge more and more on all aspects of interior decoration. Tropical hardwoods, for instance, are a no-go area unless you can be sure they are from properly managed plantations. Buying second-hand is a good way to encourage the saving of resources – this can encompass a range of sources, including fine antiques, junk-shop bargains and salvage. And an increasing amount of furniture these days is actually made from recycled materials, whether it be wood, washing machine parts or even plastic bottles and chopping boards. Lean, clean and green – those are the basics of the contemporary home.

This kitchen is a good example of contemporary simplicity combined with subtle sophistication. The quality of the finish counts for a great deal.

Summing up the style

1 The smooth whiteness of these walls is very typical of the contemporary look – an ideal background for areas of sharp colour and the sculptural outlines of designer furniture.

2 A shiny, blond wood floor reflects light and looks extremely clean and modern. At least four or five layers of varnish make the surface highly durable.

3 Recessed, low-voltage halogen spotlights are understated, while providing clear, bright light by which to cook and eat.

4 A neat breakfast table demonstrates unstudied simplicity, as does the fibreglass chair next to it – though this is, in fact, a classic by Americans Charles and Ray Eames.

5 Duck-egg blue paintwork, a stainless-steel splashback and a chunky wooden worksurface add up to an attractive kitchen working area. The elegant brushed aluminium handles are both good-looking and tactile, a thoughtful finishing touch that makes all the difference.

6 A vase of bright, fresh flowers is often all that is needed in the way of contemporary accessories.

Global styles

The grander English country house has a style all of its own. Popularized after the Second World War by decorator John Fowler, the 'country house look' has become one of the most important decorating themes of the late twentieth century. Influenced by nostalgic visions of a better way of life, the look has come to stand for a particular type of comfortable elegance, combining dissimilar types of period furniture and unmatched patterns and colours with an eye for balance and proportion. The result is often described as 'shabby chic', the aim being to create an impression of fine furniture and fabrics having been lovingly collected and lived with over the course of generations.

This interpretation of English country is most often applied to larger, even stately, homes. At the other end of the spectrum, meanwhile, is the very much more down-to-earth look of a period peasant's cottage, so unselfconscious it could hardly even be termed a style, which concentrates on the notions of warmth and shelter from the elements, with hard flooring, little furniture and a spartan but pleasing appearance. In earlier times such dwellings would have had no running water or artificial light, their owners possessing few of the home comforts we have come to expect today except, perhaps, for touches of bright paintwork and some hand-stitched textiles.

Somewhere between these two extremes is the English country look to which most people aspire. It is comfortable without being luxurious, pretty without being fussy, familiar without being predictable. It is a look that is unchanging and timeless – indeed, although it is never truly in fashion, it is never out of fashion either. It is the look that evokes the England of cricket on the village green, strawberries and cream for tea, new-mown hay and church bells on a summer's evening.

Who hasn't dreamt of escaping the rat race for a life of rural bliss? A thatched cottage with roses round the door, chickens in the back yard and cakes baking in the range oven? There could be no more perfect image of an idyllic lifestyle than traditional English country.

Having evolved over the centuries, this very appealing style is the perfect complement to vernacular houses made of local materials – whether brick, timber or stone – built to good but modest standards, with thick walls, small windows and beamed ceilings. Crackling log fires make such homes warm and welcoming in the winter, while in the summer months they are open to the fresh air, allowing the garden outside to merge with the furnishings inside. Interiors are harmonious and restful, with soft, distemper colours, squashy sofas, pretty fabrics and an eclectic taste, putting, for example, Indian rugs with tartan upholstery, Chinese porcelain with English country chairs. This is a look that is idiosyncratic and confident, using colour, pattern and scale to full advantage while at the same time appealing to all the senses. Touch, especially, is important – the textures of English country are pleasurable and evocative, from cool, hard stone to warm wood, rough wicker to soft wool, comforting velvet to delicate lace, chalky plaster to thick felt.

CREATING THE LOOK

The English country look can range from plain and bare to pretty and fresh or even rather elegant. Choose sympathetic, natural materials, mixing old and new, junk-shop finds with antiques – just remember not to be too slick and modern. Don't over co-ordinate, be comfortable without being cluttered, and remember that it's better for everything to look a little worn than absolutely brand new.

Walls

For once, don't worry if your walls are uneven or unfinished in appearance – for this look, the more crooked the better, while lumps and bumps only add character. Bare brick has a marvellously elemental feel to it, while crumbling plaster can look fantastic – but do make sure there are no structural or damp problems causing this decorative effect!

When painting walls, try to use distemper and old-fashioned matt oil rather than modern synthetics as far as possible. There's nothing wrong with expanses of white, as long as it's not bright, modern white. Alternatively, pastels are suitably pretty, and stronger colours can create a cosy atmosphere. Broken paint effects such as sponging, stippling and ragging add the right sort of interest and depth to wall surfaces, but make sure they look casual and hand-done rather than too deliberate. Simple wood panelling up to dado level is both insulating and attractive, with the upper part of the wall finished with either paint or wallpaper. There are a variety of wallpaper styles from which to choose: narrow stripes, polka dots, trellises, small all-over geometric designs and, of course, flowers – either tiny and delicate for a small room, or blowsy and full-blown in a room of larger size. If any further decorative touches are needed, finish off a painted or papered wall with a pretty, contrasting border of wallpaper or stencilled motifs.

Floors

Fitted carpets are warm and practical in a draughty cottage, but beware of them looking too modern and luxurious. It might be better to stick to natural floorcoverings such as sisal, jute or coir, which come in a range of patterns, weaves and textures, from rough and hairy to smooth and soft. Otherwise, throw down a range of rugs – oriental, Indian, Middle Eastern, rag rugs, flat stripes or needlework: if they are uncoordinated and a

LEFT A warm, earthy red on roughly plastered walls makes this fireside nook warm and inviting. The flooring is of ancient bricks, topped by a worn rug.

RIGHT Earthenware jars with neutral, drum-shaped shades create a soft, understated glow in this Kent cottage. The uneven wooden beams are set off perfectly by the whitewashed walls.

little threadbare, all the better – on top of hard flooring in the form of flagstones, brick, slate, quarry tiles or wooden boards. Planks are preferably old and worn (reclaimed boards are good for this look, and limewashing makes new wood look older) and should be matt-varnished, waxed or oiled, or else painted if really poor quality. For utility areas, consider linoleum, which is a natural material and can be used to create the right sort of functional, hard-working feel.

Lights

Lighting should be informal and atmospheric, warm and welcoming. It would be ideal to avoid artificial light completely and keep to the ambience of old-fashioned candles or the flickering flames of a log fire. For practicality's sake, however, you will need to add some form of electric task lighting. Try to avoid, if possible, central ceiling pendants, unless in the form of a simple wrought-iron coronet; instead, a combination of wall brackets and table lamps is a flexible and attractive solution. Steer clear of any shapes that appear at all modern or complex, and stick to wrought iron, brass, turned wood, plaster or ceramics – such as oriental ginger jars or plain earthenware pitchers.

Shades should be similarly understated, in coolie, square, empire (slightly flared) or drum shapes, and made of paper, raffia or fabric. Pleated silk makes for a softly diffused light, but simpler chintz and gingham also work wonderfully with this sort of

COLOURS

While English country colours can be strong, they should not be too bright – John Fowler's trick was always to add a touch of black to every paint he mixed in order to tone it down. Stick to the natural tones of the countryside, and of the traditional cottage garden – rose pink, deep raspberry, sunny yellow, dove grey, faded blue, moss green, apricot, lilac, cream and magnolia. Richer notes can be added with indigo, ochre and deep reddish brown.

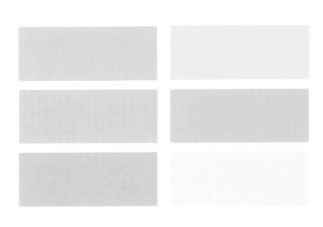

LEFT A delicately pretty country bedroom, with bedlinen and curtains that mix pale floral designs for an informal look.

look, while plain fabrics can be decorated using stencils or stamps with a countryside theme. Overall, aim for an eclectic mix of lights that don't quite match, and you'll be well on your way to creating a friendly, informal and relaxing effect.

Soft furnishings

Patterns and colours that look too well matched are wrong – aim for an unstudied mixture, using inexpensive new fabric and pieces picked up in second-hand shops and jumble sales, or unpicked from old clothes. If they look gently worn that is all the better, and anything that appears overly bright and new can be soaked overnight in cold tea for an instant ageing effect.

The fabric that is most closely associated with the country look is chintz, with its colourful, complex designs of full-blown roses, parrot tulips, peonies, lilies and other flowers. Too much chintz, however, can be overpowering, and it's not suited to the more elemental, hard-working country look. You might also want to consider tweed, with its natural colours and interesting weave, tartans,

which are bright and warming, or plain and simple ginghams, or a selection of narrow stripes and tiny spots. Or how about paisley and other 'ethnic' fabrics; tapestry and crewel-work; fruit patterns; or plains in linen, wool, fleece, chenille, velvet, mohair and cashmere? And don't forget the last word in home-made pleasure – knitting and crochet. Even beginners can get instant gratification from making small squares in different colours and sewing them together.

Window treatments should, essentially, be fairly simple – just a pair of curtains, with a lace or muslin net underneath, generously gathered or pleated and perhaps with frilled edges. Pelmets suit grander, larger rooms; otherwise just use a wooden or wrought iron pole with pretty, understated finials. If your windows are draught-proof, leave the curtains unlined for a light, casual effect. As an alternative, you could use prettily ruched Austrian blinds, while the decorative potential of roller blinds can be increased by adding a contrast border, a shaped bottom edge or stencilled patterns. Soften the look with a shaped pelmet or sham curtains.

FABRICS

For the epitome of country charm a broad mix of fabrics is desirable – the aim is for them to work well together without looking too co-ordinated. Choose cosy tweed and chenille, strong tartans and pretty lace for a variety of colour, pattern and texture, adding checks and, of course, a few floral patterns, all in nature-inspired, soft and faded colours.

RIGHT The bold, all-over rose pattern and deeply frilled valances of this plump armchair and footstool are echoed in the festoon blind at the window of this welcoming, comfortable room.

With this style there's no harm in upholstery that's a little worn, even sagging, and loose covers in chintz, corduroy or simple, plain canvas will do wonders to disguise a modern suite. Cover every sofa and armchair with piles of cushions, preferably with ones that don't match at all – use covers made from remnants, knitting, old blankets, kilims and so on. They should be as plump as possible, and if made of flowery fabric, you might want to add frilled edging. Then layer on a few throws, in the form of blankets, patchwork, paisley shawls or whatever takes your fancy. Cover side tables with floor-length fabric and use shirred material (gingham is especially nice) to replace the doors of cupboards and wardrobes. Bedlinen, too, looks best when it's piled layer upon layer. For the full effect,

start with flowered or coloured sheets, then add embroidered, lace-edged or flowery duvet covers, soft blankets and pillowcases with old-fashioned button- or tie-fastenings. Finally, top with a knitted bedcover or a pretty patchwork quilt.

Accessories

There are any number of extra touches that will transform most homes into a comfortable, cosy cottage. Piles of ancient hard-backed books, or even old Penguin classics, add an informal literary touch, and on the walls hang framed needlepoint samplers, hunting prints, watercolour landscapes and woodblock illustrations. On all available surfaces gather family photographs in silver or wooden frames. You could arrange floral or blue and white china,

ABOVE A dresser, however simple, allows you to display country-style crockery in assorted colours and styles. Distressed paintwork adds to the effect.

creamware or spongeware on shelves and dressers in rows or attractive groups. Display home-made jams, chutneys and pickles, along with jelly moulds, copper pans, cider jars and bread crocks. Gardening equipment can be attractive as well as useful – consider trugs, a cast iron wellington boot remover, a metal watering can and a besom broom, for example. Use wicker baskets of all sizes and shapes for storage – fruit, magazines, logs for the fire; show off any old-fashioned toys such as a rocking horse or a doll's house; use boxes and bowls to hold pine cones and pot pourri and, finally, arrange plenty of fresh flowers in simple containers – jam jars or enamel ewers, for example – to give you a scent of the country, wherever you happen to live.

Furniture

English country furniture is hard-wearing, honest and effortlessly attractive. The essential look is a combination of Georgian and Victorian, updated with more recent pieces – simple, sturdy and not too delicate. The aim is a handed-down, faded appearance that looks both well-loved and lived-in, so you can mix antiques with junk-shop finds, old with new. Arrange them around the fire or in casual groups, and if things get a little knocked-about, don't worry. Mend rather than replace, and cover anything that's badly battered with a layer of paint.

Avoid materials that are too twentieth-century – matt black, chrome and plastic should be banned – and try to find old pine rather than new as it is so much more solid and good-looking. Oak, elm, mahogany and cane are also appropriate. Look for comfortable, squashy sofas in timeless styles, mixed with armchairs that have room enough to curl up in, rocking chairs, ottomans, and plain wooden settles and stools. Dining chairs can have ladder, splat or spindle backs, and are best gathered around a huge, scrubbed-pine table, while a large, open dresser is pretty much an essential.

There are various ways to cheat in order to achieve this style, and if you haven't got a dresser a good idea is to hang rows of shelves above a wooden cupboard. Distressed paintwork is most effective for an instantly worn-out (but attractive) surface finish, and limewashing has a similar feel. Further tricks include lining the insides of cupboards with floral or polka-dot wallpaper, and replacing solid doors with chicken wire or gathered, checked fabric. Good quality pieces, however, should always be left untouched.

In the bedroom, a wooden four-poster or a Victorian metal bedstead are really attractive and in keeping, but a modern bed can easily be disguised with layers of flouncy bedlinen. Bathrooms benefit from the unfitted look – a deep, cast-iron roll-top bath is perfect, but modern bathrooms with standard suites can be transformed by the clever use of fabrics, accessories and the odd piece of freestanding furniture such as a wooden towel rail or a washstand complete with pitcher and bowl.

In the kitchen, choose cupboards with plain or panelled doors, large metal hinges and round, wooden or ceramic knobs. The most appropriate worksurfaces would be made of wood or tiles, complemented by a butcher's block, splashbacks made of brightly coloured ceramic tiles (farmyard scenes are particularly suitable), a large Belfast sink with brass taps and a wooden plate rack. Hang mugs, pans and implements from hooks and, if there's room, a central rack. If you are lucky enough to have a range oven, make the most of it, as it really does epitomize the country style.

For an idyllic English cottage look, there's nothing better than pale colours, floral patterns and a comfortable arrangement of unpretentious furnishings.

Summing up the style

1 Creamy walls are relaxed and attractive, and complement the soft colours of the furnishings.

2 A soft carpet underfoot can be essential for warmth and comfort in this type of interior. Dark floorboards are also very appropriate.

3 This hanging light is simple and charming; the table lamp on the chest of drawers to the left has more obvious prettiness. The fact that they don't match is an advantage rather than a problem.

4 A patchwork throw combined with floral upholstery is nicely informal and the cushions fit in well without looking deliberately co-ordinated.

5 These dining chairs are of a totally timeless 'farmhouse kitchen' style. Neither they, nor the old-fashioned armchair, the dresser or the chest of drawers match, giving a sense of family furniture collected over the years.

6 A collection of crockery displayed in a cabinet is really appealing. Other lovely touches are the prints, the basket and pitcher (in the background) and jugs of fresh garden flowers.

French Chic

Picture a French woman walking down a tree-lined boulevard in Paris. Her tailored clothes are effortlessly elegant, her shoes well polished, her make-up is immaculate and there's not a hair out of place. And all this without seeming to try. Exactly the same is true of the French home. Every element is thought through to the very last detail, from proportions and scale to the placing of a vase of flowers. And although not everything may be brand new, expensive or ultra-fashionable, like the stylish French woman it is poised and confident, sure of its place in the world and of its own inimitable attraction.

French interiors have a rich history from which to draw, centuries of evolving styles which have been highly influential both at home and abroad. After Louis XIV built the splendid palace of Versailles in the 1670s, for example, the Baroque style of heavily carved furniture, extravagant fabrics, gilding and glass was copied by courts all over Europe. In the eighteenth century pretty, light-hearted Rococo, with its curving, asymmetrical forms and luxurious gilding, glass and mirrors, was followed by the balanced restraint of neo-classicism, which emphasized symmetry and proportion rather than carving and ornament. Under the rule of Napoleon, the Empire style became the official style of France, employing dark mahogany furniture and rich fabrics that were sumptuously draped, sometimes over a whole 'tent room'. Later French designers pioneered the sinuous style of Art Nouveau (see pages 75–81) and, in the Twenties, the dramatic colours and clean lines of Art Deco (see pages 91–7), an exciting expression of a new era and a major influence on interiors both in Europe and the United States.

Although French people, on the whole, have great respect for the past, no single one of these historical styles has emerged to dominate French

There's a certain *je ne sais quoi* about French style. It appears effortless, nonchalant even, and succeeds in being smart and sophisticated yet simple and eminently comfortable – an innate *art de vivre* that is envied and imitated all around the world.

style. Rather, the best from each has been taken, modified for modern times and mixed with various other elements to form a contemporary fusion that works perfectly as a way of life.

This is not the Provençal, hens-scratching-at-the-door look of the French countryside, but a more urban, chic style. The starting point is often architectural – a house with high ceilings, tall windows, grand fireplaces and good quality flooring and finishes. Whatever the background, however, the most important part of the interior is the Gallic flair that combines disparate pieces in a pleasing way.

Traditional features such as delicate ironwork, patterned tiles, pretty lace and copper cooking pans may mingle with Venetian glass chandeliers, huge, imposing mirrors, rich fabrics and classically shaped furniture, along with family hand-me-downs and modern pieces in pale woods and with bold outlines. There are likely to be just as many flea-market finds as *objets d'art*, each piece as valued as any other and all contributing to the overall feeling of comfortable but refined good living that sums up French life.

CREATING THE LOOK

French style is not hung up about making things match, and although there is a strong sense of tradition, personal taste is paramount. Hunt around antiques shops, even junk shops: the French love flea markets, and are not snobbish about origin when it comes to finding interesting furnishings. The final result should be smart and sophisticated, with a sense of order and refinement but at the same time warm, friendly and enjoyable.

ABOVE Hard flooring is the norm in French homes, and polished parquet is especially popular. Pale walls and understated lighting are elegant but not overly obtrusive.

Walls

A strong treatment on the walls is a key to establishing this style, so don't be afraid to make a bold visual statement. Fabric-lined walls, for example, are a trademark of the Napoleonic Empire style, and really do look marvellously sumptuous. Fabric should be stretched across wooden battens which are attached to the walls – richly coloured and patterned damasks, silks, brocades and toiles de Jouy look most effective, but if you are using such an expensive material it would be wise to hire a professional to do the job for you. A simpler and cheaper way to create a similar look would be to take panels of heavy fabric and suspend them from slender poles, making a feature of their borders and the loops from which they hang. Tapestries and rugs featuring classical designs make excellent wall-hangings, too.

There are certain wallpaper designs which immediately evoke a French feel. The most typical styles originated in the late eighteenth century, and feature arabesques of ribbons, garlands and swags on a pale background. Reproductions of these are available today, and you could also look out for delicate patterns of flowers, twining leaves and vines, blue-and-white chinoiserie styles and bold stripes. Painted walls are best either in strong colours or a restrained cream or taupe, and perhaps featuring a subtle but interesting border such as a Greek key pattern or black and white checks.

For security that looks attractive, metal door and window grilles are very French – choose a fanciful, curly style and paint the bars grey for an authentic appearance.

Floors

Generally speaking, wall-to-wall carpets don't particularly appeal to the French. They are sometimes found in bedrooms, in a soft, pale colour, but elsewhere the preference is very much for solid floors. Where possible, then, and depending on your budget, aim to use flagstones, slate, marble, brick, terrazzo or ceramic tiles – black and white chequered tiling, in particular, is typically French, as are unglazed quarry tiles, in a variety of shades from pinkish-red to honey to quite a deep brown. You may even wish to use reclaimed terracotta tiles for an attractive, irregular look.

Polished wooden boards and parquet are highly suitable, too, and look extremely elegant when topped with an oriental, Indian or Turkish rug. Antique French Aubusson and Savonnerie rugs are an expensive but very tasteful choice. Aubusson rugs are flat-woven in Baroque and Rococo designs, often in dusty pink, powder blue and brown on a neutral background, while Savonnerie rugs are knotted, with typical patterns of scrolls,

floral swags, fleurs de lys and acanthus leaves. If you do choose a fitted carpet, the best option is to use either an unobtrusive plain colour or a natural matting, but choose one of the finer, softer textures, such as a wool mix, rather than anything too rough and unsophisticated.

Lights

To create the right mood of both refinement and warmth, aim for a mix of ceiling pendants, wall lights and table lamps. Use natural materials in dramatic but elegant shapes and don't be afraid to combine old with new. Antiques can look wonderful mixed with contemporary styles, but avoid a mismatching clutter by selecting pieces that have certain features in common, whether it be their shape, colour or fabric.

Chandeliers, with delicate glass droplets or made of curving wrought iron, epitomize the French style, and can be as simple or as grand as you like. You may wish to choose examples that are slightly over-scaled in proportion to the size of your room in order to create an impressive effect. If you prefer, pendants with coolie-shaped shades made of metal, fabric or paper give a more subtle but appropriate look. Tall, thin standard lamps could be made of wood or iron, with small conical shades in plain fabric, while table lamps in wood or brass, with a drum-shaped shade made of pleated silk, might have a classical feel. In addition, you could choose Art Nouveau or Art Deco styles of lighting, both of which have remained very popular in France.

COLOURS

French colours are smart and strong, but never garish or over the top. Ochre, burgundy, bright green, deep terracotta and, of course, French navy, are all classically good-looking and make a dramatic impact. Combine them with neutral shades – dove grey, stone, eau de nil and taupe, for example – for a sophisticated contrast, and you may also want to choose one or two paler colours (but not wishy-washy pastels) such as lemon, apricot or mint.

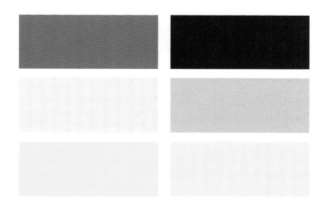

LEFT A panel of lace at the window, a very French touch, contrasts with the strong colours and classically inspired patterns of the bed drapes. A white bedspread prevents this look from becoming overwhelming.

RIGHT Minimal yet attractive, this metal and wicker stand displays food and basic, cream-coloured crockery to good advantage.

Soft furnishings

Though fabrics are very much an important part of the French home, they are never overly elaborate. The emphasis is on quality and detail rather than creating a sumptuous or fussy effect. The look is rather less abundant than a typically English style, and the preference is very much for natural fibres and a tailored, understated feel.

The most quintessential of French fabrics is toile de Jouy, which originated in the late eighteenth century in Jouy en Josas, near Versailles. There, pictorial, Rococo-style designs were printed on to cotton in one colour on a neutral background. Today, toiles are available in a huge range of designs, some historical, some modern, and can be used in a variety of ways, from cushion covers and throws to upholstery and blinds (remember that the pattern is shown to its best advantage if the fabric is used flat rather than gathered). Other

fabrics to choose include damask – which gives a subtle, classic look – brocade, velvet, tapestry, raw silk and linen.

Wooden window shutters are very often found in French homes, and sometimes they take the place of a fabric window treatment. If you do use curtains, however, you should aim for a look that demonstrates sophistication and restraint rather than fuss or frills. Flat panels made of lace are the French version of English gathered nets; second-hand shops are a good source of suitable remnants to use, or you could opt for the plainer style of unpatterned, stretched muslin.

One very attractive form of window treatment would be a roller or Roman blind, paired with cream-coloured cotton or linen that is draped over a pole above the window, held back at either side and flowing on to the floor. Alternatively, hang pull-curtains with smart pencil or goblet pleats, and give them plain, contrasting borders and tie-backs. Fringes and tassels, if used at all, should be unobtrusive.

The same restraint goes for upholstery styles, which should be square and straight, using piping to emphasize the tailoring, and box pleats rather than gathers. Table linen may come in various colours and fabrics, though nothing looks smarter than freshly laundered white damask, popular in France since the seventeenth century. Bedlinen, too, is often predominantly white, although strong colours and classic patterns can sometimes make an appearance. The aim is for a crisp and cool

FABRICS

French fabrics are refined and elegant. Toiles, velvets and damasks in subtle colours are highly suitable – ivory, taupe, cream, French navy and mid blue make good options. Stronger notes, such as crimson, mustard and 'Chinese' yellow can be introduced with care, especially in designs incorporating small geometrical motifs, stripes, oriental flowers, Romanesque medallions and Rococo-like ribbons.

effect with subtle detailing. What appears from a distance to be a plain duvet cover or bedspread, for example, might turn out on close inspection to be covered in exquisite white-on-white embroidery, or to feature delicate lace panels or borders. For a really accurate French style, and the sort of detail that makes a big difference, buy square pillows rather than rectangular ones, and use bolsters to support them.

Accessories

Many of the finishing touches you can make to a French-style interior centre on the kitchen. The French are serious about food, and their kitchen equipment, from Sabatier to Le Creuset, is second to none. A set of these distinctive, heavy orange pans, for example, makes a useful as well as good-looking addition to any cook's possessions, and will last a lifetime. Enamelware and sets of china containers with suitable labels – *sucre, café, thé,* and so on – will also help to create the right look. Displaying crockery on open shelves is a nice touch, and faïence (earthenware pottery with an opaque glaze) is especially appropriate and attractive. Last, but definitely not least, show off your food by transferring it into glass preserving jars and stack bottles of wine (*rouge*, *blanc*, *rosé* and, of course, champagne) in baskets made of delicately curved ironwork.

ABOVE A solid, large, but unfussy bed works well in this room, which combines simplicity and sophistication with typical French subtlety.

Furniture

Making the most of what you have is a key part of the French style, and this goes for furniture just as much as anything else. Family hand-me-downs and heirlooms, antiques, second-hand items and new, designer pieces can all mingle happily for this look. On the whole, French furniture tends to be rather large and formal – long sofas, grand beds, imposing mirrors, oversized wardrobes – imparting a sense of grandeur which is counterpointed by arranging rooms informally and comfortably.

A typical French necessity is the *armoire*, an enormous wardrobe, usually made of fruitwood or walnut and often given as a wedding present and handed down through the family. It can be intricately carved or painted, and is put to use to hold china, glass, bedlinen, clothes or food. Also closely associated with France is bentwood furniture in the style of Michael Thonet, whose simple chairs still grace thousands of cafés throughout the world. Fortunately, such pieces are reasonably priced and relatively easy to get hold of. You can add a classical touch with chairs and tables in a 'Louis' style, and one or two low, comfortable *bergère* armchairs. Leather-covered chairs strike the right note of luxury, while wicker is more suited to a less formal room. Choose sofas that aren't too squashy and, for a modern look, you might want to add cantilevered, chrome-and-leather chairs in the style of Modernist designers Le Corbusier and Charlotte Perriand, or perhaps some sleek, shiny Art Deco pieces. Other typical furniture includes day beds and chaise longues, marble-topped tables and ornate, gilt mirrors.

French beds come in all shapes and sizes, from the peasant-style *litoche*, with a scalloped headboard and posts at the foot, to romantic, curly metal affairs, canopied beds and *bateaux lits* – literally, 'boat beds' – which are shaped like a sleigh. In the bathroom, salvaged French sanitaryware is now much sought-after. If this appeals to you, then try to find large baths with a central tap (designed for two people!), chunky, D-shaped pedestal basins, old-fashioned nickel-plated taps, hinged towel rails, marble-topped vanity units and mirrors on concertina supports. Accessorize with nickel-plated tooth mugs, Rococo-style mirrors and lace-trimmed or embroidered white towels.

Finish by focusing your attention on the kitchen, the centre of French family life. Although this room should be efficient and functional, it should never appear clinical; add warmth and colour with displays of hanging saucepans, china on open shelves and delicious fresh food. A large dining table is a must, with curving bentwood, country-style ladder-back, classical or modern chrome and leather. You might add a butcher's block, plate racks and metal bakers' shelves for attractive free-standing storage.

Poised and elegant, this room is striking in an understated way. A high ceiling and large windows help create an airy feel despite the large scale of some of the furniture.

Summing up the style

1 A restrained wall colour provides a plain backdrop for this room, though a bolder hue would work equally well.

2 The graphic black-and-white checks of this modern rug are an effective contrast to the soft colour of the timber boards, which are so typical of French homes.

3 The classic shape of this tall table lamp, in brass and silk, is just right for creating a refined atmosphere.

4 This is a deceptively simple window treatment that manages to appear both informal and smart. The pelmets are not overly gathered, there are no tie-backs to break the line of the curtains and the gauzy fabric lets in plenty of light even when drawn.

5 French furniture is both practical and good-looking. This chair, for example, combines a square, upright shape with a padded seat, while the shapely chaise longue simply invites relaxation. Oversized bookcases with glass doors complete the look.

6 There are no fussy finishing touches here; just a couple of classical busts, which are dramatic without being over-imposing.

Mediterranean

The traditional houses of the Mediterranean share many typical features, including roofs of curved terracotta tiles, wooden shutters, elaborate wrought-iron window grilles and, especially, whitewashed walls – so that whole villages, undulating up and down hillsides above fields of vines, sunflowers, olives or oranges dazzle brightly as they reflect the blinding sunlight. Inside, furnishings are not intended to impress, but solely to be comfortable and convenient. Key features are a lack of clutter – fussy decoration is not too high on a hard-working farmer's list of priorities – and the use of practical, tough materials such as terracotta, stone, iron, wood and wicker.

Perhaps the epitome of Mediterranean style is found in Provence, which has come under the influence of so many different cultures, including the Greeks, Celts, Romans and Spanish, before eventually becoming a province of France. Here are found the elements that make up the very essence of the Mediterranean home, including thick wooden roof beams, heavy front doors with ironwork studs, hinges and keyholes, flagged or tiled flooring in stone or terracotta, unpretentious fabrics and solid peasant furniture, sometimes carved or painted but on the whole as plain as possible.

In Italy, the archetypal farmhouse is built of stone, with thick walls for coolness and spacious, symmetrical rooms. Classically inspired pediments, architraves and pilasters may add a hint of grandeur to even the humblest abode, while in southern Spain the architecture reflects the influence of the Moors, who landed from North Africa in 711AD and ruled more or less uninterrupted until the end of the fifteenth century. Inner courtyards with palm trees and flowing water are one example of the Arabian influence, while

From dramatically vibrant tones to whitewashed pastels, colour is the most striking element of a Mediterranean interior. The delicious shades of the surrounding landscape are combined with charming country furniture in wood and metal to make homes that are unpretentious, inspiring and genuinely appealing.

horseshoe arches, calligraphic or scrolling motifs and geometrically patterned tilework are other important features. This North African feeling is echoed in the buildings of certain parts of Greece, a country where the favoured colour is clear blue in shades of turquoise, azure, sapphire, cobalt and cerulean, combined with a particularly brilliant white paint that makes for a sculptural, incandescent effect.

With living areas sparsely furnished, the true centre of every Mediterranean home is the kitchen. Warm and cosy for family gatherings and endless cooking sessions, it features a huge fireplace, tiled worksurfaces, a large, basic sink and plenty of hooks or rails for hanging copper pots or fresh herbs. The region's warm climate means, however, that a great proportion of daily life is carried on out of doors, from working in the fields to a leisurely evening meal, or simply sitting and watching the world go past the front door.

CREATING
THE LOOK

This is a look that should have an air of simplicity and definitely no appearance of deliberate design. It is not an expensive style to achieve, since finely made pieces would simply not fit in. Limit furnishings to the bare essentials, concentrating on colour and texture, and complement cool stone, tiles and metalwork with the warmth of wood, wicker and brightly coloured paintwork, rugs and textiles.

Walls

The perfection of neatly papered walls is definitely to be avoided for this look; instead, leave brick or plasterwork rough and ready and, using chalky distemper, simply paint it either white or a Mediterranean shade of, say, pink, blue or yellow. A colourwash treatment also creates a very attractive and effective surface. For a particularly Italian finish, paint a pretty *battiscopa*, a wide stripe of a contrasting colour, along the bottom of walls and around doors and windows, or you could choose a Moorish look by stencilling borders of inter-linked motifs, such as scrolls, leaves or calli-graphic designs. Alternatively, use the beautiful patterned tiles from the region, both inside and out. Islamic ceramics are known for their rich colours and twining geometric patterns; majolica –

from Spain and Italy – is hand painted in bright colours on to a white background; and Provençal tiles are famed for the unique depth and variation of their soft hues. Tiny mosaic tiles, too, give a Mediterranean feel while being attractive and con-temporary in style.

Floors

Hard flooring makes an excellent choice for a Mediterranean-style home as it is cool underfoot, hard-wearing and easy to clean. You can achieve a wonderful look with tiles made of terracotta – square, rectangular or hexagonal – and sealed with linseed oil; stone slabs (marble, slate or lime-stone, for example); or wide, wooden planks, scrubbed rather than varnished. If you must have a fitted carpet, a natural floorcovering such as

LEFT In this shady courtyard, rough quarry tiles contrast wonderfully with a colourful ceramic wall panel and curly-metal gates.

RIGHT These antique carriage lamps, in wood and metal, have a strikingly elemental style well suited to a Mediterranean look. The warm orange of the plaster wall seems to glow all by itself.

sisal, jute or coir will create a suitably unsophisticated effect. For warmth and comfort, add woven straw matting or rugs in a variety of colourful designs. Flat-woven kilims from the Middle East have been imported to the Mediterranean for hundreds of years, while striped, multicoloured rag rugs are typical of a simple Greek cottage. Modern, western-style rugs would suit, as long as they feature simple, bright designs and don't give the impression of being too luxurious.

Lights

The emphasis here is on practical but pretty rather than overly ornamental, with clean lines and natural colours blending into the background instead of making a strong statement. When you don't need a great deal of light for reading or working

by, candles are very appropriate, in a variety of holders from chunky wood to metal, terracotta or pottery. Otherwise, Greek-style hanging oil lamps made of punched metal, or tin-and-glass wall lights are both simple and attractive, or you could choose a French-style wrought iron chandelier or wall bracket. In the Moorish style would be iron or brass lanterns with coloured glass panels, ranging in size from the tiny to the enormous and sometimes in an elaborate star shape, or else lattice-work wall lights made of terracotta, either left bare or painted with a matt emulsion. Terracotta can also be used for rustic-looking lamp bases, as can wrought iron, embossed tin, stone or simple turned wood – finished off with a plain shade in unbleached fabric or wicker for a nicely laid-back look.

COLOURS

Reflect the bright hues of the Mediterranean landscape with a range of nature-inspired colours, from the earthy tones of terracotta, burnt sienna and yellow ochre to brighter sky blues, lavenders, geranium reds, aquamarine greens, sunny yellows and peachy pinks. It's important that the texture is chalky rather than glossy, and remember that the colours look just as wonderful when faded to sunbleached pastels as at their freshest and brightest.

Soft furnishings

The strong sunlight and high humidity of the Mediterranean region are hard on cloth, and consequently textiles are not used in great abundance. Keep your scheme simple and pretty, in natural fabrics such as cotton, linen, canvas, wool and maybe some aged leather. Look for stripes and checks, or plain fabrics in bright Mediterranean hues or earthy, vegetable tones – perhaps with an interesting weave to add some texture. Alternatively, flower prints in vivid colours can really lighten and brighten a room, and if you're confident enough to team together a variety of complementary patterns the effect can be quite stunning.

Upholstered furniture is fairly minimal in a Mediterranean home, so avoid fussy sofas and armchairs and instead choose loose covers in cool cream or white canvas. Alternatively, lovers of pattern will enjoy peasant-like Provençal prints with their brilliantly coloured little flowers and geometric designs. Another upholstery option would be to use kilims, which can also be adapted to make wall-hangings and rough-textured cushion covers. Large cushions on top of a solid wooden chest have the added advantage of providing extra impromptu seating.

In Greece, striped rag rugs are sometimes hung on the walls, as are decorations made of lace and embroidery. Known as *kendima*, these are also used as tablecloths and for bedlinen, while a pretty type of bed enclosure made of embroidered curtains hung from a round frame is called a *sperveri*. A mosquito net or some delicate muslin draped around a bed will always give the distinctive feel of a hot country, and you could add a boldly coloured Spanish shawl as a throw over a bed, sofa or chair. Keep bedlinen either crisply white, perhaps with added embroidery, or in vegetable colours, and for winter you could throw on a quilt (known in Provence as a *boutis*) made from scraps of patterned fabric.

At the windows, hang a panel of lace and just add some very simple pairs of unlined curtains, made from unbleached calico, cotton or linen, or else in a flower pattern, hung from a wrought iron pole with curly finials. Use simple gathers, not too full, or a looped heading, and don't be tempted by complicated swags, pelmets or tie-backs. Rather than curtains, however, Mediterranean houses frequently feature wooden shutters, which are most effective in keeping rooms cool in boiling summers. These are often louvred in order that the amount of light and heat coming in can be controlled, and may be left bare or painted in a bright shade of emulsion. Split cane blinds, on the other hand, make an inexpensive alternative, while Roman or even roller blinds in an appropriate fabric would be practical and fit in well with this charming, country look.

Accessories

Without the pretension of consciously adopting a style, the Mediterranean home contains the minimum of decoration, though functional items often have their own charm that is highly pleasing. The rule is not to go over the top, but to allow just a

ABOVE Open displays of food, crockery and cooking implements help create a Mediterranean feel in a kitchen. The small green and white tiles were hand made in Seville.

FABRICS

Natural fabrics such as cotton and linen are ideal for simple Mediterranean soft furnishings. Neutral colours work well with stripes, ginghams and simple floral designs in vivid colours. You should also be able to find pretty Provençal designs (here, cherries with leaves and olives with trailing flowers) which are very typical of the southern French region and look marvellous used alone or in carefully chosen combinations with other fabrics.

few items to make an impact with their vivid colours and hand-crafted shapes.

Colourful ceramics are typically Mediterranean, and a much-loved example of the creative fusing of the useful and the beautiful. The range is broad, from Provençal faïence in deep, glowing colours to Italian majolica, Moorish-influenced Spanish tiles to the splashy, exuberantly patterned tableware from Portugal and Greece, but what they have in common is an unselfconscious vibrancy that arises from their hand-made forms and uneven glazes. Whichever type you choose – and you can mix the different styles with ease – it is delightful used as informal tableware, jugs, vases, serving dishes, candle holders and lamp bases.

Chunky, uneven glassware, in the form of drinking glasses, vases or even storage jars, is the perfect partner for bright ceramics. Add roughly woven wicker baskets and ornamental metal pieces, in the form of French-style wirework such as wine racks, egg baskets, mirror surrounds and shelves, heavy Spanish hooks, hinges and locks, or Greek fishermen's galvanized tin lanterns.

Complete the picture with plenty of terracotta pots in all shapes and sizes – they make great kitchen storage or, filled with aromatic herbs or cheerful geraniums, evoke the Mediterranean in an immediate and inimitable way.

Furniture

There is no great tradition of fine furniture in the Mediterranean – in fact, pieces may often by quite roughly made, their appeal arising from their solid form and weathered texture rather than any ornate decoration. Just occasionally a family would have been able to afford to pay for furniture with carved detailing, or perhaps bothered to paint some brightly coloured flowers on to a chest or dresser front. This is an easy way to decorate your own furniture in a country style, or you could use a distressed paint technique, which gives a wonderfully worn, antique effect.

Choose furniture for its unsophisticated looks and basic construction. Dark or mid-coloured woods are most appropriate, and reclaimed pine is particularly nice for its ready-worn feel and rich colour, while new pine can be stained without too much difficulty. Look for typical furniture such as rush-seated, Greek taverna-style chairs and stools, huge, plain tables and dressers, French-style *armoires*, or wardrobes, for food and clothing, and storage chests in all sizes to hold blankets, bedlinen, clothes, kitchenware and jewellery. Don't get carried away, however, as this style relies on a lack of clutter for its functional appearance, and just a handful of carefully chosen pieces (they look nicer if they don't match) will do the trick.

Though wood is the predominant material used for Mediterranean furniture, metalwork is also found everywhere in the region. This can range from a wall light to a window grille and all types of furnishings in between, including curly shelving, marble- or tile-topped tables with wrought iron bases, and large straps and locks on chests and doors. Beds, too, are often made of elaborately twining wrought iron, though a simpler version would be in the form of a banquette which doubles as a sofa during the day.

Small pieces of metal furniture come in handy as a means of creating the right atmosphere in the bathroom, too. A set of shelves or a wire rack is both useful and attractive, or you could add a small, tile-topped table if there's enough room, along with a free-standing towel rail. A white suite will look wonderful against brightly painted walls or vividly coloured tiles.

Finally, concentrate your efforts on creating a warm, welcoming atmosphere in the kitchen, the heart of every Mediterranean home. Here, surround a huge old pine or oak table with assorted wooden chairs and stools, and use open, wooden shelves or metal racks to display bright crockery. For worksurfaces and splashbacks use either terracotta tiles or Mediterranean-style multicoloured tiles laid in checked patterns. You can use wicker baskets or metal hooks for storage, and kitchen cupboards, fronted with lattice to allow air to circulate, should be painted in bright colours so that the overall effect is lively and welcoming, cheerful and easy to live with.

Believe it or not, this whitewashed Italian kitchen was once a stable. Its look is eclectic and casual, typical of the relaxed Mediterranean lifestyle.

Summing up the style

1 Though these walls have been kept as plain as possible, a little more colour – and perhaps an interesting, textured wash – would not go amiss in this type of interior.

2 Brick-shaped reclaimed terracotta tiles, laid in a herringbone pattern, are hard-wearing and have a lovely warm homeliness.

3 A simple idea makes for a very unusual and effective form of pendant light – two inverted flowerpots. Candles in the plainest of metal sconces provide additional atmospheric lighting.

4 Basic but colourful checks are put together with dense floral patterns. Mediterranean fabrics are minimal, usually printed cottons, but nevertheless bright and breezy.

5 The heavily distressed patina of this wooden cupboard really suits this style. Note how the open shelves above give it the look of a one-piece dresser. Banquette seating and rush-seated stools and chairs are casual and comfortable, and give a down-to-earth impression.

6 Cooking implements, fresh vegetables and a large woven basket are strung from the beams, forming an attractive and useful finishing touch.

Scandinavian

Scandinavian style combines country charm with understated grandeur, warmth and simplicity with elegance and an uncluttered sense of space and light. Although inspired by the past, it is contemporary, too, and is not only pretty but also extremely practical.

The forces of nature are at their most impressive in the Scandinavian countries of Sweden, Norway, Iceland, Finland and Denmark. Here, extremes of landscape and climate are the norm – endless forests and vast fjords, snow-capped mountains, boiling geysers and the Aurora Borealis. Not surprisingly, making best use of light dominates all aspects of life: these may be the lands of the midnight sun, but in the long winters daylight is a fleeting pleasure. In the more isolated, northernmost regions, especially, the need to keep warm brought about a distinctive vernacular architecture: houses with thick log walls, small, south-facing doors and windows, and thatched or birch-bark roofs, sometimes topped with living turf.

Vividly coloured decoration in these cottages provided some relief from the gloom of night and the expanses of gleaming snow. During the long winters, it was customary for men to carve while women wove, filling their homes with intricately chiselled spoons, bowls, cups and chests, and bright cushions, rugs and blankets. Furniture would be painted in the style of Norwegian *rosmålning* (literally, 'rose painting'), a technique that uses strong colours for stylized flowers, scrolls and teardrops, or Swedish *kurbits*, where outsized flowers surround scenes of village life or Bible stories.

The spare lines and light colours most often associated with Scandinavian interiors, however, originate in a style that emerged under the influence of King Gustav III of Sweden (1771–92). This appropriated the strict neo-classicism of Louis XVI, merged it with Rococo gaiety and gave it a gentler, more accessible edge that was distinctly Swedish. The Gustavian style's main features were a considered symmetry, the use of subtle, pale colours, ceramic-tiled stoves, ribbons and floral swags, glass chandeliers, gilding, mirrors and delicate wooden furniture. Although developed by the nobility, a new capacity for mass production meant that it was soon in use at all levels of society – a democracy of style that is essentially Scandinavian. The same appreciation of craft skills and natural materials marks the work of modern Scandinavian designers, whose fusion of traditional and contemporary gives their furniture, lights and accessories wide appeal.

The typical Scandinavian home today combines folk arts with an easy-going Gustavian style and an open-plan love of light and space. This unique mix was largely created by one man, Carl Larsson, a Swedish artist whose influence on Scandinavian design has been incalculable. In the 1890s Larsson and his wife, Karin, decorated their rural cottage in a highly innovative way that combined traditional Nordic styles, British Arts and Crafts, Art Nouveau and japonisme. When Carl's watercolours of the house were published in 1899, the public response was immediate and overwhelming. The style was accessible, bright and airy, robust and pretty, and its timeless attraction has ensured that it has never gone out of fashion.

CREATING THE LOOK

Scandinavian style can range from the earthily rustic to the strikingly sophisticated, and you could opt for one extreme or another, or a Larsson-like combination of each. Distinguishing elements are clear colours, clean lines and unfussy, natural materials, put together in a way that emphasizes light and space. Steer clear of clutter, and pick pale woods, sheer or checked fabrics, painted furniture and lots of sparkling glass and mirrors.

Walls

To set off painted furniture, walls should be interesting but not overpowering. Tongue-and-groove is a most appropriate covering, up to dado level, to the tops of the walls or even across the ceiling, creating a sauna-like effect. You could leave the wood in its natural colour, just adding a coat of varnish for protection, or paint it with a typically Scandinavian hue. Plaster walls, too, could be painted in one plain colour, but there are also a variety of paint techniques which both recreate this look and add a touch of individuality. Marbling, spattering and trompe-l'oeil were all once widely used throughout Scandinavia, but it is stencilling which typifies the style of the region. Use matt paint in traditional colours to scatter garlands of flowers, leaves, ribbons and tendrils liberally from

ABOVE Painted walls in pale colours give a definite Scandinavian feel, while the curving glass and metal candle holder is typical of the style.

floor to ceiling, or as a frieze along the top of a plain wall. Wallpapers with soft-toned and small-scale leaf and flower prints are pretty, while fake classical panels are very Gustavian. Wall-hangings, in bright colours and folk designs, are not only attractive but also act as insulation in living rooms and dining rooms, while blue-and-white tiles featuring historical patterns are highly suitable for kitchens and bathrooms.

Floors

Vast areas of Scandinavia are covered in forest, and its people's love of timber practically knows no bounds. Wooden floors, then, are almost *de rigueur* – large areas of pale boards that are light, bright and extremely easy to keep clean. Rough-cut, stripped planks are down-to-earth and rustic, while polished parquet is more sophisticated and elegant: it is up to you which you prefer. If you are installing a new wooden floor, avoid dark woods such as oak and opt instead for beech or ash; existing floors, if too dark in appearance, could be lightened by limewashing. Equally, painted floors are very attractive – a good choice would be an off-white base with diamond patterns or floral borders.

Alternatives to wood include vinyl or lino, cushioned underfoot yet still hard-wearing; honey-coloured quarry tiles; or tightly woven natural matting, such as sisal or coir, in a light golden colour. Fitted carpets are not particularly appropriate, but you could get away with a one-colour, neutral style if it's not overly luxurious. Adding a selection of narrow, flat-woven rugs and runners will give a great deal of authenticity – these could be in cream, ivory or taupe for a sophisticated, modern look, but would be more typical in vivid colours and folk patterns.

Lights

Adequate artificial light is essential in northern European homes, counteracting the long evenings and dark mornings of winter and creating a welcoming, warm and homely atmosphere. Scandinavian style demonstrates a mastery of the use of light, making the most of reflection and refraction

COLOURS

Choose colours for their ability to reflect light or add splashes of heartening colour – 'Falun red', a mix of copper pigment and linseed oil, is traditional in Norway and Sweden and makes an attractive accent, while other folk colours such as apple green, straw yellow and mid blue make for a bright, country look. Larger areas are more restful if treated with paler, pearly Gustavian tones, which include white, cerulean blue, slate, grey-green, pink and silvery grey.

in glittering glass and metal, resulting in a look that is highly functional and also extremely attractive. The most typical Scandinavian light fitting is the eighteenth-century-style chandelier made from glass and brass, easy to find today in reproduction form, either pleasantly simple or complex and

ABOVE Imitation candle bulbs can help create a suitable lighting effect, as this minimal wrought-iron chandelier demonstrates.

ornate in design. Mirror-backed wall sconces in a curvy Rococo style are another way to add sparkle to your home, while table and floor lamps could have shades made of traditional pierced paper, which also help increase light levels while creating an attractive pattern. Other shades could be made of checked fabric in white and one or two bright colours. Add plenty of candlesticks, made of wood, glass, pewter, silver or brass, and perhaps one or two old-fashioned lanterns. As a simpler

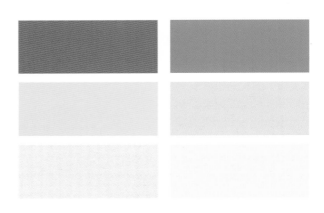

alternative to glass, brass and mirror, wrought-iron fittings are very peasant-like, or you could choose streamlined modern styles such as recessed spotlights or wall-mounted uplighters, which fit in surprisingly well with the Scandinavian aesthetic.

Soft furnishings

The exuberance of Scandinavian painted walls and furniture should be combined with natural fabrics that feature relatively simple designs. Cotton, wool and linen make the best choices, and texture is important – twills and loose weaves, for example, create a pattern of their own. Generally, soft furnishings should not be too overstated, instead contributing quietly to the overall effect of prettiness and practicality.

Scandinavian fabrics tend to use just one or two colours on a white background. Checks both large and small are the most typical, usually in blue, red or brown with white, and it would be easy to create a wonderful scheme based solely on combinations of checks in various sizes and colours. Stripes and delicate floral designs may also be used. In the 1730s cotton began to be imported to Scandinavia from China and India, to be printed with complex patterns inspired by the flora of Asia; these exotic flowers and twining tendrils were immensely popular, used for all types of home from up-market town houses to peasant's cottages.

An easy way to evoke the Scandinavian style would be to make tailored slip-covers for sofas and chairs in checked fabric, or to use an ivory-coloured fabric and complement it with cushion covers in various checks and ginghams. Make seat covers for dining chairs, perhaps with pleated 'skirts' that extend halfway to the ground, and layer tablecloths made of a variety of checks and plains, or else embroidered geometric patterns in white, red, blue or black on white. A narrow table runner with beaded fringing is typical of the Larsson look.

Bedlinen could be in plain white, or with a self-stripe or colourful embroidery. A gingham border would be pretty, while all-over checks or floral sprays make more of a statement. If you like the elaborate look, create an impression with a four-poster hung with floral-patterned fabric, or suspend pretty drapes from a central coronet.

Window treatments can make a big difference to this style, as they have such an immediate effect on the quality and amount of light in a room. Simplicity is of the essence, and any treatments that smack of the grand, the elaborate or the pretentious have no place here. Wooden window shutters are often used in Scandinavia, and where curtains are needed they tend to be unlined and ethereal, with the gauzy, floaty feel of muslin or voile. If you need a heavier fabric, use plain or checked cotton or linen. Create a straightforward style with pairs of gathered, pencil-pleated or tab-headed curtains, hung from a wooden or metal pole and perhaps with a softly draped fabric pelmet – Karin Larsson made flat panels embroidered with red and green on a

white background. A Roman or roller blind, or a ribbon-tied panel, can be given a decorative surround by swirling a length of voile around a pole and draping it each side.

Accessories

The inherent elegance and simplicity of the Scandinavian look would be ruined by the addition of too many fussy accessories, so ensure that anything you choose works well with this type of decor and has the appearance of functionality rather than pure ornament. The Nordic countries are famous for the spare lines of their beautiful glassware, silver and ceramics – etched drinking glasses, smooth silver platters and white-glazed porcelain beakers and vases would make an understated and yet attractive display in any room. Mirrors with carved and gilded frames, in curving Rococo shapes, are another way to add a touch of pretty glitter, while pale wood-framed mirrors make a more basic alternative. Further wooden items can be added in the form of spoons, bowls and cups – carved wooden spoons, in particular, are a traditional Scandinavian lover's gift, offered by a man to the object of his affection and, if accepted, taken as evidence of an interest in romance. Other folk

FABRICS

The Scandinavian look is light, bright and airy, and this theme is continued strongly with soft furnishings. Unbleached muslin, for example, is suitably ethereal, especially for windows, while blue, yellow, green and scarlet are good colours to use all over in cotton, linen and wool. Patterns may be fairly robust – ginghams and strong checks, for example – or pretty and delicate, perhaps in the form of tiny, trailing florals.

ABOVE The decorative carving on this table and elegant shape of the armchair are typically Scandinavian, as are the gauzy curtains and the bright geraniums on the window sill.

crafts that would make useful and attractive features include woven willow baskets and wreaths; oval or round wooden boxes, with lids and painted decoration; painted clocks, chests and trays; and delicate *scherenschnitte*, cut-paper love tokens, in a wooden frame.

Furniture

Hand-crafted Scandinavian country furniture is well-made and pays attention to detail. It is often ornately carved and nearly always features a coat of protective paint which can itself be a work of art, as demonstrated by the hand-painted pieces in Carl and Karin Larsson's home, Lilla Hyttnäs. The most basic type of Scandinavian furnishings are built-in box beds, tub chairs – made by hollowing-out tree trunks – and stools whose legs are natural timber forks. For your scheme, however, English country pieces – splat- or panel-backed chairs, sturdy tables, simple chests of drawers and dressers, blanket boxes and hanging cupboards – will make an excellent base for decorative painting, whether it be marbling, distressing or wood-graining, a trompe-l'oeil, *rosmålning* or *kurbits* finish, or a simple covering with one colour of wood stain or matt paint.

The Gustavian style has a greater elegance that lends itself to contemporary homes. As living rooms in which to entertain guests evolved in the eighteenth century, so new pieces of furniture came into being, including the circular tea table, the tray table with a detachable top and the gate-leg dining table. These pieces, along with desks, chairs, bookshelves, cot-style sofas, bedside cabinets and chests of drawers, were made in a distinctive style that employs gentle curves, delicate tapering legs, upright shapes, subtle carved details and pale paintwork. The typical sofa, for example, would have an exposed frame with removable seat, back and arm cushions and tapering, turned legs; the Gustavian dining chair would have a spoon-shaped or rectangular back with pierced splats, plus carved floral decoration and fluted legs; while a desk would have elegantly tapering legs and pretty brass decoration in the form of handles and key escutcheons.

Reproduction Gustavian-style furniture is becoming easier to find even on the high street, and you can approximate the look by painting sugar-almond colours on plain yet elegant wooden chairs, tables, chests, shelves and glass-fronted cabinets. The overall effect should be easy and unfussy, mixing antiques with new pieces, junk-shop finds with valued family heirlooms. Aim, too, for a clean-lined and pared-down look – this furniture needs space in which to breathe, and rooms should be uncrowded and verging towards the sparse, although at the same time retaining a welcoming and comfortable atmosphere.

A huge window helps give this dining room the exceptionally light and airy feel that is an integral part of the Scandinavian look, enhanced by the slender and elegant furnishings.

Summing up the style

1 Wood panelling, painted a creamy colour, is most appropriate for a Scandinavian room.

2 For a typical taste of Scandinavia, pale, polished boards such as these are just right. They reflect the light and are easy to clean, as well as looking stunning.

3 This curving iron chandelier is very much in keeping. It is light and pretty, without being overly refined, and its curving shape reflects that of the chair backs.

4 Quiet fabrics in pale colours are best for this style, and this simple pair of gathered curtains is very easy to emulate. The tied cushions on the dining chairs, with their ruched edging, are charming, too.

5 These Gustavian-style chairs are very Swedish in both form and colour. Open backs such as these increase the feeling of lightness and brightness.

6 Scandinavian glassware is renowned for its beauty. Modern silverware and ceramics in bold, simple shapes would also make attractive accessories.

Russian

The palaces of imperial Russia, with their fanciful ornamentation, copious gilding and striking, onion-shaped domes, stand as lavish symbols of the grandest elements of the nation's cultural heritage. For ordinary people, however, folk values are summed up by a type of Russian dwelling that could not be more different: the *izba*, a traditional peasant cottage in a style that has been in existence since as early as the ninth century.

Made of roughly cut logs of pine, fir or spruce, the walls of the *izbas* were held together with wooden dowels or spikes, any gaps plugged with moss. As protection against potentially dangerous forest spirits, the peasant builders carved decorative wooden figures on the gables, beams and cornices of the cottage roofs. Beautiful carvings also frequently extended across much of the exterior of the cottages, especially the balconies, window frames, shutters and roof edgings. In deep relief, and picked out in white paint, this intricate decoration resembled embroidery in wood, and made a dazzling and unexpected contrast to the harshness of the environment.

The insides of the cottages were dominated by an enormous stove, constantly alight during the severe winters and around which all activities took place. It sometimes vented through an ornately carved wooden pipe in the roof, but when poverty meant that a flue was unaffordable, the insides of the *izba* would be covered in soot; unsurprisingly, these were known as 'black' cottages.

Apart from the stove, almost everything else inside the *izba* (which was most often one single, shared, multi-purpose room) was made of the nearest and cheapest material to hand – wood from the surrounding forests. Lack of space meant that much furniture was built-in – movable furnishings were a later, bourgeois development –

Russian peasant cottages were simple and basic, but protecting and comforting against the harshest of climates. With rich, deep colours and carved or painted furniture, this is a folk look full of welcome and warmth.

including benches for sitting and sleeping near the stove. Beds were a sign of distinction and rarely seen in an *izba*. Instead, straw mattresses were the norm, with the elders sleeping on a bench above the stove and children in the loft. One of the few exceptions to the purely practical, however, was the *krasny ugol*, or 'beautiful corner', which marked the entrance point for spirit visitors and which was usually beside the family dining table, opposite the stove. Here, constantly burning wax tapers or oil lamps formed an altar around an icon, with a shelf for offerings and an embroidered ceremonial cloth as decoration.

Today, the traditional Russian peasant's way of life has all but disappeared. Perhaps this change is just as well – *izbas* were undoubtedly crowded, dark, damp and smelly, poorly furnished and austere, offering a harsh and unpleasant existence. Elements of the *izba* lifestyle, however, such as embroidered fabrics, holy shrines, wonderful woodcarving, and a determination to create warmth and individuality through colour and pattern, have lived on, ensuring the Russian folk look a permanent place in people's hearts worldwide.

CREATING THE LOOK

To recreate some of the elemental simplicity of the Russian peasant's home can provide a welcome relief from the complexity, sophistication and frenetic activity of modern-day western life. Make wood your primary material, and choose sturdy country furniture, embroidered fabrics – especially in red and white, two deeply symbolic colours – and traditional Russian accessories such as samovars, painted wooden eggs and nesting dolls.

Walls

Wooden tongue-and-groove walls are the obvious choice for a Russian peasant-style scheme. The planks can be run either horizontally or vertically, and left bare for the very simplest of effects which delights in the colour, grain and texture of timber. If you wish, however, you could wash the wood with a stain or with tinted matt varnish – darker colours would be best. A plain plaster finish can be whitewashed or painted in a subtle, natural colour, making an understated background against which to display the bright embroideries and accessories that characterize this look.

Some *izbas* featured painted motifs on their walls, as either friezes or vertical panels. Using relaxed, flowing, roughly sketched lines, you could add this type of decorative element to any

room by painting flowers, fruit and trees in panels, along the tops of walls or around doorways. This effect looks particularly nice in kitchens, where you could adapt the motifs for use on cupboard fronts or above cookers.

Floors

Laying wooden boards is really the best way to authentically recreate the style of a Russian peasant home. They should, against all current convention, be quite rough and ready looking, and be left untreated as much as possible – glossy varnish, in particular, would be a mistake. Try to choose wood that is mellow in tone, but not too pale in colour – you could use a wood stain or tinted matt varnish, where necessary, to create a more authentic colouring. The wider the planks the better, giving an old-fashioned, rustic air. You may get away with using a wood laminate flooring, but this is one instance where wood-effect vinyl will probably not work. As an alternative, use stone flags or quarry tiles, which offer a similar feel of hard-working, uneven simplicity.

Flat-woven runners in simple stripes of bright colours (toning rather than garish) are perfect on top of all this hard flooring. You could, equally, use stripy rag rugs, which are common to many folk interiors and create a cosy, peasant-like atmosphere. And perhaps, if you like the hunting-lodge effect, you may even want to add one or two animal skins – fake, of course.

Lights

The basic conditions of the *izba* would not have been improved by their lighting, which was minimal and barely adequate. Today, the aim is to reproduce the essentials of the look without being forced to live with its lack of comfort, so with this type of scheme is will be necessary to combine a few folk elements with modern fixtures that are capable of providing proper illumination for a present-day lifestyle.

Izba-style lighting would include some carved and painted wooden candlesticks or candelabra in very simple shapes, iron wall sconces and metal and glass lanterns of plain construction, which

ABOVE Candles in a three-branched, wrought-iron candlestick have a low, soft glow. Lighting for this style should be kept as simple as possible.

you could use as pendant, wall or table lamps. If you wish to be a little more ornate, you could add some brass fittings, perhaps a very restrained, curved chandelier, or else one or two wall lights. To build up adequate task and general light, use discreet modern fittings, which could include hidden spotlights or hemispherical plaster uplighters, painted the same colour as the walls. The plain wooden bases of table and floor lamps could be painted in vivid colours, and their ivory-coloured card or fabric shades stamped or stencilled with appropriate folk motifs.

COLOURS

Red and white are the two predominant colours of the Russian folk interior. Red, the colour of life itself, is also associated with beauty – in fact, the Russian word for 'red' is the same as the word for 'beauty'. White offsets this intense scarlet in the form of lace, embroidery and carved-and-painted wood. Ochre, black, brown and dark, mossy green are also suitable, while touches of gold make for a slightly grander look, and bring to mind the glow of icon paintings.

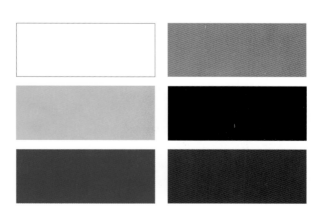

LEFT Hours of work would have gone into making this beautiful lace window panel and bright patchwork tablecloth. The effect is bold without being grandiose.

Soft furnishings

Vivid colour was used by the Russian peasants to enliven their harsh lives, and nowhere was this more in evidence than in their love of textiles. Long winter evenings were filled by completing home-made embroidery, patchwork and lace, which warmed and brightened their cottages. In vibrant colours and natural fibres such as cotton and wool, the results were hung from beams and around cornices and doorways, and used for seat covers, wall-hangings, table linen and bedlinen.

Most characteristic of all Russian textiles is pretty, detailed embroidery, often in cross-stitch, which has, from as long ago as the twelfth century, embellished ordinary domestic linen (such as sheets, bedcurtains, towels and aprons), wedding gifts and ceremonial cloths (in the form of special towels and small squares of fabric known as *chirinkas*). The usual colour of the stitching is red on a white background, although sometimes white-on-white is employed for particularly prized pieces, and other vivid colours occasionally play a part. The motifs

FABRICS

Red and white is the all-encompassing theme of the Russian country home, though you can add variety with the occasional use of vivid yellow, green, blue or black. Gingham and lace are universal country-style choices, while bold abstract motifs or delicately printed flowers and fruit are also suitable. Introducing some small embroidered motifs makes these soft furnishings even more authentic.

depicted are many and various: flowers, foliage, birds, eight-pointed stars, suns, mythological humans and other figures, lions, unicorns, stags, peacocks, galloping horses, firebirds and zigzags, among others.

To emulate this unsophisticated use of fabrics, start by trying to find examples of cross-stitch embroidery in red on white (antique textiles specialists may be your best source) or even stitch your own, if you have the patience. Use it to add deep borders to sheets and bedcovers, to trim shelves, to make tablecloths and place mats, to cover cushions and to form beautiful pelmets. You can also use plenty of pretty white lace and drawn threadwork – a technique in which threads are pulled from the fabric and the remaining threads rearranged to form lace-like patterns – for the same purposes.

When you are using printed fabrics, you should combine colours and patterns with naïve abandon. This looks especially effective for bedlinen which, traditionally, should be piled high on top of the bed with layer upon layer of pillows and quilts. Patchwork quilts worked in very straightforward patterns offer a colourful finishing touch, while a fake fur throw over a bed also gives a suitably warm and raw effect.

In the *izbas* it was not unusual to find sprigs of cranberries and mountain ash berries arranged as

an alternative method of window decoration, the light from inside filtering through them to give a welcome glow to visitors and passers-by. Any other form of window treatment was certainly never ornate, so your curtains should be in a delicate, rather minimal style, with simple pairs of slightly gathered panels hung from a wooden or basic iron pole. White cotton is an ideal fabric, left plain or embroidered along the bottom, preferably in red cross-stitch. Edge with a deep panel of lace, and top with an embroidered panel, again in red and white, as a pelmet.

Accessories

Though there was little in a Russian peasant home that was purely decorative, even the most hard-working of items was given lavish embellishment in the least subtle of fashions. As was the case with folk craft in many different regions, wooden implements were often carved and painted – for your scheme you could choose spoons, ginger-bread moulds, laundry beaters, salt boxes, egg dishes and bowls, all covered with freehand floral patterns, to make bright displays on open shelving. Metal trays and are typically Russian: they, too, are often brightly painted, in a style not dissimilar to British canal art. And, if you can find one, that ubiquitous Russian tea urn, the samovar, would deserve pride of place.

Further attractive displays can be created with groups of painted glass tumblers and flasks. This is a technique you might like to try for yourself, using thinned enamel paints and inexpensive glassware, following traditional folk patterns, such as hearts, stylized flowers or naïve human figures. Lacquered papier mâché boxes and brooches are another typically Russian craft, painted in tempera (a paint made with egg yolk) and gold, and depicting fairy tales, legends or folk heroes.

On a more practical note, you could also include a variety of simple earthenware pots and wooden barrels, which were essential in the *izbas* for all types of storage. Fill bowls full of painted wooden eggs, which originated from Orthodox Easter celebrations, add some carved wooden children's toys (naïve horses on wheels, for example) and finish the look of with, of course, a set of brightly painted nesting Russian dolls, called *babushka*, the Russian for 'grandmother'.

ABOVE A roughly painted chest, in remarkably vivid colours, would have held sheets and other linens. Such a piece would be quite easy to recreate today.

Furniture

For centuries, *izba* furniture consisted of built-in benches and tables, plus some storage chests, a sideboard, a loom and a spinning wheel. Later, more movable furniture was added, but it was still fairly rudimentary and not exactly designed for comfort. While this basic look may be admirable in its own place, its rough and ready austerity is hardly desirable for modern-day life, and if you wish to create this sort of scheme you will undoubtedly want to make some compromises in favour of a little more luxury.

In general, aim to keep furniture as simple in structure as possible, in strong shapes and solid wood. The best pieces to choose are sturdy, planked benches, square tables, chests and chairs, and some boxy cupboards. The occasional piece – perhaps a sideboard, chest, bedhead or chair – may be carved in fanciful peasant patterns, forming an echo of the lace-like carvings that adorned the exteriors of these cottages.

To add another decorative element, you may also want to paint some items of furniture – this is a look that is never monotonous but always bright and cheery, despite its relative lack of finery. Use quick-drying, acrylic colours in strong tones, and either wash a solid colour over chairs, tables, shelves and cupboards, or create interesting designs by emulating traditional Russian motifs such as flowers, suns, trees and horses. Use a distressing technique, or sand down once you have finished, to give an attractively aged and worn effect to the paintwork.

Some plain iron furniture can, if you wish, be introduced to this very wood-orientated environment. Though not strictly authentic, it adds interest in the way of colour and texture, and gives you the opportunity to vary your furnishings just a little. Some simple metal seats, for example, or an iron bedstead, would not be totally out of place. Most *izba* beds (when separate beds existed, which was rare) were boxed in and surrounded by curtains – not just to keep out the cold, but also to maintain privacy in these overcrowded surroundings. Try to recreate this look by hanging fabric around beds, either from the bed posts (if you possess a four-poster) or from wooden rails attached to the ceiling or adjacent walls.

When it comes to upholstered furniture, you will need to work hard to make sure that it fits in with this look. The best course of action is to choose pieces that are very unadorned and that display as much of their wooden frame as possible. Avoid overstuffed and deeply buttoned upholstery, and choose plain fabrics in colours that are typical of the region. An additional disguise would be to cover with an all-enveloping fake fur throw, or a large embroidered panel in cheerful red and white cross-stitch (see Soft Furnishings for further details).

The predominant reds of this cosy, down-to-earth sitting room are what give it such warmth and vigour, reminiscent of a Russian *izba*.

Summing up the style

1 Bare brick walls have the right sort of rough-and-ready feel. For a slightly less rustic look, however, there would be nothing wrong with painting them.

2 A huge, flat-woven Middle Eastern rug has been chosen for its scarlets and blood reds glowing out of the black patterning.

3 This earthenware table lamp, with a plain paper shade, is neutral enough not to be too noticeably out of place. Overall, lighting levels are quite dim, which adds to the feeling of all-embracing comfort.

4 The colours and patterns of these fabrics have been mixed with joyful abandon, though the overall impression is of a vivid scarlet. Nothing looks too pristine or new, which is just as it should be.

5 A bench-like sofa such as this is simple yet made comfortable with its scattering of plump cushions. The other pieces of furniture are simple, too – note the large wicker chest used as a coffee table.

6 Woven baskets in a variety of shapes and sizes, and bunches of herbs, are all hung from the chunky ceiling beam, typical of a peasant's cottage.

Indian

A vast region that stretches from the snows of the Himalayas to the tropics of Sri Lanka, covering lush river valleys and parched deserts, with a population of more than a billion people speaking scores of different languages, it is no wonder that the subcontinent of India is a land of excess.

To define a style that is purely Indian, Pakistani or Bangladeshi is not a straightforward matter: not only do craftsmen continue to produce furniture and textiles in centuries-old designs peculiar to their particular region – even their particular village – but it is also essential to remember that the original Hindu inhabitants of the region have had to assimilate the influences of a number of foreign cultures, including the Muslims, the Moghuls and the colonizing French, Portuguese, Dutch and British.

What has come to be regarded as 'typically' Indian includes various features. Highly decorated arched entranceways, for example, give an unforgettable greeting to visitors and may involve incised stucco, rich woodcarving, pressed terracotta, intricate paintwork or complex tilework – sometimes all at the same time. Wrought iron window grilles are echoed in shape by carved wooden or stone screens, known as *jali*. Hindu motifs that are frequently seen are peacocks, parrots, intertwining exotic flowers, the elephant-headed god Ganesh, Krishna and other figures from the Hindu epics. By contrast, beautiful, brightly coloured tiles are often covered with intricate geometric designs, or with Arabic inscriptions, scrolling arabesques or swirls of flowers and leaves, all reflecting the important influence of Islamic culture.

One of the most influential periods of art and architecture in India was that of the Moghul dynasty, established in 1526 by the cultured

The images of India are always highly evocative. Luscious colours and a laid-back atmosphere come together with a wealth of decoration that owes its style to many different influences.

Emperor Barbur. By the mid seventeenth century the rulers had amassed great wealth, and they became enlightened patrons of the arts, architecture (the Taj Mahal was built in this era) and crafts. Imperial workshops employing expert artisans from India, Persia, Central Asia and Europe produced painting, fine textiles, lacquerwork, carpets and tapestries, precious metalwork, decorative tilework and gorgeous animal trappings, in a style that blended Indian and Islamic motifs, the sensuous lyricism of Persia and influences from China and Europe.

From the sixteenth century onwards European traders began to make their mark along the Indian coast; by the mid eighteenth century the British East India Company effectively ruled most of the subcontinent until the British government took control in 1858. And so yet another ingredient was added to the cultural mix: the unique colonial fusion of Victorian with Indian, an influence still strongly felt in this style of interior. Darkened rooms with ceiling fans, chintz, heavily carved furniture and animal skins formed the backdrop to tiffin and big game-hunting, tea parties and gin and tonic – the days of the Raj may be over, and the British may have left India, but these evocative images will never truly be lost.

CREATING THE LOOK

Indian style is relaxed, comfortable and easy to live with, and can be given a very individual flavour. It works especially well in Victorian houses, but can also look highly contemporary. Combine an array of woven rugs with the subcontinent's rainbow colours, rustic wooden furniture and gleaming metal accessories for an eclectic, soulful feel.

Walls

Voracious ants and inclement weather are the enemy of wallpaper in this region, so for walls in Indian style it would be best to choose colourful paintwork or tiles. Be bold and juxtapose varieties of intense colour on different planes or, alternatively, paint delicate, intertwining flowers and leaves, especially as borders at the top and bottom of walls and around doors and windows. You could even include elephants, parrots, peacocks and dancing figures, or copy the exquisite, jewel-bright miniatures of Moghul times. Including some mirror and mother of pearl, if possible, would increase the decorative feel even further. For a colonial feel, a background of whitewashed walls is more restrained, although you might want to nail one or two fake tiger skins to the walls,

ABOVE Mustard yellow walls and a wooden floor topped with assorted colourful rugs are ideal for an Indian look. The quirky accessories strike the right exotic note.

made of *faux*-painted canvas or printed fabric, to create a visual joke. An exuberant, over-the-top look, well-suited to lovers of kitsch, can be attained by creating collages using pictures cut out from travel brochures, Bollywood posters and magazines, with one or two prints of Indian deities and a selection of sequins and glued-down sweet wrappers thrown in for good measure.

Floors

Indian floors are extremely simple, often no more than smooth beaten earth – since wood is tempting for termites. In more temperate climes you could, however, use stone or old wooden boards, striving to avoid a feeling of overt luxury. Alternatively, natural coir or sisal would be the best type of carpeting for this scheme.

Top with rugs in a variety of styles. Felted-wool rugs, for example, are used in several areas of Pakistan, while the *gabba* is a Kashmiri floorcovering made of thick woollen cloth which has been cut and appliquéd in layers. Dhurries, or flat-woven cotton rugs, are easy to obtain and vary in pattern from nineteenth-century floral designs to plain blocks of colour – so it should not be hard to find one that suits your personal taste. Kilims are an equally good choice, especially the faded, antique versions, which can look absolutely stunning, or choose Moghul-style rugs that are densely covered with elaborate, twining, floral designs. Fake animal skins, used in moderation, may work well with a certain Victorian/Indian look – a reminder of colonial hunting parties but without the danger to indigenous wildlife.

Lights

Rooms in colonial India were often dark and gloomy, dimly lit with smoky oil lamps, their wooden shutters kept closed to avoid harsh sunlight. Today, however, it is possible to have the best of both worlds: authentic-looking, attractive fittings that are wired for electricity to give adequate light whatever the occasion. The fitting that most sums up Indian style is the melon pendant lamp, a fluted, inverted bell jar made of glass and suspended from the ceiling by three chains. One or

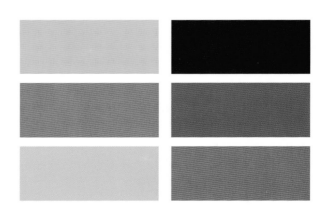

ABOVE A star-shaped, pierced-metal lantern with added glass baubles casts a strangely wonderful shadow on walls and ceiling.

two of these will give a pretty, soft glow and go a long way towards establishing the right effect. Glass and metal hurricane lamps, either as pendants or placed on side tables, also set the right tone, while pierced-tin lanterns are particularly Indian in style. Star-shaped pendant lights are unusual and eye-catching, and not too difficult to come by, while wicker or raffia shades help give the correct feel to a western-style lamp base. Finally, add one or two candle holders, made either of wrought iron or of wood; the latter will create a grand impression in the style of the monumental carved candlesticks that grace many an Indian temple.

COLOURS

The richness of decoration that is associated with Indian style comes from a unique use of saturated colour. It was once said that 'pink is the navy blue of India', and bright hues are, indeed, a way of life, used to differentiate castes and symbolize religious occasions. Confidence, imagination and a no-holds-barred attitude are essential, the range of hues including crimson, mustard, orange, saffron, purple, pink, terracotta, indigo, lime green, olive, emerald and ochre.

LEFT Colourful roman blinds such as these can be easily made from panels of bright fabric, bordered with mirrors, ribbons and appliqué, and pulled by means of an oversized tassel.

Soft furnishings

Indian textiles are known for their high quality and versatility of design, and have been prized throughout the world for centuries. In the different regions of the sub-continent, craftspeople produce a wide variety of hand-woven, embroidered, brocaded and appliquéd cloth, often of great complexity. Fabrics range from cotton (the most predominant natural fibre), calico and jute to silk, muslin and wool, and they come in a delicious rainbow of hues, thanks to an enormous number of native dye plants and minerals. It is possible to buy antique Indian textiles (from specialists), modern-day imports, or western interpretations of traditional Indian fabrics and patterns.

Paisley is probably the best-known example of an Indian fabric that was appropriated by another nation. These teardrop-and-floral patterns originated in the sixteenth-century Moghul court, and were imported to Britain in the eighteenth century, where they became immensely fashionable. They were imitated by weavers in the Scottish town of Paisley, from which the pattern gets its name. Chintz, now seen as typically English, also began as an Indian pattern, named from the Hindi word *chint*, meaning 'variegated', because of its vivid, multicoloured floral patterns.

The Moghul legacy is patterns of elaborate arabesques and large-scale flowering motifs, sometimes within an arched niche. Crewel-work, which features chain-stitch embroidery in softly coloured wool on a linen backing, is a traditional Kashmiri skill, while Pakistani textile artists produce elaborately embroidered costumes, accessories and animal adornments featuring delicate stitching, mirrorwork – to deflect the evil eye – and silk tassels (or sometimes buttons, shells and wool pom poms). Appliqué and quilting, too, are ancient methods, with Gujerat particularly renowned for its appliquéd ceremonial hangings. And, of course, the entire sub-continent is famous for its wonderful silk saris, some with a contrasting warp and weft to give a shot appearance. Often the colours are shockingly intense, and the lengths of fabric may be adorned with metallic thread for an even more mesmerizing effect.

Whether you prefer paisley, crewel-work, tie-dying or shot silk, there is certainly no shortage of choice when it comes to Indian soft furnishings. You could choose any of the above or even an exotic print which features elephants, peacocks, parrots and twining flowers. Indian-style quilts make wonderful (and warm) bedcovers, while resist-dyed fabric can be used for throws, blinds or curtains, table linen, wall-hangings or cushion covers. With cushions, in fact, you can really go to town – even if the rest of your scheme is fairly restrained, emphasize pattern and colour by using vivid fabrics embellished with mirrors, sequins, appliqué or embroidery, plus silk tassels on the corners and around the edges.

At the window, choose wooden Venetian blinds or shutters made of wooden fretwork, or else use panels of beautiful fabric (sari lengths or dyed muslins are especially appropriate) made into slightly gathered curtains or Roman blinds, adding a large tassel on the end of their pull-cord. The traditional Indian embroidered or appliquéd friezes called *torans*, arch-shaped or with a pennant-like bottom edge, can be used as highly decorative pelmets, though their customary use is to hang above doorways, where they will also add an intrinsically Indian flavour to your scheme.

Accessories

The crafts and traditional artefacts of this region are so many and various that you will have no problem at all in finding suitable accessories. Try to avoid, however, the very cheap, mass-produced tourist nasties, and instead collect interesting and unusual items with a personality or some sort of history. The traditional textiles of Pakistan, for example, include small, colourful, woven or embroidered animal trappings, horse headcovers, purses, and storage bags, often with mirrors, tassels, sequins and beads, which can either be framed or simply made into a fascinating display on a small side table or window-ledge. They could

FABRICS

Vivid colours are the hallmark of Indian fabrics, creating a superb atmosphere of exoticism, intense excitement and liveliness. Spice colours such as turmeric, chilli and cayenne are mingled with shocking pink, electric blue, indigo and deep green, with geometric patterns and bold checks making an appearance too. Glinting metallic threads add the final, unrestrained note of decorative excess.

ABOVE Brass accessories, such as this shapely teapot and tiny cups and saucers perched on a metal tray, can really evoke the Indian style.

also be teamed with ceremonial bells and small items of lacquerware from Rajasthan or Kashmir. Beaten metal, either brass, copper or pewter, is one of the signatures of Indian style – look for bowls, dishes, cooking pots and *lotas*, small, round-bottomed water-pourers. Earthenware pots, not too delicate or fine, are similarly distinctive, as are silver-plated boxes in various shapes and sizes. Wooden lattice-work can be employed as mirror or picture frames, or else across the top of a door-way or window. For a little colour, you could hang some miniature Moghul-style paintings of mytho-logical or domestic scenes, animals or plants, in pure, vibrant colour, and add wine goblets adorned with colourful glass 'jewels'. Even chang-ing the handles on cupboards and drawers to coloured glass or flower-patterned ceramic knobs will add to the desired bright, decorative and com-plex overall effect.

Furniture

Indian furniture comes in a range of styles; sim-plistically, however, it can be divided into just two varieties – ethnic and colonial. A large proportion of original Indian furniture comes from Rajasthan or Gujerat and was made in the late nineteenth or early twentieth century. Rustic in flavour, it has Arabic and Hindu influences, demonstrating high-quality workmanship and featuring a marvellous patina of age. Although modern reproductions are

available, if you choose these quirky, hand-made, antique pieces you will find that they have a spe-cial character all of their own.

Colonial furniture is Anglo-Indian in style, a combination of the Victorian forms specified by the colonials and the native decoration and tech-niques used by its Indian designer-makers. When furnishing a colonial-type room, the look can be summed up by a relatively small number of pieces. These include, in particular, folding drinks tables (for a gin and tonic at sundown); steamer chairs, light and foldable for long boat journeys; planters' chairs, a form of non-upholstered chaise longue with extended arms (for the master of the house to rest his legs on while the servant pulled off his boots); and four-poster beds hung with mosquito nets. Upholstered furniture can seem a little out of place so, instead, use bamboo or rattan sofas, armchairs and dining chairs with loose cushions.

In your choice of ethnic pieces bear in mind that, as in the Far East and North Africa, India is a floor-oriented culture. Furnishings are used sparsely and are often lower than we are used to. Look out, in particular, for short-legged tables made of teak, camphorwood, rosewood or mahogany (remembering to check that new pieces are made of wood from properly managed planta-tions), perhaps featuring some decorative chip-carving. Bed rolls and floor cushions are also typical, while an antique Indian door, protected by a sheet of glass, makes an excellent coffee-table top. Small, upright chests and boxes from north-west India are often painted with Moghul scenes and floral imagery. Armed with delicate brushes, acrylic paints, a pot of clear varnish and a library book for reference, recreating this look on a plain, panelled chest could make an enjoyable weekend project. Another typically Indian chest possesses hundreds of tiny drawers for storing medicines, and makes a useful jewellery box or unusual spice cupboard. And a very distinctive and attractive piece is the bar-fronted 'prison' cupboard, wardrobe or cabinet – why not adapt this style for practical kitchen units, a bathroom towel cup-board or even workspace storage?

The shimmering colours and patterns that conjure up India are very much in evidence in this exotic sitting area.

Summing up the style

1 Carved openwork screens such as these make wonderful room dividers; they can also be used as window grilles, doors and, with a piece of glass placed on top, coffee tables.

2 A natural matting such as this, with a fairly wide, rough weave, makes an ideal floorcovering for an Indian room. You could also add a kilim or Moghul-style rug for extra colour.

3 The rainbow colours and varied designs of Indian textiles are renowned the world over. Spicy hues such as these vibrant silks make a good choice, in a confident mix of stripes, large flowers, zigzags and small repeats. Also typical of Indian soft furnishings is the use of embroidery and appliqué, with mirrors, sequins and tassels providing extra adornment.

4 Rustic Indian furniture has a very individual character and, like this coffee table, it often combines simplicity of construction with a decorative quirkiness. The nearby chest, with its many drawers embellished with brass knobs, is also typical.

Oriental

The allure of the east has been a part of western consciousness for many hundreds of years. Yet an attempt to classify the 'Orient' as a single, distinct culture is unwise and, ultimately, impossible – vast and varied, it encompasses the icy wastes of Manchuria and the tropical spice islands of Indonesia, Thai houses on stilts and Japanese homes with paper walls. Nevertheless, there are certain elements common to the diverse styles of the countries to the east of India: an appreciation of natural materials, a veneration for fine craftsmanship and a strong sense of tradition, with all aspects of life imbued with an inherent spirituality and symbolism.

The traditional Japanese home employs bamboo, natural matting, stone, lacquer, paper screens and unpainted wood to create an atmosphere of refined quietude. Furnishings are pared down to the barest of essentials but the result is not austere, simply meditative and calming. The method of decorating, where the squares and rectangles of walls, mats, screens, windows and futons echo each other in a repeated and pleasing rhythm, is governed by *shibui*, a Zen Buddhist concept of restraint. Gardens reflect this cult of understated perfectionism, a partnership of manicured pebbles, gravel and water, their precise arrangement according them meaning and significance.

In China, a vast land covering enormous contrasts of climate and landscape, an underlying order is expressed through the concept of yin and yang, opposing forces which must achieve balance in order to establish harmony. Traditional crafts such as embroidery, intricate cut-paper, woodblock prints and painted clay toys are created to help celebrate a variety of festivals, in particular the Chinese New Year. Pattern and colour are seen as highly symbolic, corresponding to ancient beliefs, among them the intriguing ancient art of

Although in many ways the nations of east and south-east Asia are ultra-modern and industrialized, they have developed a look that embraces their ancient cultures in a way that is unequalled in the west – the perfect antidote to the hustle and bustle of the modern world.

geomancy, or *feng shui* – in which the aim is to enhance health, wealth and happiness by living in harmony with the environment. Yin and yang, cosmic breath, wind and water, dragons and tigers are all part of this complex blend of mysticism, folklore, common sense and astrology, which is used on a day-to-day basis in the east and now becomingly increasingly popular in the west.

Although other nations of the Far East have a rather more decorative attitude to life, the same basic adherence to natural materials, simple furnishings and open, airy spaces is still very much in evidence. Bamboo, in particular, is found everywhere in the region, used as a building material, for food, and to make an incredible number of domestic items. In Indonesia, bamboo strips form the usual flooring of native wooden houses, while in Thailand it is woven to make walls that can withstand both monsoon and excessive heat. Flashes of colour and pattern are then added with batik or ikat textiles, jewel-like silks and exquisite lacquerwork and gilding.

CREATING THE LOOK

Today's 'oriental look' stands for understated individuality, with hand-crafted, good-quality pieces that enhance an interior with an aura of spirituality. Aim for a clean-lined, functional Japanese mood or a sophisticated fusion of east-meets-west, achieved by keeping spaces light and airy, colour schemes unified and furniture simple.

ABOVE This is not a style that works well with casual clutter, as is evident from the pared-down furnishings and graphic lines of this wood-floored bathroom.

Walls

Japanese walls, though well crafted and perfectly finished, are sometimes given extra interest by mixing tiny grey or white pebbles, crushed shells or hemp fibres with the plaster. It may be possible for you to reproduce something close to this texture by using sand or fine grit mixed with emulsion paint (experiment on a small area first to get the mixture right). Otherwise, simply use a white, ivory or pale bamboo-coloured paint and stipple it on for a textured effect.

The controlled, understated look of this style is easiest to achieve against white or neutral walls but, used with care, spice tones can provide an interesting backdrop for oriental furniture and accessories. Or break the neutrality but retain the mood with a richly coloured silk kimono suspended from a pole pushed through the sleeves.

Wallpaper does not immediately spring to mind when planning an oriental style, but tactile papers that imitate, for example, hessian or rice paper would be a natural complement to a minimalist look. An 'oriental' wallpaper will produce a busy background, but if you like these designs, especially in the traditional shades of blue and white, you may wish to hang separate panels of these papers, each of them showing traditional motifs such as pagodas, flying cranes, bridges or waves.

Floors

An essential element of Far Eastern style is plain, hard flooring – so choose elegant planks of wood, elemental stone, earthy terracotta or a natural fabric such as jute, coir or sisal. In Japan, floors would be covered with *tatami* mats, made of compressed rice straw, about 5cm (2in) thick and with the edges bordered in black linen tape or a colourful brocade. The *tatami* mat comes in a standard size (equivalent to about 1.8x1m or 6x3ft) and is traditionally used to indicate the size of a room:

an estate agent might describe a small flat, for example, as having 'two-*tatami*-mat rooms', while a larger property may encompass twenty *tatamis*. You can easily achieve the wonderfully graphic *tatami* effect by buying small rugs made of natural matting (a ribbed surface is best) with ready-bound edges. A softer approach would be to lay down oriental rugs, with their thick pile and gentle tones of pink, cream, moss green and sky blue. Tibetan rugs, in particular, though hard to obtain, are especially beautiful, featuring traditional Buddhist symbols such as lotus flowers, dragons, snow lions and the mandala, or wheel of life. They will be particularly effective if they provide the only pattern in the room.

Lights

There's nothing more oriental in style than a paper lantern, and they come in an enormous variety of shapes and sizes. For a genuine modern classic, the designs of Isamu Noguchi were inspired by eastern principles and have powerful presence in any room. Less expensive, however, and easier to find by far, are the ever-popular, simple and serene spheres that are available from many chain stores and lighting shops. Look out, too, for cube, bee-hive, drum and box shapes, and although your general preference should be for a natural parchment colour, you may wish to experiment with other hues for different lighting effects. Lanterns made of metal are appropriate, too, while a metal tea caddy could be adapted as an interesting and unusual lamp base. The same goes for ceramic

ginger jars, with their distinctive bulbous outlines and blue-and-white patterns. Coolie shapes are, of course, the best type of shade to choose. Many modern light fittings would also work well in an oriental interior – choose sleek outlines or, for a minimal statement, concealed lights.

ABOVE Coloured paper lanterns are typically oriental, and their soft glow will give an attractive lighting effect in just the right style for minimal outlay.

COLOURS

With this style you can revel in a variety of natural colours: woody bamboo green, dark teak, subtle stone and parchment, deep blue-grey slate, jade green and dark indigo. Off-white, pale grey and a muted wicker yellow can be used anywhere, while touches of black or lacquer red can be used to create a very graphic statement.

Soft furnishings

The use of indigo-dyed fabrics or natural, unbleached colours are very typical of the Far East and, especially, Japan. Textiles produced from native hemp, cotton, wool and silk are traditionally dyed using plant extracts and hand-woven on a backstrap loom, which means that the fabrics are narrow in width and therefore perfectly suited for adaptation as wall-hangings, blinds, throws or cushion covers in a western home.

For an attractive and typically oriental textile, choose cloth treated with a resist-dye technique such as tie-dye, batik or ikat. Perfected in Java centuries ago, batik is a method of printing where hot wax is applied to cotton which is then dyed – the wax prevents the dye from saturating the material, and the result is a delicate, refined and

ABOVE A bamboo-framed bedhead and woven-wicker ceiling are unusual features in this oriental bedroom, against which the richly coloured silks make an effective contrast.

often intricate pattern. This is a simple method of fabric treatment which you can try out yourself quite easily, using equipment available from any craft store. Ikat, on the other hand, is a complex technique in which patterns are dyed on to silk or cotton yarn, again using a resist method, before it is woven. The designs created have a very recognizable blurred edging. Whichever you prefer, all these fabrics create a striking effect used as bedcovers, wall-hangings, throws, cushion covers, table linen or even simple blinds. Graphic black or navy on an unbleached background makes a good choice for fabric colourways; if, however, you prefer more vibrant tones, add a selection of oriental silks. These will make a spectacular statement against the natural tones of bamboo, wood, stone, sisal and paper.

Complex fabric window treatments are uncalled for with this look. In the tropical countries of south-east Asia it is common to dispense with glass entirely, and there is certainly no effort at creating an ostentatious effect with draped curtains and elaborate pelmets. Choosing wooden shutters or split-cane blinds, then, will go a long way towards achieving an oriental effect, while blinds or very simple curtains, perhaps in a sheer, coloured muslin, would make a subtle and restrained alternative choice.

Accessories

The grace and subtlety of an uncluttered oriental home is attained as much from what's left out as what's put in, so you should choose just a handful of exquisite pieces and arrange them carefully in order to contemplate the intrinsic beauty of each one. Blue-and-white porcelain, red or black lacquer-ware, kites, painted masks and jointed shadow puppets, for example, all typify this look, and just one or two examples will really stand out. A statue of Buddha instantly sums up the style you are seeking, as does Chinese calligraphy, sweeping black brushstrokes on a beautiful panel of paper. Continuing the paper theme, why not buy several sheets of hand-made paper and frame them as you would a picture? Raku and stoneware pottery, with textured surfaces, natural colours and symbolic painted imagery, is very evocative of the east, and so are bamboo-handled teapots, brass or wooden bowls, boxes with mother of pearl inlay, carved jade, beautiful woven baskets and oversized clay storage jars. An elegant vase can be used to display a single branch of plum or cherry blossom. Finally, pick out some *feng shui*-enhancing artefacts: a pair of carved-wood mandarin ducks to improve marriage prospects, fish (real or porcelain) to symbolize wealth and prosperity, or a small water fountain for general good luck.

FABRICS

For a wonderfully understated oriental look, black, white, indigo and unbleached naturals are typical colours, used in sheer muslin or more substantial cotton. Patterns, also, are restrained, and if there is an ikat-like quality in the ragged edges of their designs so much the better. A self-stripe bamboo tone and mustard-coloured silk, as shown here, add relatively muted colour while providing contrast with interesting and varied textures.

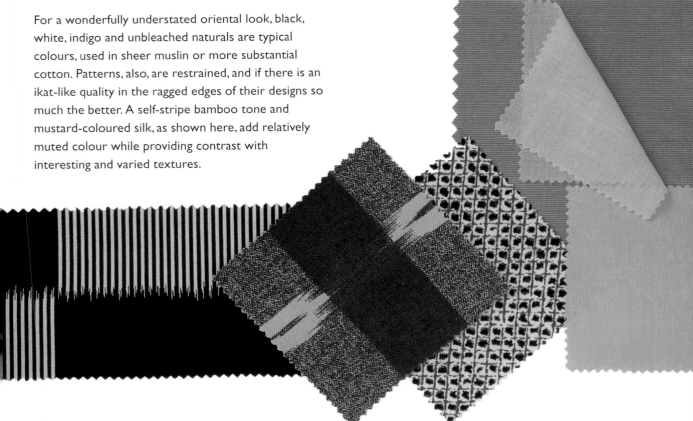

ABOVE A lacquered chest with beautiful, intricate inlays would make an interesting addition to an oriental-style room in which you wished to avoid a very minimalist effect.

Furniture

Eastern cultures are floor-based, so the rule when choosing furniture is to keep everything near the ground: look for large, low coffee tables, long benches, simple stools, huge floor cushions and so on. The less there is, the better – a little goes a long way with an oriental look – and remember that overstuffed upholstery is entirely out of place, so it's best to disguise any squashy sofas or armchairs with a well-placed length of suitable fabric.

Hand-carved teak and other tropical hardwoods are typical, but do try to ensure that such pieces originate from a properly managed plantation or, better still, are made of reclaimed or recycled wood. Generally speaking, keep wood unadorned and unpainted, unless with layers of gleaming black lacquer. Bamboo and rattan – sofas and chairs, side and coffee tables, chests, wardrobes

and beds – are light and inexpensive alternatives that are perfectly suited to this look. They create a wonderful impression in a conservatory or bedroom, but may be harder to integrate into a western living room. To avoid this problem, choose solid, well-made examples and link with other furniture by using similar cushions and throws.

Uncommon only a few years ago, futon mattresses are rapidly becoming a popular choice of bedding in the west. For maximum adaptability and space-saving (paramount in Japanese city homes) you can sleep on your futon on the floor, rolling it up and tucking it away in a cupboard during the day. For a more permanent bed, however, there are plenty of styles of futon bases – both as beds and sofabeds – to choose from. If you find a futon uncomfortable, choose a wooden bed with a clean-lined design (no padded headboard) and perhaps increase the eastern atmosphere with a mosquito net draped above.

Like the futon, a screen is another ingenious way of making the most of space, and they are often found in Far Eastern homes in the form of wooden fretwork panels, decorated with oriental designs or as minimal bamboo-and-rice-paper constructions. You could ask a carpenter to make you a hinged screen out of MDF (medium density fibreboard or particleboard), leaving it bare (for a very restrained look), washing with a solid colour or painting with oriental patterns. Or, for the ultimate in simplicity, buy lengths of bamboo from a garden centre, tie securely into a frame with string, then finish by attaching sheets of rice paper.

Bathing in Japan is more a ritual than a routine, and often takes place in a special deep wooden tub. For the genuine experience, you should shower and wash first, then simply relax in the very hot water of the tub – a temperature of 43–55°C (110–130°F) is normal. Even without the traditional tub, however, the atmosphere of the orient can be obtained by keeping fittings as simple as possible and adding a few typical accessories such as loofahs, wooden brushes and natural sponges. This is a look to which a standard modern bathroom suite often adapts well.

Only the absolute necessities of life remain in this austerely attractive bedroom, emphasizing the spiritual and promoting an atmosphere of calm contemplation.

Summing up the style

1 The wall's gridded shape and contrasting black framework and white paper infill contribute to the room's oriental atmosphere.

2 Neutral flooring such as this works well; black-bordered *tatami* mats would add even more to the repetitive geometry of the room.

3 The ultimate in simplicity: an oval paper lantern in a natural colour, suspended from the ceiling. Such fittings are inexpensive yet utterly authentic.

4 This graphic fabric has a real flavour of the east without straying too far towards the decorative, which would be out of place in such a pared-down environment.

5 With a simply shaped seat and delicate legs, this woven chair, though not specifically oriental, has a style that fits in well here. The futon bed which has been rolled out on the floor, on the other hand, is an authentic and practical contribution to this style.

6 The small potted plant on the windowsill, symbolizing nature, is the only form of ornament.

Moroccan

Stretching from coast to desert, oasis to mountain range, Morocco is an ancient crossroads for trade, a melting-pot of peoples, colours, crafts, patterns, religions and traditions, all of which have contributed to the nation's incredibly rich culture – and to its interiors, both religious and domestic, which are legendary for their visual sophistication. First settled by the Berbers, a blue-eyed, fair-skinned race of tribal nomads, North Africa was colonized by the Romans in the first century AD and then, 600 years later, conquered by the Arabs, who introduced Islam and settled in Morocco, from where they set out to invade southern Spain. The Arab reign in Spain lasted 800 years; when forced out, they returned to Morocco, among them an enormous number of skilled artisans who brought back a Hispano-Moorish tradition which is still very much in evidence.

Today, the Berber people make up between a third and a half of the population of Morocco, the remainder being Arabic, and there is also a fair sprinkling of European émigrés, drawn to this fascinating nation with its intriguing and rich artistic tradition. Berber customs, though endangered by changing lifestyles, are still valued today. Weaving is a way of life for these tribespeople, and their traditional nomadic tents, for example, are made of woven sheep's wool and goat hair in stripes of black, brown and off-white, insulated with rugs on walls and floors and decorated with woollen embroidery. Berber strongholds in the country, by contrast, were built to last, made of pounded red earth reinforced with straw. They seem to grow out of the ground, distinguishable only by their decoration of incised patterning and whitewashed motifs around doors and windows.

Moroccan town houses are equally plain on the outside, featuring flat roofs and bare façades with

Colonnades leading to cool courtyards, mysterious contrasts of light and shadow, colours combined in a captivating, compelling way: this is the intense, sensual sophistication of North African style.

thick, arched doors and small, iron-grilled windows. Inside, however, is a riot of elaborate embellishment, and it is unusual to find a surface area that has not been decorated in some way. Intricate, interlocking motifs can be seen in the form of fretted wood, wrought iron, chased brass, painted furniture and, especially, colourful small tiles or *zelliges*, covering walls, floors, ceilings, doors, shutters and many types of furniture. Woodwork, textiles, ceramics and jewellery are inspired by the Arabo-Muslim architecture of mosques and palaces, and the repertoire of designs includes not only geometric patterns of squares, triangles, diamonds, crosses, eight-pointed stars, spirals and circles, but also flowers, leaves and animals (which may be abstract or representational), human hands and eyes, and Arabic calligraphy. These shady rooms glow with colour, and typically lead from a courtyard containing palm trees and a burbling fountain – a magical space evoking the Koran's description of paradise as 'a garden flowing with streams'.

CREATING THE LOOK

Moroccan style is extremely versatile, and can be adapted as an all-over, *Thousand and One Nights* look or, equally, a more contemporary aesthetic, with just a few dramatic pieces. The backbone of the scheme is intense colour, especially in paint, tiles and textiles, to which is added carved wood, intricately patterned metalwork, piles of rugs, and traditional crafts such as tooled leather, Berber jewellery and woven baskets.

Walls

Wall decorations are an important feature of a Moroccan home, the simplest being bare plaster, sealed and left as a beautiful, glowing shade of pink. You could, equally, introduce a stronger colour by emulating the hues of *tadelakt*, a treatment in which a tint is mixed with plaster and sand and the resulting surface polished to a dull sheen – the usual tones are oxblood, rust, grey, tan or yellow. Add more complex adornments by painting Arabic script in elegantly flowing lines – you could write your name and the date, or spell 'welcome' above a doorway, using an Arabic dictionary for reference. The geometric patterns of Islamic tiles are ideal to take as inspiration for repeated stencil motifs in dusty desert colours. Panels of leather (one of Morocco's best-known crafts), dyed or painted, make unusual hangings, and kilim rugs, too, look wonderful whether against just one wall or all around a room.

ABOVE A bold use of colour, strong but chalky, on these plaster walls, means there is no need for elaborate furnishings in order to make an impression.

The ideal choice for walls, however, if at all possible, would be the startlingly beautiful tilework that is seen everywhere in Morocco from palaces and mosques to ordinary homes. Intricate and polychromatic, this makes a wonderful covering for an entire bathroom, works well as a splashback or cupboard fronts in a kitchen, and can be used for panels, door and fire surrounds, skirtings and on the lower portion of walls anywhere else in the house.

Floors

Zellige tiles, either in simple brick shapes of varying colours or incredibly intricate geometric patterns, make the ideal Moroccan-style floor. As an alternative, brick or terracotta both make a good choice, while wooden boards, neutral carpets and natural matting can blend into the background reasonably well. If your floor isn't highly patterned, you can recreate the North African mystique by throwing down a selection of woollen rugs. Tightly woven *hanbels*, or floor-blankets, often have alternating bands of intricate pattern with plain red, while other rugs feature designs such as eyes, flowers, octagonal medallions, palm trees, the hand of Fatima or the tree of life. The Berber varieties are very distinctive, either flat-woven with lozenge, zigzag and diamond patterns, made with graphically stylized pile designs, or as straw mats with woven-in red wool. Black and white pile rugs with a banded or checked pattern emulate the tribal rugs of the North Atlas mountains, while other kilims employ either repeated, all-over motifs or a central medallion in a field surrounded by borders. If you are unable to find these traditional styles, simply choose kilims in bold stripes and strong colours, particularly shades of red, orange and saffron.

Lights

Moroccan light fittings are works of art, their intricate designs adding yet another layer of complexity to the lavish and sumptuous interior atmosphere. The most notable lights to look out for are filigree lamps, lanterns, pendants, chandeliers and uplighters in brass, iron or copper, which may be fitted with glass or be left as openwork. This glass can also be plain or multicoloured, the latter giving an even more elaborate effect. Some

ABOVE A brass lantern with coloured-glass panels is typical of this region. First made for candles or oil lamps, today they can easily be wired for electricity.

of these lanterns are quite small, suitable for a side table or propping on a mantelpiece; others are enormous, and have the potential to dominate a room so much that it barely needs any other furnishings. Look out, too, for candelabras hammered with designs of pentagrams, rosettes or arabesques, and lights in the form of spheres, stepped shapes and hanging stars – the latter are most fashionable and blend well into even the most contemporary of homes.

COLOURS

The colours of Morocco are unforgettably vibrant and varied. This is a palette that will bring the warmth and intensity of the North African landscape to any home. Choose mustard, saffron, ruby red, emerald, orange, turquoise, deep purple and cobalt blue (believed to ward off evil spirits), mixed with earthy terracotta, warm brown, verdigris and umber. Brilliant white will provide relief and make these jewel-bright hues really stand out.

Soft furnishings

Moroccan textiles are dazzling, impressive and distinctive, in all shades and patterns ranging from the naïve to the sophisticated, from silk brocade and fine embroidery to rough, utilitarian linen, cotton and wool. Some fabrics may feature clashing patterns and polychromatic colours, perhaps embellished with metallic threads, while others are restrained and subtle, in simple stripes and natural tones. Traditional motifs include rosettes, eight-pointed stars, tulips, eyes, crosses, camels, zigzags, diamonds, cypress trees, scorpions, centipedes and the hand of Fatima.

Such variety gives you the option to create a scheme either based around saturated colourways and complex patterns, or else involving plains and stripes with muted, earthy hues. Berber weaving, for example, is renowned for its use of the natural

ABOVE An abundance of cushions in a multitude of colours, aided by sumptuous swathes of fabric hung from the ceiling, creates the atmosphere of a bedouin tent.

colours of sheep's wool – cream, brown or black – together with dyes made from saffron, madder, pomegranate and indigo. A striped Berber blanket, warm and functional, makes a wonderful bedspread evocative of the region, and such weaves could also be adapted as cushion covers or heavy curtains.

Though these are the best-known Berber designs, the nomads of North Africa have a varied textile tradition stretching back centuries, and they are capable of producing fine tapestry weaves in glowing colours, wonderful embroidery and vivid *ha'iti*, panels of appliquéd fabric in many different colours which are used to decorate the insides of festival tents. Specialist shops may be a source of such unusual fabrics, but if you are unable to buy originals you could create your own appliqués using scraps of fabric cut into typically Moroccan motifs. They can be adapted for use as bedcovers, throws, table runners, curtains, blinds or cushion covers, depending on their size.

Perhaps the simplest way to achieve a Moroccan look is to use plain fabrics in intense colours, mixing a range of spicy tones to create an all-over environment, from window treatments to table-cloths, cushions to bedlinen. If one or two are shot through with metallic threads it will add a touch of exotic glamour, while stitching bright silk tassels along the bottom of pelmets, around cushions and as edges to blinds produces the right kind of densely decorative feel.

Upholstery can be treated in a similar way, although perhaps the best choice would be to have your sofas and chairs covered in kilim fabric, with its rhythmic geometric or stylized floral patterns in many different colours. Kilims also make great cushion covers, which will contrast well with plain upholstery. At the window, although Moroccan homes generally employ fretwork shutters, you could use lightweight cotton or muslin, either in a brilliant hue, or in plain white to offset the bright colours elsewhere. Make up into pairs of tab-headed or slightly gathered curtains, and hang from an iron pole, tying them back with an over-sized silk or wool tassel.

Accessories

Moroccan culture has been steeped in craft production for thousands of years, giving you broad scope to display a multitude of different artefacts which readily call to mind the North African way of life. Moroccan metalware, for example, rarely comes without a hammered pattern, and you could group silver-plated, lidded boxes in various shapes (octagonal, barrel, circular, square, oval and teardrop) as a most attractive display. Wooden accessories might include huge bowls, thuya-wood boxes, and carved mirror or picture frames with an arched outline. Painted glasses, for the ever-present

FABRICS

Spice-like colours with metallic glints make the Moroccan palette deliciously different, dazzling and enticing, particularly when employed for soft furnishings. Silk, cotton, canvas and chenille can all be used, and including one or two plain colours will provide a balance for a variety of patterns, especially in the form of traditional geometrical motifs such as chevrons, ziggurats, crosses and stars.

ABOVE This shimmering Moroccan metalware is dazzlingly beautiful. The effect is enhanced by displaying so many pieces together.

sugary mint tea, can be matched with silver- or brass-plated trays, teapots and tea-glass holders. Add woven baskets, utilitarian Berber jars, heelless leather slippers (known as *babouches*), coloured glass vases, camel saddles and *tagines* – cooking dishes with a conical lid.

Finally, search for Moroccan pottery which, typically, comes in a myriad of colours and an infinite number of patterns. Fez is famous for its enamelled pottery, usually blue and white, while Safi, where the country's oldest kilns are still in operation, produces plates, bowls and vases in a deliciously strong turquoise, yellow or cobalt blue, bordered with metal to prevent them from chipping.

Furniture

Moroccan styles of furniture encompass the very simple and the extremely elaborate; what they have in common, however, is being near to the ground – think of eating couscous sitting cross-legged on the floor and you'll get the picture. Mix dark woods with the gleam of chased brass and the honest patina of iron, looking for shapes that are essentially geometric – squares, rectangles, hexagons, octagons and circles.

Star-shaped stools, for example, are one attractive form of seating; another is long banquettes topped with rows of plump cushions. Tables, too, can be star shaped, or perhaps octagonal, with a panelled base featuring intricate cut-out motifs. An ingenious way to create another type of side table is to rest a circular brass tray on a central stand (a solid cube of wood would do) – but do ensure that it is stable before using it. A brass four-poster bed would fit in with this look, while brass fittings on chests and cupboards help to summon up the mood. Continue the use of all-over pattern with elaborately carved wood, which in Morocco is frequently used for doors, screens, shelves and table tops. One distinctive type of woodworking is *moucharaby*, an openwork design most commonly made of cedar. Created either by making elaborate pierced openings or by glueing or nailing turned knobs into a grid, this acts as a mysterious window covering that allows Muslim women in traditional households to look out on to the world without being seen themselves. You could use this type of fretwork as attractive shutters, bath surrounds, radiator covers or the fronts of kitchen units.

If your furniture is rather plain, however, no matter. Moroccan wood is frequently painted, in designs that echo the complexity and virtuosity of *zellige* tilework. This technique is known as *zwaq*, and you can emulate it by painting wooden table tops, chair backs, cupboard doors, chests and so on with intricate, multicoloured geometric patterns. Sanding back the paint a little once it has dried will give a delightfully distressed finish that is most suitable for this look. There is one type of wooden furniture, however, that is left unpainted. Thuya, which is similar in appearance to walnut, is exceptionally attractive and popular both for furniture and accessories; it can be plain or burled, and is glossed to a high sheen using vegetable oil, needing no further embellishment.

Another option would be to avoid solid furniture altogether, and just use informal floor cushions or bolsters, huge and comfortable, covered in kilims, appliqué, embroidery or leather. If, however, for the sake of comfort or convenience, you wish to add one or two pieces of European-style furniture, choose examples that are low and solid, preferably showing off their carved-wood or chased-metal construction, and that look and feel comfortably solid.

**The colour and
pattern in this room
combines with many
examples of
Moroccan
craftsmanship. The
bite-shaped arched
doorway is authentic,
as are the wooden
screens around the
lower seating area.**

Summing up the style

1 The restrained, pale sheen of these
walls is very restful: a good choice
when everything else in the room is so
full of interest.

2 A variety of kilims are thrown down
over the hard flooring. They provide
warmth with their texture and strong
colours, and are a typically Middle
Eastern touch.

3 A superb lantern in metal and multicoloured glass throws off an attractive
spectrum of light. Though it is quite
large in size, it is well suited to the
scale of this room, which has very high
ceilings.

4 Bright colours and busy patterns are
offset by natural tones. Rich woven
kilims also makes a good choice for
upholstery and for covering large floor
cushions.

5 An octagonal table with a fretted
apron is typically Moroccan, as are
the banquette seats. Occasional tables
like these are an opportunity to
introduce decorative woodwork
techniques such as marquetry and
mother of pearl inlay.

6 This room is crammed with
Moroccan artefacts. They look
particularly good displayed in the wall
niches, which have been made in
varying sizes.

Mexican

The varied landscape of Mexico, from seashore to city, mountain to canyon, jungle to desert, is matched only by its varied history. Here lived the great ancient civilizations of the Toltecs, the Mayas and the Aztecs. Creative and sophisticated, the Mayas were architects, muralists, sculptors and potters, while the Aztecs built monolithic, gloriously extravagant structures and produced rich textiles, precious-metal artefacts and many styles of pottery. When, in 1519, Hernán Cortés' army of Spanish soldiers arrived at the Aztec capital city of Tenochtitlán, they marvelled at the sight of its pyramids and palaces. This did not stop them, however, razing it to the ground within two years in their search for conquest, gold and Catholic converts.

For 300 years the Spanish ruled the country, their occupation bringing new forms of architecture and furnishings that fused with native Indian traditions to produce a uniquely Mexican style. Grand churches, monasteries and cathedrals were designed from memory of European forms but built by Aztec craftsmen who added their own interpretations. Colonial town houses were based loosely on a Moorish style (Spain had been part of the Moorish empire for 600 years), with walls punctured by small, iron-grilled windows and a heavily studded wooden door, enclosing an inner courtyard which often featured a fountain and colonnades. These essential elements remained more or less unchanged for hundreds of years, though in the early eighteenth century the Baroque style which had swept across Europe (see page 35) was adopted enthusiastically in Mexico, employed unrestrainedly in churches and city houses.

In the countryside, on the vast estates handed out to the Spanish conquistadors, a different style emerged: that of the *hacienda*. Practically self-sufficient communities, these buildings were on a

Colour is at the heart of Mexican life, together with exuberance, energy and a raw, passionate intensity. The Aztec and Spanish cultures come together in a style that is an uninhibited celebration of the nation's highly decorative folk heritage.

massive scale, with thick red walls, huge columns, stone-paved courtyards and grand furniture to reflect the conquerors' wealth and taste.

Independence from Spain was won in 1821, and in the second half of the century Mexico flirted with the European styles that were introduced by the Emperor Maximilian during a brief period of French occupation. Neo-classical, Art Nouveau and Art Deco were all popular, but after the revolution of 1910–20 a new spirit of nationalism emerged, and the Mexicans were encouraged to reclaim their indigenous ancestry. A government-sponsored muralist programme promoted these traditions, and a cultural renaissance was led by the painter Diego Rivera and his wife, Frida Kahlo. Their home in Mexico City is symbolic of the Mexican folk movement, filled with clay idols, flower embroidery, hand-blown glass, straw toys, Day of the Dead skeletons, masks, colourful tiles and folk jewellery. With its wild colours and rustic crafts, the house, called Casa Azul because of its cobalt blue paintwork, celebrates all that is best about twentieth-century Mexico, embodying the spirit of this fascinating country.

CREATING THE LOOK

Mexico's most famous architect, Luis Barragán, described his buildings as 'scenery for the theatre of life' – and a strong sense of drama is vital when creating your scheme. The hand-made look is very important here, and rustic crafts displayed in a carefree way can make all the difference to a room. Furniture should be solid and massive, and colours intensely bright – the key to this vital and inventive look.

Walls

Roughly plastered walls make the best backdrop for Mexican style. Simply seal and leave them bare, or paint in blocks or bands of different chalky tones for a dazzling blast of colour. An alternative ideal wallcovering would be in the form of *azulejos*, the very typical tin-glazed Mexican tiles, which feature hand-painted flowers and geometric patterns in vivid colours. The art of making these beautiful tiles was brought to Mexico by the Spanish, who learnt it from the Moors, who learnt from the Persians, who were, in turn, originally taught by the Chinese! In

ABOVE A collection of animal masks gives this multicoloured wall a dramatic appearance. The lamp base is painted in the gaudy colours so typical of the region.

Mexico, glazed ceramics are known as *talavera*, after the town in Spain where they were originally produced; during colonial times, the most important centre for *talavera* production was the town of Puebla, and Mexican tiles are often described as 'pueblo tiles'.

Use the tiles anywhere, both inside and out, in combinations of patterns and plains, or as an all-over, spontaneous mix of joyful designs with a dense, patchwork-quilt effect. They work particularly well as splashbacks in a kitchen or bathroom, but can also make a wonderful wall panel in a living room or bedroom, or below dado level in a hallway or flight of stairs. As an alternative to tilework, you could stencil splashy fruit, flower or geometric designs, or simply cover walls almost completely with ceramic plates, portraits of saints, punched-tin candle sconces, mirrors, sombreros, painted masks and other characteristic artefacts; it's a tradition, too, for Mexican kitchens to feature displays of miniature earthenware pots all over their walls.

Floors

Hard flooring is ideal for this style, giving a tough, basic look that is hard-wearing and attractive in a rough-and-ready way. Honey-coloured, glazed terracotta tiles are very typical of Mexico, and can be square, brick- or lozenge-shaped, or hexagonal. Decorative insets in the form of *azulejos* look really stunning, but remember that they need to be laid fractionally lower than the rest of the floor so as to minimize wear and tear. Stone flags, bricks – laid in rows or a herringbone formation – or dark wooden planks are also suitable. If your floorboards don't look dark enough, or if the quality is poor, you may want to paint them: use gloriously bold colours – bright yellow, for example, is traditional in peasant houses as an insect repellent – and add stencilled borders of Mexican motifs. Then throw down a selection of rugs to soften the hard feel underfoot.

COLOURS

Colour is what characterizes the Mexican look. It can be used as impressive planes against a backdrop of pure white or mixed in a kaleidoscopic swirl of pure cheerfulness. Earth and terracotta make good base colours, while yellow and blue is a favourite combination – the traditional deep azure is believed to ward off evil spirits. Splashes of bubblegum pink, magenta, violet, orange and indigo make for a carefree confidence that is utterly typical.

Natural mattings such as sisal, coir, rush or jute, in their undyed colours of toffee, gold, beige or greenish-brown, have a calming effect amid all this vivacity, or you may prefer to layer on yet more colour in the form of flat-woven wool rugs with native Indian-style, dramatically contrasting stripes, chevrons, diamonds and squares.

Lights

Wrought iron chandeliers and wall lights, in simple, imposing shapes and with plain shades, have a naïve grandiosity that is just right for a scheme of this nature. Tinware, too – crimped, punched and embossed in angular patterns – is perfect for lanterns, wall-mounted sconces and free-standing candle holders. You could introduce a Hispano-Moorish note with hanging lanterns, perhaps with stained-glass panels in various different colours, star-shaped metal and glass pendants, and heavy, wooden candlesticks (carved and/or painted) that resemble the oversized fittings in Mexico's Baroque churches and cathedrals.

Another style that would be perfectly in keeping is a ceramic base with a parchment or plain fabric shade, either square or drum-shaped, or you could adapt a gourd or clay pot to make an unusual lamp base. The last word in over-the-top decoration goes to the fantastic, huge candelabra that are among the most striking of all Mexican folk crafts. Made of polychromatic glazed pottery, they depict festive scenes or, very often, a tree of life burgeoning with Adam and Eve, devils and angels, assorted animals, birds, fruit, flowers and leaves.

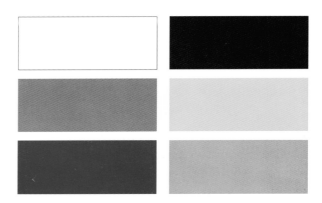

Soft furnishings

The Mexican love of ornamentation is never more evident than in their bright and lively fabrics, so vibrant in colour that they seem to shimmer and glow. Traditional textiles are woven on a backstrap loom and thus have a predetermined width – approximately that of the human body – which is perfect for adaptation as throws, wall-hangings, table runners and cushion covers. Techniques include brocade weaving, ikat dying, where threads are tie-dyed before being woven to give a characteristic pattern with blurred edges; embroidery in brilliant shades; drawn-threadwork, where threads are

cotton and wool weaves or prints featuring such designs, and choose a bold mixture of the brightest colours you can find.

Wonderful wall-hangings, bed covers, throws, cushion covers and the like can be made from two traditional Mexican garments – the men's *sarape*, a rectangular blanket with a slit for the head, and the women's *rebozo*, a rectangular shawl. The *sarape* is practically a symbol of the Mexican identity, and comes in vivid stripes or complex geometrical designs, usually in cotton or wool, but sometimes made of silk with added gold and silver thread. *Rebozos* can be plain-woven, embroidered

LEFT Some Mexican fabrics favour restrained white-on-white; more often, though, the aim is to use as many hues as possible, in an exciting extravaganza of colour.

pulled from the fabric and the remainder rearranged in a lace-like pattern; and appliqué, which often involves the use of brightly coloured ribbons.

Cotton and wool are the most typical Mexican fabrics to use: indigenous cotton comes either in white or a naturally occurring toffee-brown (called *coyuche*), and wool weaving was introduced when the Spanish imported sheep to the region. The conquistadors also brought Moorish designs with them, which were, eventually, blended with native Aztec motifs to result in typical fabric patterns including diamonds, stripes, lozenges, chevrons and jagged outlines. When choosing soft furnishings, then, seek out natural

or resist-dyed, and are sometimes finished with deep fringing at the edges.

Bright stripes, of varied width and colours, make an excellent option for upholstery, as does brown leather or, perhaps, plain white to act as a relief to the shock of colour everywhere else. Keep table linen white, too, in the form of drawn-threadwork, delicate crochet or white cotton with small, brightly coloured motifs embroidered around the edges – flowers, animals, geometrics and religious images are all suitable. Bedspreads, too, could be either embroidered or crocheted.

Windows in Mexico are most often wooden-shuttered, so keep curtain treatments fairly unfussy and unsophisticated. Rough, unbleached canvas looks great, or else pick a typical striped weave in vivid tones. Hang curtains from wrought iron or wooden poles – if you choose the latter, try painting the poles and rings in several different colours that echo those of the fabric below. And Mexican style frequently involves the addition of light-hearted, multicoloured trimmings to all sorts of soft furnishings to create delightful extra adornment. Bedeck throws, bed covers, curtains and cushions with tassels, pom-poms, sequins, beads, crochet, lace, ribbons, buttons or macramé fringes, throwing caution to the wind in favour of liveliness and abundance rather than conventional good taste.

Accessories

A delight in decoration is what characterizes Mexican style, and you can give your interior irresistible charm with the addition of an over-abundance of attractive crafts – this is, after all, one of the most creative cultures in the world. Consider displaying hand-blown glassware, huge terracotta urns, bulbous earthenware pots, mirrored balls and baskets in various shapes and sizes. Dried, hollowed and painted gourds make marvellous storage, and tinware in all forms is synonymous with the nation's decorative tradition: use it for cut, punched or gaudily painted mirror surrounds and picture frames, Christmas decorations and animal, heart or flower shapes to hang on the wall. Into this mix you could add a collection of cacti or sombreros, some squat clay idols, naïve but dramatic wooden masks, bowls of fake fruit, brightly painted pottery figurines and perhaps strings of chillies in the kitchen.

FABRICS

Striking chevron patterns make a very appropriate choice for Mexican-style fabrics, in colours ranging from strong contrasts to a more muted palette; gold, too, comes in to play as part of this exuberant look. Stripes in varied colours will always work well, while bright silk, though unpatterned, is equally full of impact.

ABOVE Don't be afraid to use accessories in abundance. On walls, shelves and mantelpieces, their vivid colours and lively forms add spirit and fun to a room.

Don't forget the spiritual element which is ever-present in Mexican life. Christianity can be represented by *santos* (figures of saints) and *retablos* (wood panels painted with religious images), or you may prefer to display the ornamental skulls and skeletons that play an important part in the Day of the Dead. Taking place on 2 November every year, this is the day when, it is believed, the dead can revisit their friends and relatives on

ABOVE Mexican furniture is block-shaped, strong and sturdy. Here, a typical *equipal* table has been arranged with simple armchairs and a profusion of terracotta pots.

earth, who pay their respects by burning incense, decorating their homes with offerings of flowers, food and drink, and sometimes even by picnicking on their ancestors' graves! Far from being morbid, however, the custom encapsulates the exact opposite: an unstudied, infectious and typically Mexican celebration of life.

Furniture

Mexican furniture is, on the whole, rather rough and ready. Solid in shape, heavy and sturdy, it is, however, enlivened by colourful paintwork and lively carving. If you can't find the genuine article, substitute 'country' furniture and cover in bright paint, rubbing it back with sandpaper for a knocked-about, distressed finish.

Once the Spanish had settled in Mexico, they began to commission furniture for their new homes. This was made by local craftsmen but designed to a Spanish style, and the results were a distinctive cross-over of the two cultures, even, in fact, bearing some similarity to medieval European furniture due to its simple, monumental appearance. To achieve this look, choose pieces that are square and plain in form, made of golden timber with leather or unbleached canvas, or featuring gently worn, flaking paint. Look out for robust chests, large tables (these could be topped with terracotta or *talavera* tiles), sideboards, dressers, bedheads, cupboards and, especially, benches, which frequently take the place of individual seating in this look.

There are, however, some chairs that would be especially suitable for Mexican style. These include upright chairs with hard wooden seats, rush-seated stools and chairs, and more comfortable, leather-covered club chairs. One classic Mexican armchair is called the *butaca*, which has an x-shaped profile, a one-piece, curved seat/back (which could be in leather, rattan, wood or upholstery), and arms that scroll down to meet the front of the seat. Another ubiquitous item, found in living rooms, bedrooms, kitchens, dining rooms and even on patios, is called *equipal*, in the form of drum-shaped chairs or tables with a criss-cross timber base and leather seats, backs and arm rests. *Equipal*-style furniture is found in practically every Mexican home, and adding one or two to your scheme would really give it a characteristic and authentic look.

Finally, kitchens can be given a Mexican-style overhaul by using thin sheet aluminium to cover the fronts of cupboards and drawers. Before you attach the sheets (be extremely careful of sharp edges if you need to cut them), embellish them with indented patterns – such as zigzags, stars, diamonds or simple rows of dots – on the reverse side, giving a typical embossed effect. An old biro is the perfect tool for impressing the pattern in the soft metal. The same technique goes for other metal accessories – sconces are particularly appropriate – anywhere in the house.

The exuberance of Mexico is summed up in this interesting room, with its huge assortment of Mexican craft items.

Summing up the style

1 A chalky whitewash covers this plaster wall; it sets off the vibrant colours everywhere else beautifully and hints at the rusticity of the style.

2 A layering of different rugs over rough stone flooring is typically haphazard, yet they work well together.

3 With so many authentically Mexican artefacts crammed together, a classically styled floor lamp like this makes a nice contrast without seeming out of place.

4 Plain upholstery has been combined with broad stripes and an intricately patterned and vibrantly coloured quilt – the ornamental effect of the latter is very Mexican.

5 This solid, square coffee table is wonderfully robust and unpretentious, as is the rocking chair in the corner. The sofa, though comfortable, is suitably unfussy in its design.

6 Displaying a 'Day of the Dead' skeleton on his *burro* is far from morbid – in fact, it reflects the Mexican love of life. All sorts of other artefacts have been accumulated in this room, and their dramatic effect comes from so many of them being displayed together – in defiance of conventional good taste.

Caribbean

Everyone knows what to expect of the Caribbean: endless beaches with coral reefs, blue skies, lush rainforest, palm trees, coconuts, yams, mangoes, delicious seafood, intoxicating rum and exotic wildlife from flamingos and parrots to turtles and geckos. But while these images are all true, what one doesn't expect is the enormous diversity of peoples and cultures that exists among these scores of islands nestled in the Caribbean Sea.

'Discovered' by Columbus in 1492 in a search for a western route to south-east Asia (hence the name the West Indies), the islands were at that time inhabited by two tribes of Indians, the peaceful, music- and dance-loving Arawaks and the war-like, cannibal Caribs. But the door was open for settlers – first Spanish, then British, French and Dutch – to take possession of the islands and exact a profit for their homelands. From the early 1600s until the mid nineteenth century, millions of enslaved Africans were transported from the newly colonized areas of West Africa to work tobacco, sugar and cotton plantations for their European masters.

The various settlers gave each set of islands in their possession an individual character and it was only later, in the nineteenth century, that a specifically Creole style emerged, a unique mix of European and African cultures and traditions. This can be seen today on the various islands, freely adapted and encompassing differing elements such as English porches, French dormer windows and very simple Spanish forms. Building materials include clapboard, concrete, palm, wooden shingles, brick and wrought iron, with structures varying from simple shacks with corrugated iron roofs to imposing, three- or four-storey plantation houses, perched on the tops of hills and dominating the horizon. With their elegant rows of

Taking its cue from the region's clarity of light and lush, tropical surroundings, Caribbean style is as happy-go-lucky and relaxing as island life. For anyone, anywhere in the world, the look will evoke lazy days in the sun, sipping rum punch.

wrought iron balconies, these grandiose homes are often painted in a mix of pretty pastel colours, resembling a delicate wedding cake.

Impossibly bright colours are, however, the norm for less sophisticated dwellings. Thick, glossy paint covers shutters, gables, doorways and window surrounds, often in unexpected juxtapositions that, nevertheless, produce thrilling effects. Other features, too, are uniquely Caribbean, especially wood-slatted shutters, wooden bargeboards carved in delicate, lace-like patterns, symmetrical façades with a central entrance door and, especially, an emphasis on outdoor living. This results in houses that are designed so as not to differentiate too much between indoors and out, with plentiful verandahs, balconies and galleried walkways, where the windows are left almost permanently open, and where colourful, tropical plants trail indiscriminately around both gardens and indoor living areas. There are no set rules for living in the Caribbean, and while the architecture instinctively incorporates certain typical features there is, equally, an unworried, ad hoc attitude, and a freedom of expression that is uniquely Creole.

CREATING THE LOOK

Use your imagination to create an individual style that reflects the Caribbean's sunny climate and laid-back attitudes. Concentrate on refreshing colours, simple but good-looking furnishings and details that conjure up life in the islands, from ceiling fans and hurricane lamps to cool, durable surfaces able to withstand the heat of the sun. Lush, exotic pot plants will help create a taste of the tropics.

Walls

Wallpaper wouldn't withstand the Caribbean's tropical climate, so in this scheme it is advisable to concentrate on paint or wood for walls. Tongue-and-groove or timber panelling are both highly suitable, the former having an attractive, casual effect while the latter is more formal, echoing a colonial drawing room. Panelling is best left unpainted, simply sealed and/or varnished, but you may wish to give tongue-and-groove a covering of typically Caribbean thick, glossy paint in an appropriate colour. It's best, in fact, to paint most woodwork, such as skirtings, window frames, doors and door surrounds, with a bright gloss, creating an eye-catching mixture of irresistible hues. Plaster walls look marvellous when painted in planes of different tones – this is, after all, a

ABOVE An open-air feel helps give any room a Caribbean flavour. Pairing hard-wearing but attractive ceramic floor tiles with whitewashed plank walls is simple but effective.

scheme where brights are predominant, and you must not be scared to combine them in unusual ways. Use a colourwash effect if you want to create extra depth and interest. If, however, you really cannot take the dazzle of all this colour, aim for a calm, sophisticated look by covering walls with pure white paint, using them as a plain backdrop for vivid fabrics and striking furniture.

Floors

For Caribbean flooring, timber – laid as boards or parquet – makes an ideal choice. Polish to a high sheen for a colonial look or, if the wood is not worth putting on display, paint with a thick colour that complements your walls. Other hard floorings, such as brick, ceramic tiles or quarry tiles are also very appropriate – you are seeking to create the effect of an indoor/outdoor world, where floors need to be tough and resistant to wear rather than overly fine and sophisticated. If you simply cannot avoid carpet, then natural matting would be best for laying wall-to-wall. Choose whichever variety you prefer, but bear in mind that rush would be particularly suitable as it thrives on humidity, and in a dry climate actually needs regular dampening in order to prevent the fibres from flaking! Natural floorcoverings can also be made into very attractive mats, which would sit well on hard flooring to create a Caribbean look. Alternatively, choose rugs in rich, deep colours, avoiding any designs that appear too oriental in origin – perhaps it would be best, in fact, to stick to the simple stripes woven by native American Indians.

Lights

Hurricane lamps scattered across every available surface are enormously reminiscent of the Caribbean style. Their curving, clear glass cylinders were originally designed to protect candles from being extinguished in high winds, though today they can be used as simply another decorative effect. They can be placed, in a range of sizes, on side tables, mantelshelves, dining tables and window ledges to form a pretty and evocative display. Oil lamps and metal lanterns are appropriate

ABOVE Glass hurricane lamps make a very suitable choice of lighting for this style, and work well in any setting, whether simple or sophisticated.

for this style, too, while brass chandeliers with curving arms will create the look of a more formal plantation house. You could also choose the typical British colonials' 'melon' lamp, a fluted, inverted bell jar made of glass and suspended from the ceiling by three chains. They give a lovely soft glow and look enormously characteristic. Add heavy, wooden candlesticks in basic styles and also, if you need to increase the overall levels of light, some lamps in timeless, placeless shapes and neutral tones – bulbous ceramic bases with a pleated-silk shade, for example, or wooden stems topped by conical paper shades.

COLOURS

Colour is the most striking element of a Caribbean home, reflecting the vivid hues to be seen in the surrounding landscape. This unrestrained, mouthwatering palette consists of bonbon pink, sunburst yellow, bright turquoise, azure blue, vivid green and hot reds and oranges. Frosted pastels are the other option, though they, too, should be used with verve and abandon, mixing pink, violet, sky blue, lemon yellow and pale green.

LEFT Generous quantities of white muslin swathed over a four-poster bed create an instant colonial effect in this light and airy Caribbean bedroom.

Soft furnishings

The Caribbean interior is, often, almost completely devoid of soft furnishings, due to fabric's inability to withstand humidity and harsh sunlight for very long. At the windows, for instance, you are likely to find hinged, louvred wooden shutters (jalousies) – which make an elegant way to regulate sunlight and emphasize the size of the room. You will find that these are available in all sizes, or can be custom-made to suit the dimensions of your windows. Leave them natural, showing the grain and colour of the wood, or paint in suitable colours that complement the rest of the scheme without being overly dominating. The same goes for wooden Venetian blinds, which create a simi-

larly cool and airy look without the fuss of fabric, and usually at less expense. The cheapest option would be bamboo blinds, which are appropriately minimal and, like wood, blend in with any of the bright colours that are typical of this style.

If you have no option but to fit curtains, make sure that they are plain and practical, just flat or shirred panels of fabric hung from the simplest of poles, and in a hardy, down-to-earth fabric such as cotton or canvas. Sheer, gauzy muslins, by contrast, create a floaty feel that is barely-there while still allowing privacy – you could choose either bright white or a vibrant, saturated colour.

Tie-dyed and batik fabrics are typically Caribbean, and both are easy to do yourself at home, using pots of hand-dye and clean, pale fabric. Printed textiles, too, can be used in order to make an unforgettable Caribbean statement. In general, you should mix vivacious colours and bold, splashy patterns to form a carefree cacophony, a far from subtle – and truly wonderful – medley. All sort of fabrics would be suitable, from cotton and canvas to synthetics, and they can be employed for upholstery, throws, table linen and, in particular, piles and piles of cushions.

Keep your bedlinen crisp, clean and white to create a cool, colonial bedroom atmosphere. You may, however, prefer a brighter, less formal feel, in which case top with a colourful bed cover – either pretty sprigs of flowers or big, bold patterns that really make an impact. An alternative would be to use a patchwork quilt, either in the precise, European-American style where repeated geometric patterns are made from small pieces of toning cloth, or in the African-American improvised style, in which left-over fabrics create unpredictable designs in bold colour combinations. All beds should, it goes without saying, be hung with plenty of diaphanous muslin to emulate the ever-present mosquito net.

FABRICS

Caribbean colour can be evoked through textiles just as much as paintwork. Use plenty of sheer, white muslin, mixed with exuberant patterns such as exotic leaves, flowers and splashy swirls in ultra-vivid, eye-catching hues that echo the surrounding tropical landscape.

Finally, no Caribbean scheme would be complete without the addition of frills of broderie anglaise and lots of lace – the more robust rather than very delicate varieties. Use both on sheets, pillows, bed covers, tablecloths, table runners and quirky shelf trims for pretty and decorative finishing touch.

Accessories

In the hot and sticky climate of the Caribbean a rotating ceiling fan to bring fresh, cooling breezes always seems not so much an accessory as an essential. The larger versions are best, in wood and brass, like those used by overheated colonials in their grand plantation houses. In the same vein, you could create a display of casual straw hats, worn as protection from the glaring sun. Large terracotta jars are commonly used as ornaments in Caribbean gardens, where they may be joined by oversized terracotta pineapples or figurines. There is nothing to stop you, however, from bringing them indoors, using jars as casual storage and the ornaments for witty doorstops or purely as a non-functioning, visual joke.

Bright tin toys, made with gleeful ingenuity, are another speciality of this region. It can be great fun to collect them, but you should remember that they are rarely safe enough to actually play with – if there are young children about, the rule should be look, but don't touch. Finally, round the whole scheme off by filling rooms with lush houseplants and vases of exotic fresh blooms, together with bowls overflowing with tasty fruits such as yams, mangoes, pineapples, bananas and pawpaws.

LEFT A pale floor and white walls make this Caribbean living room bright and light. The cane furniture – an inexpensive yet attractive option – is extremely comfortable and evocative of tropical island life.

Furniture

Caribbean-style furniture should be sturdy and comfortable, with broad arms, wide seats and loose, lightly stuffed cushions. The most common wood used in the region is mahogany – thanks to its termite-resistant qualities – but today you should avoid buying tropical hardwoods unless you can be sure that the wood you are buying comes from a properly managed plantation. In your scheme any mid- to dark-brown wood would look the part, especially if buffed to a glossy sheen. Look for suitable pieces in antiques shops, junk shops, even jumble sales, bearing in mind that some judicious staining and varnishing, and a change of cushions, can work wonders to transform even the most unlikely of pieces.

Colonial-style furniture is quite distinctive, and would include typical pieces such as a large rocking chair, with a wicker seat and back, and a planter's chair with swing-out arms and generous dimensions. Imposing wooden or iron four-poster beds provided rest after a hard day managing the fields; but four-poster or not, swathing your bed with muslin to resemble mosquito netting will result in an attractive, and also appropriate, effect. Continue the colonial theme with large, solid tables and chairs, stout chests and cupboards, heavy wardrobes and the like. The furniture you choose could be self-consciously grand, but not necessarily very fine. Dark wooden units would be perfect for kitchens, while in the bathroom you could add cabinets, shelves, towel holders and so on in a similar style.

Some of the more elaborate items of Caribbean furniture are boldly carved, often in the form of twisted rope and pineapples. If you can find furniture that features these details it would add greatly to the authenticity of your scheme. Another way to create a hot, tropical look is to buy inexpensive, sturdy country furniture and paint it in bold, glossy hues. And, if you want, you could stencil pineapple motifs on the backs of chairs, on table tops, shelves and cupboard doors. Or, for a clean, cool brilliance, cover pieces in bright white paint – a marvellous way to unify different woods and mismatching shapes.

An alternative, which works just as well with a striking Caribbean colour scheme, is bamboo or rattan furniture. Sofas, chairs, tables, chests and even wardrobes are all easy to find and give a look that is lighter and more modern-looking than wooden furniture, yet equally Caribbean in style and with the advantage of being widely available and relatively inexpensive.

This is an example of a grand plantation house, decorated in clean, pastel colours to offset the room's sophisticated furnishings. The lacy door-tops have a romantic quality which is typical of the architecture of this type of building.

Summing up the style

1 As a plain backdrop to the room, and to promote a sense of a cool retreat from the heat, walls have been painted an all-over pale colour.

2 Though it is in a neutral shade, this carpet has a texture that provides subtle interest.

3 The elegant silks of this upholstery would be equally at home in a European interior – evidence of the Caribbean settlers' British, French and Spanish origins. This room would have quite a different look if more vibrant fabrics were used – in fact, changing cushions covers is an easy, inexpensive and instant way to transform an interior.

4 A wood and wicker planter's chair such as this is very much at home in a Caribbean-style environment. The large-scale wardrobe, too, suits the scheme very well, with its brass hinging reminiscent of a sea-chest.

5 A ceiling fan makes the perfect finishing touch to this style of decorating, and a few large, frondy potted plants help evoke the atmosphere of the Caribbean.

Shaker

The United Society of Believers in Christ's Second Appearing was a Christian sect – known as the 'Shakers' because of their practice of dancing, flapping, writhing and shaking during worship – which was founded in Manchester in the mid eighteenth century. When one of the followers, 'Mother' Ann Lee, was imprisoned for 'disturbing the Sabbath' in 1770, she experienced a vision of a new way of life and in 1774 she led a small group of followers to the New World. They established their community in New Lebanon, New York, three years later. Although few converts were made at first, eventually the Shakers' numbers began to grow, and by 1860 there were about 6000 men and women living in Shaker communities across New England and in the west of America.

The Shakers believed in celibacy, equality of sex and race (a most unusual concept at the time) and common ownership of property. Their communities were divided into families, who lived together in a 'dwelling house', the men and women – known as brothers and sisters – sleeping in separate dormitories. They worshipped together in a communal meeting house and worked to a strictly organized rota. It was a pure and simple life, spiritual, self-sufficient and purposeful, with a great emphasis on hard work and efficiency. Only the best was good enough, and all their produce, from furniture to food, was of the very highest quality: Mother Ann's guidance was to: 'Do all your work as though you had a thousand years to live and as you would if you knew you must die tomorrow'.

Despite their withdrawal from the world, the Shakers were by no means naïve. In fact, they were frequently ahead of their time, and have been credited with numerous inventions, including the circular metal saw, the automatic washing machine and the apple corer. They were quick to

'Beauty rests on utility,' said the Shakers, and the elegant simplicity of their unpretentious style has remained unchanged for 200 years. The harmonious sense of proportion, high standards of craftsmanship and perfect unity of form and function give this look a timeless and universal appeal.

realize that selling what they made would supplement the income from their farms, and for many years furniture (including seven different types of chair), herbal medicines, textiles, garden seeds, preserved fruit and other foodstuffs, baskets and storage boxes were sold from shops within their communities. They even exhibited at trade fairs and operated a mail order service.

However, during the late nineteenth and early twentieth centuries the Shakers began to suffer. Their celibate lifestyle meant that the communities relied on new members joining from the outside world, and gradually fewer and fewer people were attracted to do so. By 1959, only three communities remained, and today only a handful of people are left living and working as Shakers, although the movement's legacy lives on with a revival of interest in its elegantly proportioned yet highly functional furniture and accessories which combine to make harmonious interiors.

CREATING THE LOOK

This is a look that has widespread appeal and can work well in both modern and traditional homes. There is an abundance of Shaker-style furniture available today, though some of it is not nearly of a standard that would have met the Shakers' own stringent requirements. Pay attention to quality of detail, good craftsmanship and a refined sense of proportion, where the attraction comes from the functional 'rightness' of each and every piece.

ABOVE Wood-panelled walls painted in matt grey-green are restrained but not cold; they and the natural floor-covering are an ideal complement to Shaker furniture.

Walls

'Beadings, mouldings and cornices, which are merely for fancy, may not be made by believers,' said the Shakers' laws, and the walls of Shaker dwellings were always exceptionally plain. A skirting gave ground level protection, and sometimes a chair rail was used to prevent knocks and bumps from the backs of chairs. The most unusual feature of Shaker walls, however, was the distinctive peg rail, which was fixed into every single wall at approximately picture rail height, the rail set flush into the wall with pegs spaced at every 20–30cm (8–12in). This neat method of storage is attractive, tidy and highly versatile: you can use peg rails to hang practically anything, including chairs, cupboards, shelves, mirrors, kitchen implements, clocks, candle sconces and gingham drawstring bags.

Most Shaker walls were simply white-painted plaster, and any woodwork, such as skirtings, peg rails and door surrounds, was washed with an opaque tint that allowed the grain to show through. This is a restrained and plain solution for showing off beautiful wooden furniture and colourful fabrics, but if you prefer a brighter background there's nothing to stop you using a paint in an appropriate Shaker colour. In hallways, tongue-and-grooved panelling up to dado height is suitably hard-wearing, while in bathrooms it hides unsightly pipework – the Shakers would have approved of this combination of practicality and good looks. An alternative for the bathroom, and useful for kitchen splashbacks, too, would be white, cream or terracotta tiles.

Floors

The Shakers never strove for comfort, and their floors tended to be very bare, made simply of local stone or wooden boards. When dining, they ate in silence, allegedly due – at least in part – to the din that would have resulted from so many people speaking at once in an uncarpeted room!

To achieve this look today, then, aim for practicality rather than luxury, and use flagstones, quarry tiles or varnished floorboards made from oak, maple or cherry, or a paler wood stained to a rich, reddish brown. Linoleum is suitable, too, and a natural floorcovering such as sisal or coir, in a mid-golden colour, will give the right impression of unadorned practicality. Alongside a bed, in front of the fire or in a hallway, add one or two rag or flat-woven rugs in strong Shaker colours, either plain or in simple, broad stripes.

Lights

The typical Shaker light was a candle sconce, made of tin – inexpensive, light and easy to work with – and hung from a peg rail. In the early days the sconces were extremely simple, and a scoop shape, with its elegant curve, high back and low front, is especially pleasing. Later, however, a more decorative approach was taken: the tin was crimped at the edges and punched with decorations in the form of hearts, stars or simple geometric patterns.

ABOVE The simplicity and practicality of this sunny-coloured hallway typify the Shaker style. Note the scoop-shaped candle sconce hung from the ever-present peg rail.

Other candle holders, such as a simple pipe shape with two side arms, stood on mantelpieces and side tables – indeed, one small circular table was known as a candle stand because it was made specifically for this purpose. Several of these tin

COLOURS

Shaker interiors were often surprisingly colourful, with woodwork and fabrics in strong hues that worked harmoniously together due to their natural origins – local clays and colourings with which the communities created home-made dyes and pigments. Creamy white makes an ideal backdrop, with shades of blue ranging from indigo and denim to turquoise or a greyish sky blue. Olive and minty green, butter yellow, terracotta and ox-blood red complete this attractive palette.

candle holders will spread a beautiful soft glow in your Shaker-style interior.

When you need brighter lighting, look for pieces made of unembellished wood or metal, with parchment-coloured fabric or paper shades in very simple shapes. A curving, wrought-iron chandelier is perfect, and plain paper globes, although a twentieth-century invention, express the right mood of unpretentious practicality.

Soft furnishings

While the brethren worked in the fields or the furniture workshops, Shaker sisters spun, dyed and wove their own fabrics, including cotton, silk, wool and linen. Very often it was completely plain, but it could also be woven into simple checks in a range of sizes, from tiny ginghams to large window checks. Today, simple and inexpensive natural fabrics, such as wool, cotton, ticking, canvas and linen, are the most appropriate for a

Shaker interior. The Shaker colour palette works harmoniously in any number of combinations, and you can use plains mixed with different checks to give infinite variations on a theme. Putting them together does not require a great deal of know-how or confidence, and the result is always fresh and pretty.

The windows of Shaker dwelling houses were sometimes left bare, and when a covering was necessary, wooden shutters were preferred to curtains. It is possible, however, to create an inexpensive window treatment that looks right for a Shaker scheme. Keep it as plain as possible, using home-spun fabric in typical colours; roller blinds, Roman blinds or simple panels of fabric that tie back on to themselves with ribbons are appropriately restrained, or you could use a pair of gingham curtains, with a looped heading, hung from a wooden or iron pole. Add nothing more than a pair of unshowy finials, shaped as a heart, a star, a gentle scroll or a sphere, and functional tie-backs, perhaps made of bands of contrasting fabric.

'Never put on silver spoons for use, nor tablecloths, but let your tables be clean enough to eat without cloths,' said Mother Ann. Despite this dictum, if your dining table is not of a suitable style it would be a good idea to disguise it by covering it with a simple gingham cloth. Plain-coloured or checked linen napkins were used by the Shakers, and although they left their own unadorned, those they made to sell were given delicate border embroideries, typically a heart shape, or else birds or flowers. They also used checked tea towels, very often in blue and white. Today, you could even adapt tea towels to make inexpensive cushion covers or small blinds.

For bedlinen, although white and plain colours would be appropriate, it is prettier to opt for an embroidered style, featuring hearts, flowers or birds, or cross-stitch borders. Alternatively, layer checks on top of each other – not just for sheets and pillows, but woollen blankets, too. Blankets can also be used as throws over upholstered furniture. Patchwork quilts are not particularly appropriate for this style, as the Shakers were not known for their quilting, but if you do want to buy or make one, choose a design of simple squares in Shaker colours.

Accessories

Nothing was too unimportant to receive the Shaker treatment, and the design of a wide range of small household items, from bread boards to sewing baskets, epitomizes their typical combination of utility and beauty.

Most reminiscent of Shaker neatness and well thought-out practicality is the oval wooden box. With a perfectly fitting lid and elegantly tapering swallowtail joints fixed with copper tacks, the boxes can today be bought in numerous sizes, plain or painted, and may be used to hold everything from jewellery to needlework, magazines to toys. Baskets of all shapes and sizes are another typical Shaker accessory, adding an air of natural homeliness. Other touches could include wooden bowls and bread boards, the latter either heart shaped or with a cut-out heart motif; plain wooden picture frames; iron latches, hooks and rails, again with a heart motif; and folk art dolls and rabbits, like those made by the Shakers out of scraps for their younger members to play with.

FABRICS

For the Shaker look the emphasis is on practical prettiness rather than artifice or fuss. To this end, muslin, canvas and cotton checks – in a variety of sizes from tiny ginghams to large windowpanes – all make excellent choices, with colours equally unpretentious, either natural and unbleached, or else straightforward brights such as red, green, blue or yellow.

ABOVE These wooden kitchen implements, lovingly hand-crafted from solid wood, would be a pleasure to use. The heart is a recurring Shaker motif.

You could also use fabric, gingham in particular, to line the insides of boxes, cover shoeboxes and make drawstring bags to hold shoes, clothes, toys or dried lavender (hung from a peg rail, of course). Overall, simply remember to avoid anything made for appearance rather than use because, as Mother Ann said: 'Whatever is fashioned, let it be plain and simple and for the good.'

Furniture

When new members joined the Shaker communities, any furniture they brought with them would be given up for general use, while Shaker carpenters would copy the designs and refine them according to the group's ideals. The result was some of the finest furniture ever produced. Each Shaker chair, table or bed was created according to the belief that 'beauty rests on utility'. Shaker furniture makers strove for a perfection that demonstrated their fervent spirituality, while efficiency of use was considered essential. Chairs, for example, were light enough to be easily moved when cleaning, with finials on the backposts in order to lift the chairs without damaging them. Dining tables were large, for communal eating, and trestle-style, braced along their length rather than their width so as not to limit the space for knees underneath. Sewing tables had underslung drawers that could be pulled out from either end, allowing a sister to work at each side, and small tables featured a slender central leg which gently widened at the base, with tripod feet slotted neatly in, giving both delicacy and solidity.

Mother Ann told the Shakers to 'provide places for all your things, so that you may know where to find them at any time, day or night,' and well-organized storage – both built-in and free-standing – was another predominant feature of the Shaker dwelling houses: one surviving room even has a bank of 860 drawers. Drawers for herbs, drawers for clothes, drawers for towels, for bedlinen, for textiles of all kinds – all were simply constructed according to what was to be kept in them, resulting in an attractive variation of shape and size.

When choosing Shaker-style furniture, look first of all for good quality, in solid wood and with well-made joints. Pieces to watch out for include ladder-back dining and rocking chairs, trestle-style tables with arching feet, small side tables with a central pedestal, desks on gently tapered legs, and large wardrobes and chests of drawers with plain, panelled fronts and round wooden knob-pulls.

The Shakers had no leisure time as such – their lives consisted solely of work and worship – so they did not have living rooms with sofas and chairs. Unless you're prepared to live in this austere way today, you will probably want to add some form of comfortable seating: the best way to do this is to choose pieces in timeless styles, with exposed wooden frames and minimal, tailored upholstery.

LEFT The natural tones of beautifully made Shaker furniture ensure an overall unity in any room. The hanging cupboard and the adjustable candle sconce are typically ingenious.

The Shaker look combines the old-fashioned with the contemporary, the refined with the charming, as demonstrated by this beautiful kitchen.

Summing up the style

1 Adding a peg rail to a wall is not only true to the Shaker aesthetic, it is also a convenient and attractive way of storing kitchen equipment.

2 Wooden boards are topped with a simple striped rug: a perfect example of the Shaker belief that 'beauty rests on utility'.

3 Tin candle stands are typical of the Shaker style. Other versions can be hung from a peg rail.

4 Plain cotton, made up into curtains in the least fussy of styles possible, suits this look well. A simple gingham check would also be appropriate.

5 Every item of Shaker furniture was designed with the aim of achieving perfection in function and appearance; the taped seats and backs of Shaker chairs, for example, are hard-wearing, supportive and comfortable. The many drawers fitted under the wooden worktop are typical – the Shakers deplored untidiness, and were very keen on well-organized storage.

6 This heart-shaped chopping board is both useful and attractive, as are the besom broom, the woven basket and the large wooden salad bowl.

Further reading

I have used a great many sources in researching this book, in particular, the National Art Library at the Victoria and Albert Museum, Exhibition Road, London SW7; the Westminster Reference Art and Design Library, 35 St Martin's Street, London WC2; and the Geffrye Museum, Kingsland Road, London E2.

Among the many books I found helpful are the following:

Nicholas Barnard, *Living with Folk Art: Ethnic Styles from Around the World*, Thames & Hudson, 1998; Geoffrey Barraclough (ed), *The Times Concise Atlas of World History*, Times Books, 1994; Mel Byars, *The Design Encyclopaedia*, Laurence King, 1994; Stephen Calloway (ed), *The Elements of Style*, Mitchell Beazley, 1996; Alan and Ann Gore, *The History of English Interiors*, Phaidon, 1995; Dinah Hall, *Ethnic by Design*, Mitchell Beazley, 1995; Elizabeth Hilliard, *Library of Interior Detail* series, Pavilion; Jocasta Innes, *The Thrifty Decorator*, Conran Octopus, 1993; Miranda Innes, *Ethnic Style: From Mexico to the Mediterranean*, Conran Octopus, 1994; Edward Lucie-Smith, *Furniture: A Concise History*, Thames & Hudson, 1995; Anne Massey, *Interior Design of the 20th Century*, Thames & Hudson, 1996 and others from the Thames & Hudson *World of Art* series; Judith and Martin Miller, *Period Style*, Mitchell Beazley, 1994; Phyllis Bennett Oates, *The Story of Western Furniture*, The Herbert Press, 1993; Ruth Pretty, *The Ultimate Interior Designer*, Ward Lock, 1997; Suzanne Slesin, Stafford Cliff and Daniel Rozensztroch, *Style Library* series, Thames & Hudson; various authors, *Essential Style* series, Ward Lock; Herbert Ypma, *World Design* series, Thames & Hudson.

Picture credits

The Publisher should like to thank the following for their kind permission to reproduce the photographs in this book:

Abode 25 (2 left), 49, 58 (16 right), 61, 64, 82, 84, 87, 89, 164; Aktiva Systems (0171 428 9325) 125; Anglepoise (01527 63771) 101; Arcaid / Richard Bryant 50, 52 (16 centre) by kind permission of 'The Mount Vernon Ladies' Association of the Union, 66, 74 (17 centre), 80 / David Churchill 18 / Richard Einzig 116 / Mark Fiennes 105 (3 right) / Lucinda Lambton 26 / Julie Phipps 31 / Bill Tingey 180 / Alan Weintraub 62; Laura Ashley (0990 622116) 152; Axiom / Jim Holmes 182 (130 right), 183 / James H. Morris 135, 148; B&B Italia (00 39 31 795 111) 102; Bona Arts Decorative (01252 616666) 95; Bhs (0171 262 3288) 77; Julian Cornish, courtesy of David Mikhail Architects (0171 485 4696) 122, 124, 129; Crown Decorative Products (01254 704951) 158; Crowson Fabrics (01825 761055) 30, 178; Design Archives (01202 753248) 54, 144, 179, 207; Dulux (01753 336959) 7, 8, 13, 57, 139, 172 (3 left), 204; Fired Earth (01295 812088) 166; Geffrye Museum, London 108; Peter Guild (01234 273372) 167; Habitat (0171 255 2545) 128; Harlequin Fabrics and Wallcoverings (01509 813112) 126 (17 right); Ikea (0181 208 5600) 159, 160; The Interior Archive / Cecilia Innes 196 (2 centre), 198, 200, 201, 202, 203 / Schulenburg 20, 36, 42, 48, 76, 81, 156, 210 / Andrew Wood 114, 208 (131 right), 211 / YMPA 194; Isis Ceramics (01865 722729) 39; Knoll International, London – Mies van der Rohe Barcelona Collection (0171 236 6655) 104; Looking East (01598 763300) 21, 29; Mainstream Photography 174, 175, 176; Malabar (0171 501 4200) 192 (131 left); Mathmos (0171 404 6605) 117, 120; Meubles Granges (01780 754721) 146; John Miller 138, 151, 153, 155 (130 left), 170, 191; Monkwell (01202 753205) 20; New England Direct (01527 577111) 45, 47; Nordic Style (0171 351 1755) 162 (9), 163; Ocean Home Shopping (0171 501 2500) 126; Original Style (013923 474059) 60; Paris Ceramics (0171 371 7778) 150; The Pier (0171 351 7100) 145; Prêt à Vivre (0181 960 6111) 11; The Royal Oak Furniture Company (01756 753378) 24; Sanderson (01895 238244) 10, 70, 140; Shaker (0171 724 7672) 212, 213, 214, 215, 216, 217 (131 centre), 218, 219; Stovax (013293 474055) 79; Tempus Stet (0171 820 8666) 37, 53; Twyfords (01270 410023) 96; Elizabeth Whiting & Associates 28 (16 left), 32, 38, 41, 44, 46, 55, 56, 65, 69, 72, 73, 78, 86, 90, 92 (17 centre right), 94, 97, 98, 100, 106, 109, 110, 112, 113 (2 right), 118, 121, 132 (3 centre), 134, 137 (130 centre), 1· 147, 168, 171, 184, 185, 187, 188, 19C 195, 206; Mark Wilkinson Furniture (01380 850004) 88; John Wilman Fabric & Wallpapers (0800 581984) 136; Wood Bros (Furniture) (01920 469241) 33, 68; Christopher Wray's Lighting Emporium (0171 371 0077) 85, 93.

Front cover: Axiom / James H. Morris centre right, Bhs centre, The Interior Archive / Cecilia Innes bottom left, Nordic Style top left, Shaker bottom centre & right, Elizabeth Whiting & Associates top centre, top right, centre left. Back cover: Arcaid / Julie Phipps left, Fired Earth bottom right, The Interior Archive / Andrew Wood top right. Front flap: Mathmos. Back flap: Etienne Bol.

Fabric credits

The Publisher should like to thank the following for their kind permission to reproduce the fabrics in this book:

Laura Ashley (0990 622116) 87, 136–7, 144–5, 168–9, 217; G.P. & J. Baker (01494 467467) 54–5, 94–5, 103; Beaten Path Studio (01556 502543) 78–9; Chelsea Textiles (0171 584 0111) 168–9; Ciel Decor (0171 731 0444) 153; Crowson Fabrics (01825 761055) 39, 209; Thomas Dare (0171 351 7991) 201; Design Archives (01202 753248) 54–5; Fired Earth (01295 812088) 22–3, 31, 39, 63; Firifiss (01202 753251) 185; Habitat (0171 255 2545) 46–7, 119; KA International (0171 584 7352) 153; Cath Kidston (0171 221 4000) 110–111; Leejofa (0171 351 7760) 31, 54–5, 87, 119, 136–7, 144–5, 7, 185; John Lewis (0171 629 7711) 22–3, 31, 39, 46–7, 119, 161, 168–9, 193, 201, 217; Mansion Textiles (0161 367 8585) 153; Monkwell (01202 753205) 136–7, 144–5, 193; Montgomery Interior Fabrics (01244 661363) 193, 209; Mulberry Company Design, Home Division (01749 340594) 201; Nordic Style (0171 351 1755) 161, 168–9, 217; Osborne & Little (0181 675 2255) 71, 78–9, 87, 103, 119, 127, 136–7, 144–5; Prêt à Vivre (0181 960 6111) 103, 161; Pukka Palace (0345 666660) 185; Scandecor (01273 820208) 94–5; Stuart Renaissance Textiles (01460 240349) 31, 39; Jim Thompson (0171 351 2829) 103, 176–7, 217; Watts of Westminster (0171 376 4486) 63; John Wilman Fabrics & Wallpapers (0800 581984) 127, 144–5; Brian Yates (01524 35035) 127, 168–9, 193, 209; Zimmer & Rohde (0171 351 7115) 119, 127, 185, 193, 209.